D1236613

# JOHN CALVIN: A STUDY IN FRENCH HUMANISM

# JOHN CALVIN: A STUDY IN FRENCH HUMANISM

By

QUIRINUS BREEN

SECOND EDITION

With a Foreword by John T. McNeill

ARCHON BOOKS

1968

First published 1931

SECOND EDITION

© Copyright 1968, Quirinus Breen

Library of Congress Catalog Card Number: 67-26660
Printed in the United States of America

Dedicated to

Helena, the wife of my youth

and to the memory of

Professor Ralph Janssen

1874–1945

# ERRATA

Kind French reviewers of the 1931 edition have offered corrections of such items as follow: the allegation (p. 3) that the Concordat of 1516 gave the French church "a practical independence"; the error of dating the founding of Louvain's three-language college as 1515 instead of 1517 (p. 62); that Calvin sent a French translation of his "Address to the King" to Francis I in 1535 is *not* certain (p. 123, note 83); besides, faulty Latin references to Josse Badius's press (p. 128) and to Erasmus (p. 169). There are a number of misspellings not caught in proof-reading, among the worst pertaining to Poggio's *Facetiae* (p. 127). Others have noted spotty passages in translations from the Latin on pp. 53–55 and 86–89. Each time I see the blunder on p. 54, l. 24, my heart faints. The misaccenting of Olivétan on pp. 23 and 40 is perhaps as disturbing to a Frenchman as giving a plural form to the Digest on pp. 103–4 to a civilian. I cannot imagine why l. 25 of p. 142 was not taken out. A line was omitted at l. 17, p. 134; it should read, "and it had been carefully recorded that three million lines or sentences were reduced . . . to one hundred fifty thousand." On p. 74, l. 13, the word "it" has no antecedent, which should be "Stoicism." Catholic scholars may forgive a pre-ecumenical insensitivity to a possible implication in ll. 5–6 on p. 1.

Quirinus Breen

# FOREWORD

The re-appearance of Dr. Breen's pioneering study of young Calvin's humanism makes available to a new generation of teachers and students what is still the best introduction to the humanist theologian's formative years. The book was hailed at the outset by grateful readers as an informed and illuminating description of the elements that combined to shape and equip the mind of the reformer-to-be. Any student of recent Calvin literature will have come frequently upon references to Breen's material and opinions. Although the newer scholars have made us increasingly aware of Calvin's importance as an historical figure, they continue to have recourse to this dissertation for guidance at significant points. In the earlier chapters we are brought into Calvin's immediate environment as an undergraduate at Paris, when the student body was beginning to stir with the new life of the Renaissance. Then we are led to Orléans and Bourges to find Calvin in his early twenties responding, with his friends, to the divergent instruction of two of the great legal scholars of the time. Later, at the end of his formal academic education, we find him absorbing the higher learning in the classics and Hebrew, and possibly mathematics, of the newly established Royal Lecturers in Paris. Under these men the modern French university was coming into being before his eyes. Calvin was as fortunate in his teachers as he was in his natural gifts. Where else in history can we find an instance in which so stimulating an environment served to enrich so talented a brain through ten crowded years?

On Breen's canvas are pictured the figures that crown the French Renaissance, among whom young Calvin moved with natural ease. His Seneca Commentary, a learned plea for humane government, was proof that he had profited by it all. But another excitement was now in the air. Men were committed to a new cause, and were dying for it. It drew inspiration in some degree from Wittenberg but also from the biblical humanism of Lefèvre. It went to the Bible for authority and instruction. Among its adherents were Calvin's cousin and old companion, Olivétan, and Etienne de la Forge in whose house he had written his Seneca study. After a protracted struggle Calvin, now about twenty-five, underwent a "sudden conversion" which made him a member of the evangelical company. He referred to this long afterward not as the culmination of his studies but simply as an act of God. There was something inevitable about what followed. His new "brethren" were devoted to Holy Scripture: Calvin had acquired knowledge by which he was peculiarly fitted to interpret it. Henceforth his commentaries would not be on classical texts but on books of the Bible and from the Bible he would shape the theology of his treatises.

But conversion, sudden or not, does not annihilate the learned convert's learning or "mastery of language", or shatter his habits of study. So Dr. Breen at the close discusses "the precipitate of humanism" in the mature Reformer. A hundred more recent investigators of Calvin's life and thought have not taken away the freshness, or the usefulness, of this book. I am happy that it is to be given a second span of life, and in this improved form.

JOHN T. McNEILL

June, 1967

# PREFACE

THE Reformation may be said to be both the child and the protector of humanism. The vivid interest in human life as it is to be lived in this world, the realization that in classical antiquity—as to art, law, religion—there was a more adequate point of vantage from which to evaluate the present, the assurance that the then modern man was mentally healthier, stronger than the medieval man,—these are common to both. All the Reformers had diligently studied the humanists. Their early religious zeal was largely a passion for intellectual honesty. Their study of the fathers of the church, their Biblical scholarship, their faith in the principle of "libre examen" and in the right of private judgment hail from humanism.

The Reformation was more than a mere continuation of humanism, of course. Over against the centrifugal force of humanistic individualism there were in the Reformation counteracting unitive ones. Humanism is aristocratic, the Reformation democratic. The genius of the one is secular, that of the other religious.

The ideals of humanism were much the same wherever it was found, but there were differences of emphasis in the various nations. So it is proper to speak of French humanism, not only as a geographical distinction but also in the sense that humanism in France adapted itself to the character of the land and the people. So, for example, the French humanists interpret the Roman law so as to give support to the absolutist claims of Francis I, while in Germany a man like Zasius opposes the absolutism of the Roman law and proceeds rather to work its principles for the regulation of social and business relations into the statutes of Freiburg. We have good reason therefore to speak of Calvin's early training as having taken place under the auspices of the humanist movement as it was found particularly in France.

In fact, the study of his early life reveals a cross-section in miniature of French humanism as such. First because it is obvious that, up to 1532 at least, he is wholly identified

with it. He stands in contact with the Italian origin of the
French movement, through Alciati, the works of Valla, and
others. He studies in Paris during the fifteen hundred
twenties when everybody is talking about Erasmus, De
Berquin, and Luther who at this time is regarded as a
humanist there. He knows Guillaume Budé, the dean of
French scholarship. He is early enrolled in that greatest
product of French humanism, the Lecteurs Royaux (1531-2).
His *Seneca Commentaries,* appearing in 1532, are quite the
thing a brilliant young humanist would have done.

There is another reason why his early life may be studied
from the point of view of the fortunes of French humanism;
it is that the movement had practically spent its force at
about the time of his conversion, which occurred perhaps
in 1534. Josse Badius would die in 1535, Erasmus in 1536,
Budé in 1540. The great masters had therefore done their
work. Besides, the Roman church was tightening the reins,
so that a check was laid upon the free play of the mind. The
domination of the classical languages was being challenged
by the new writers,—Marot, Marguerite, Rabelais, and
others. The pure intellectualism of humanism became almost immoral in the face of the social fact of the suppres-
sion of the rights of the common people to think and speak.
So Calvin's conversion, though religiously motivated, is his
turning from pure intellectualism to a concern about the
common man. It is followed by making use, with progressing
facility, of the French language. Moreover, his conversion
did not alter his mental "set." To escape the domination of
the Roman Church meant freedom to employ his critical
apparatus with respect to the text of Scripture; he is at one
with the then modern spirit of questioning the official histories of the church; he extends his search into such dangerous fields as the absolutism of monarchy. The spirit of
humanism is slowly leaving the classical age, dealing now
with questions that burn in every breast.

Two documents have proved exceptionally useful. The
first, Duchemin's *Antapologia,* in the composition of which
Calvin appears to have had a hand. It certainly contains his
sentiments about the matters therein found, for he wrote
the Preface and saw the book through the press. In any
new edition of the complete works of Calvin it should have

a place, just as Nicholas Cop's Rectoral Oration.[1] The second document is of course the *Seneca Commentaries*, the importance of which is so obvious that it is not disproportionate to devote two chapters to it as we have done.[2]

It were ingratitude to send this thesis into the world without acknowledging the help received from Dr. J. T. McNeill, my advising professor, whose exactness and erudition and not least whose friendship have given the ideal auspices under which to work. I owe a debt also to the Virginia Library of the Presbyterian Theological Seminary of Chicago, the Newberry Library, the Libraries of the University of Illinois, and especially the Libraries of the University of Chicago, whose invaluable help has been extended with unfailing courtesy.

THE AUTHOR.

July, 1931.

---

[1] See Chapter III, Section 2, Appendix: Duchemin's *Antapologia*.
[2] See Chapters IV and V.

# CONTENTS

# PROLOGUE

Though the Reformation took place in a secular context, its genius was religious. The secular environment affected many of its aspects; but no social, political, economic, intellectual factors can by themselves or in combination account for such religious springs as sin and grace in Luther or Calvin's awe of God. The environmental conditions have changed, but the spiritual energy of the Reformers endures.

This having been said, it has an importance of its own to consider the Reformation as a Renaissance phenomenon.[1] The preeminent scholarship of the era was the humanistic, a preoccupation with the study of classical literature, mainly philological and rhetorical. The question of how deeply it influenced the Reformers is apropos, for the Renaissance (including its humanism) has been under attack by some theologians, and even the Reformation has been charged with being infected by its evil virus.[2]

The effort of the present volume has been to show how fruitfully Calvin was influenced by humanism. Since its first printing (1931), other studies have appeared.[3] Moral philosophy was a favorite theme of most humanists,[4] which, as was recently shown, is strikingly reflected in Calvin's *Institutes*.[5] In the Epilogue to this book is a discussion of Calvin's defense of humanistic, i.e., secular, studies. Of significance is that it is religious defense, made boldly and eloquently. He nowhere apologizes for applying the humanistic philological methods to Bible study.[6] He must have shared with good scholars the conviction (often un-

---

[1] "Religious aspect of the Renaissance" is J. T. McNeill's pregnant phrase in "The Reformation's Debt to the Renaissance," *Religion in the Making*, II, 2–7.

[2] See Herbert Weisinger, "The Attack on the Renaissance in Theology Today," *Studies in the Renaissance*, II (1955) pp. 176–189.

[3] See A. Veerman, *De Styl van Calvijn in die Institutio Christiana Religionis*, Utrecht, 1943; more significant was A. M. Hugo, *Calvijn en Seneca: Een inleidende studie van Calvijn's Commentaar op Seneca De Clementia*. Groningen, 1957; F. L. Battles and Hugo will soon publish a critical edition of the Commentary on Seneca, with translation and elaborate notes; Q. Breen, "John Calvin and the Rhetorical Tradition," *Church History*, XXVI, 1957, pp. 5–21.

[4] See P. O. Kristeller, *Renaissance Thought, Its Classical, Scholastic, and Humanistic Strains*, New York, 1961, p. 10.

[5] See below, note 5 of Epilogue.

[6] See below, p. 154.

spoken) that any document, and also the Bible, has (so to say) a moral right to be accurately copied, translated and understood in the light of its times.

There was a broader Renaissance humanism than that concerned with the philological and rhetorical study of the classical literature. This had to do with any effort and art to explore and express the potentials and actions of man as man; such as were manifested in Renaissance poetics, drama, the arts of painting and sculpture, mathematics, philosophy.[7] It is a useful distinction. If, in their confrontation of the church, the Reformers, so to say, meant to restore to man the "Sabbath [that] was made for man," surely, this was a humanism broader than philology and rhetoric. In this sense the Reformation may be considered as humanistic par excellence.[8]

Of Calvin studies the end is not in sight. A score of works published or reprinted since 1960 alone include authors such as A. Biéler, H. Daniel-Rops, J. T. McNeill, R. M. Kingdon, J. H. Rilliet, and F. Wendel.

For much counsel and constant encouragement my deepest gratitude goes to Dr. J. T. McNeill, once my major professor and always my father in Calvin.

Grand Valley State College
Allendale, Michigan
March, 1967

---

[7] The challenge of Biblical philology by over-zealous heresy-hunters during Calvin's student years at Paris is exemplified by Beda, on whom Walter Bense has a doctoral dissertation (Cambridge, Mass., 1967), *Noel Beda and the Humanist Reformation at Paris, 1504–1534* (typescript). Though blind to the importance of Biblical philology (of Le Fevre and especially Erasmus), it appears Beda was neither ignorant nor wanting in principles.

[8] Professor P. O. Kristeller has championed the distinction between a philosopher as such and a humanist who pursues studies of classical literature philologically and rhetorically. This was my cue for extending the distinction for other broader kinds of humanism. See *Istituto Nazionale, Firenze-L' Opera e il Pensiero di G. Pico della Mirandola della Storia dell 'Umanesimo*. Convengo Internazionale (Mirandola: 15–16 Sep. '63) Vol. I pp. 32–3, 134–7. In his *History and Character of Calvanism* (N.Y., 1967), Professor J. T. McNeill has a chapter on Calvin's Conversion (pp. 107–118), whose analysis of it bodies forth Calvin's finding of himself as a man (in the sense already mentioned). In "Humanism and the Reformation," a chapter in *Essays in Divinity* (Chicago, 1967) I enlarge on the said distinction; in the section on Calvin's conversion, the part played by philosophy should be understood to take into account McNeill's larger context.

# JOHN CALVIN: A STUDY
# IN FRENCH HUMANISM

# CHAPTER I

## GENERAL BACKGROUND

### Section 1. France

IT is important to realize that John Calvin was born in a country with a highly-developed national state.[1] While the Roman church was the only one recognized by the State, France retained a sense of her national importance to such an extent that she did not allow the church to reduce her to serfdom.

Under the Capetians the monarchy had become well consolidated. Each decade France became more sensitive about her rights over against the claims of the Roman pontiff. The French clergy themselves reflected the pride of the nation (and too often its avarice). In June, 1438, representatives of the Gallican church convened at Bourges, and adopted for use in the realm the principal decrees of the Council of Basel, which, after some retouching were promulgated by Charles VII under the name of the Pragmatic Sanction (July 7). The heart of the document was that the Council is superior to the Pope. In several ways the papal prerogative in appointments and finances were seriously abridged. It is almost needless to add that the Pragmatic Sanction defended the French Church against the King with less hardihood.[2] In October, 1472, Louis XI both "abolished and reëstablished" the Pragmatic Sanction; that is, under the pretext of returning to the See of Peter the rights taken from it in 1438, he signed a Concordat which "put the highest dignities of the French clergy at the mercy of the royal authority."[3] Finally came the famous Concordat of 1516 under Francis I, a compromise with Rome, but not at all to the disadvantage of the Crown.[4]

---

1) SMITH, P., *The Age of the Reformation*, p. 182 f.
2) RENAUDET, A., *Préréforme et Humanisme à Paris pendant les premières guerres d' Italie (1494–1517)*, p. 4 f.; VALOIS, N., *Histoire de la Pragmatique Sanction de Bourges sous Charles VII*, pp. xciii–cxxvi.
3) RENAUDET, *op. cit.*, p. 4; COMBET, J., *Louis XI et le Saint-Siège (1416–1483)*, p. 102.
4) THOMAS, JULES, *Le Concordat de 1516, ses origines, son histoire au XVIe siècle* (2 vols., Paris 1910).

The result of this strong national consciousness was obviously of benefit to France. For, troubled as the church was by a worldly and grasping clergy, disorganized as was its discipline,[5] the Roman See's dealings with the French crown and church were characterized by a considerateness equalled nowhere. The epitome was the Concordat of 1516. Again, the French independence toward the papal court was to the latter's advantage as well. For, though there would be threats and outbreaks of revolt against the whole papal system, yet there was to be no decisive break with Rome in the kingdom of France. There was no general hatred of the Roman curia as, for instance, in Germany. Like Italy, France was to remain officially Roman Catholic. Rabelais, like Boccaccio, remained a son of the old church. The humanists of France, save a very few, were to remain Roman Catholics. So, too, reformers like Le Fèvre, Briçonnet, Roussel. And Calvin himself was to be slow to break with the dominant French tradition. Not until a series of events that were to prove too powerful for him, was he to become the radical reformer of the *Institutes.*

It must be assumed that his interest in Protestantism was growing every year, yet up to a few months before his conversion we find him steeped in classical studies, and, according to all appearances, carving for himself a career as a professional man of letters. There are reasons to think that this was to an extent a studied effort to evade the then paramount religious issue. To be like Budé, the dean of French humanism, was to him more desirable than to be like Luther. To remain loyal to the church seemed a price not too great to pay, though he must already have been offended by its corruptness. More than all, he must have wanted to stay on French soil. It meant certain death or exile to be a Protestant.[6]

---

[5] RENAUDET, *op. cit.,* pp. 1–21.
[6] Even after his conversion, he found refuge in *French* Switzerland, Geneva. He speaks lovingly of France as "nostra Gallia" Cf. Comm. on *De Clementia,* Opera Calv. V, 54. His contact with France is so vivid that by 1560 he can count his followers by the hundreds of thousands. (PIPER, O., Vom französischen Protestantismus; *Zeitwende,* März, 1930, p. 251). One of his ideals remains to improve the French language. H. BOSSERT, (*Calvin,* in *Les grands ecrivains français,* p. 211 ff.), exhibits Calvin's care in bettering his French style. Comparing the first chapters of the French editions of the Institutes of 1541 and 1560, he discovers such improvements, e. g., as *pensée* for *cogitation, sagesse* for

France and the French tradition, humiliation of it and all that, were too dear to him. The result is the two volumes on the *De Clementia.*

## Section 2.   Francis I, Marguerite, and the Court

The king of France during Calvin's youth and early manhood was Francis I, sometimes called the Great (1515-1547). Not particularly a strong character, he was favorably enough situated at Maringan (1515) to break the coalition of the pope with the king of Spain, the dukes of Milan and the Swiss against him, so that he could force the conditions of the Concordat.[7] Thus the French church, retaining its practical independence, had a constitution by which it was to live till the Revolution. Thanks to this victory France breathed more freely, and the king enjoyed such a popularity as few have had before or since. Even the defeat at Pavia, 1525, did not diminish it permanently.

The king, successful in war, beloved by his people, felt that he could afford to encourage research and letters. This alone was sufficient reason why he deserved, in the eyes of Beza, the title of "The Great."[8]

---

*sapience, moquerie* for *contumélie, enquête* for *inquisition.* His pains were rewarded, for Calvin disengaged his French from Latinisms more successfully than some of his greatest contemporaries. "Beaucoup plus que son contemporain Rabelais, plus même que Montaingue qui est venu quarante ans après lui, il se rapproche de la prose du XVII siècle. Au point de vue du developpement de la langue, il sort de la suite chronologique et se place immediatement avant Pascal."

The high Germans, e. g., the Marburgers, never liked him, nor he them. Perhaps there were national as well as theological reasons why they were at odds. Much as he owed to the German reformers he appears never to have taken pains to learn the German language. cf. KOLF-HAUS, *Die Verkehr Calvins mit Bullinger,* (Calvin-Studien, [Editor, BOHATEC, J,—1909], p. 104), who says that Calvin estimated Luther's view of the Eucharist more favorably "als sie in Wirklichkeit sei, und führte zum Beweise einzelne Aussprüche Luthers an, die Calvin wegens *seiner Unnkenntnis des Deutschen fremd waren'* (Italics mine). (Cf. also NIESEL, W., Verstand Calvin Deutsch, *Zeitschrift für Kirchengeschichte,* xlix Bd., III Heft, 1930, pp. 343–346.)   He remained a Frenchman to the last, but a Frenchman in exile, a symbol of what his conversion implied for him as a son of beloved Gallia.

7) RENAUDET, *op. cit.,* p. 580.

8) DE BEZE, THEO., *Histoire ecclésiastique des églises reformées au royaume de France* (Ed. Vesson, 1882).   After picturing the significance of Budé's contribution to the revival of learning in France de Bèze proceeds to show that the French Renaissance was equally much indebted to Francis I: "Pour revenir à Budé, il fut si heureux, en son erudition, que de recontre un roy d'excellement bon esprit, & grandement amateur des' bonnes letres encores qu il n' eut congnoissance que

To improve and to lend greater glory to French jurisprudence, he paid the famous Italian Andrea Alciati double
the salary he had at Milan, to lecture at the University of
Bourges.[9] The king also founded the Lecteurs Royaux,
chiefly at the instigation of Budé, and against the opposition
of the Sorbonne. This institution was of great significance
for the training of Calvin.

Not only did the king not fear the displeasure of the
Sorbonne in establishing the Lecteurs Royaux, but he had
protected, more than once, men who suffered from the
heresy hunting of the Theological Faculty of Paris. Lefèvre
and Louis de Berquin were among those who had enjoyed
the royal good will.

Withal, men of letters, artists,[10] innovaters of new ways
of thinking were rather fortunate to live under Francis I.
Before his time there was no strong cultivation of art and
letters in France. For example, the French language was

---

de sa langue maternelle, à savoir Francois, premier du nom, auquel aiant
dédié cest excellent livre, intitulé les Commentaires de la langue grecque
il luy persuada non seulement que les trois langues, & les bons livres
escrits en icelles, se devoient les és escoles & universités de son royaume,
mais aussi d' establir certains excellens personnages, qui luy furent
nommés, pour enseigner à Paris avec bons & honnestes gages, en intention de bastir un magnifique Collège de trois langues, avec bon revenu,
pour y entrentenir bon nombre de regens & escoilers. Ce néanmoins le
bastiment de ce collège ne peut jamais venir a effect: mais bien furent
establir plusiers professeurs, entre lesquels furent les plus renommés,
pour la langue hébraïque, Agathius, & François Vatable, ausquels fut
adjoint puis après Paul Paradis, juif, de nation; pour la langue grecque,
Pierre Danès & Jacques Tusan; & pour les mathématiques Oronce Finée;
de forte qu'en peu de temps tout de royaume de France se sentit d'un
tel bien: aiant rendu la memoire du roy François premier si recom-
mendable a la postérité à cest esgard, que d'un tacite consentement de
tous le surnom de grand luy en a esté attribué plustost que pour aucun
autre exploict."

[9] DOUMERGUE, E., *Jean Calvin*, I, 141–149.

[10] Thus BENVENUTO CELLINI (*Memoirs*, [Trans. by Miss Macdonell])
expressed his intention to "set out for France . . . to seek another country and better luck," (Bk. I, sec. 94); he mentions a pressing invitation
from Francis I to come to France (Bk. I, sec. 101); he recalls Francis
examining a vase and basin, and saying, "Verily I believe even the ancients never saw such a beautiful piece of work. *For I well remember to
have examined the masterpieces of the best artists in all Italy*" (Italics
mine) (Bk. II, sec. 9.). Cellini remarks that this king had made the
same provision for him as he had done for Leonardo da Vinci (Bk. II,
sec. 12); Francis bestowed on him such honors as calling him by the intimate name of "nom ami" (Bk. II, sec. 19); toward the end Cellini shed
"tears of regret. . . . that I ever had left France," (Bk. II, secs. 75, 90).
Cf. also Bk. II, secs. 15, 25, 37, 39, 41 for further indications of Francis's
enthusiasm for art.

all dialects, an "inepuisable polychronie."[11] Very significant was the promulgation of the famous "ordonnance de
Villers-Cotterets," as a contest against the religious "juris-
dictions" that used Latin. But it had also a social and
literary effect. The language of l' Ile-de-France became
uniformly the official language of the whole kingdom, and
it became the universal language of French literature.[12]

The wars with Italy gave stimulus to letters and art. The
de Valoises had contested the possession of the Duchy of
Milan with some Italian princes. Hence periodically the
Alps had to be crossed. The kings took with them their
nobility. It was for these "barbarians a revelation, and
irresistible enchantment..... They returned conquered by
all the luxury of the vanquished..... Every year toward the
end of the century some three or four hundred young men
went thither, and the Italians reciprocated........ With
Catherine de Medici, who took with her a throng of adven-
turers, the court was entirely Italianized."[13]

Francis I, coming into his kingdom when this fraternizing
of French and Italians was in its youth, himself having
grown up in a court that rang with the tales of Italian greatness, could not but be an enthusiast for Italian learning and
art.[14] This explains his persistent promotion of these
interests in his own country.[15]

11) STROWSKI, F., *Histoire de la nation française*, Tome XIII; *Histoire des lettres, Deuxième volume* [*De Ronsard à nos jours*] par For-
tunat Strowski (Ed., Gabriel Hanotaux [Paris, 1923], p. 1 ff.)
12) STROWSKI, F., *op. cit.*, p. 3, " . . . ailleurs, n'avait-il pas prouvé sa
(the language of l'Ile-de-France) superiorité sur tous les autres dialectes,
en servant à un Calvin, à un Marot, à un Rabelais pour écrire des chefs-
d'oeuvre?" Again, unity of taste followed the unity of language.
Francis I had such a radiance that writers and artists asked no greater
reward than to be approved by him and by the lords and ladies of the
court. "Et quand il mourut, il n'y avait plus en France pour eblouir les
jeux et pour attirer les poètes, que la cour!" *Ibid.*, p. 3 f. On "l' edit
de Villers-Cotterets" see LAVISSE–RAMBEAUD, *op. cit.*, p. 228.
13) STROWSKI, F., *op. cit.*, p. 4. Cf. also RONZY, PIERRE, *Un humaniste
italianisant, Papire Masson (1544–1611)*, Paris, 1924, Book II, chap. I.
"Masson et Hotman: La querelle des Italogalles et des Francogalles."
Masson was the author of Vie de Calvin, a studiously impartial biog-
raphy. The literature on the French invasion of Italy, and its cultural influence, is vast. Any good hand book on French literature discusses it, e. g., LANSON, G., *Histoire de la littérature Française*, 1922,
p. 222; note 1, p. 223 provides a convenient bibliography. See also
CLARK, WM., *Savonarola, His Life and Times*, Chicago, 1891, p. 47 ff.
14) CELLINI, B., *op. cit.*, Bk. II, secs. 9, 12, 19.
15) See also DE BBANTÔME, *Oeuvres complètes*, (Paris, 1838), Tome I,
pp. 243–247: "Il fut appellé Pere et vray restaurateur des arts et des
lettres."

Of no less importance for the cultural history of France is the king's sister Marguerite.[16] She was born April 11, 1492, two years before Francis. Both children were educated by their mother, Louise of Savoy, who was a superior woman, despite her reactionary religious policies in old age. Their father, Charles of Orléans, Count of Angoulême, had died in 1496. Marguerite learned Greek, Latin, and Hebrew, and spoke Italian, Spanish, English, and German well. She early developed a taste for philosophy and poetry. At twelve she was at the court of Louis XII who espoused her to Charles III, Duke of Alençon, whom she married in 1509. In this she submitted to her mother and the king (Louis XII), "but she gave her heart to God, since her husband did not have it," and she adopted as her device "une fleur de souci tournée vers le soleil avec cette legende: Non inferiora secutus."[17] Personally chaste, she was, however, broadminded. With Marguerite and her group the famous French court manners begin.[18] Louis XII had had a Platonic affair with Thomassine Spinola, but Marguerite introduced into the manners of her times "ces alliances toutes spirituelles." She invented the names "de frère et de soeur d'alliance," and thus she stamped her court at Alençon and that of her brother. It is said that the famous Charles de Bourbon had been in love with her, but that she had not reciprocated; yet she had sought to protect him against Louise de Savoye. Her visit to her sick brother at Madrid to negotiate for his release is a celebrated one. To her belongs the credit for the reforms in Bearn with respect to agriculture and jurisprudence.[19] She held court at Pau and Nérac. Here she gathered poets, painters, etc. Clément Marot, the satirical Bonaventure Des Périers, the elegant translator Claude Gruget, Antoine Du Moulin, De la Haye, were there. "She embraced with sympathy the hopes of philosophers

---

[16] Known variously as Marguerite de France, Marguerite de Valois, Marguerite d'Angoulême, Duchess de Berry.

[17] LACROIX, PAUL, "Notice historique sur Marguerite d'Angoulême reine de Navarre," pp. i–xxxvi, in *L'Heptaméron des nouvelles, par Marguerite de Navarre*, (Ed., Paul Lacroix, Paris, 1880).

[18] LACROIX, *op. cit.*, pp. v–vi. "La lecture des anciens romans de chevalerie avait introducit à la cour ces habitudes de tendre et innocente familiarité entre les deux sexes, et leurs relations continuelles créaient des lors cette sociète françoise dont le bon gout et la politesse devaient faire plus tard l'admiration et l'example de L'Europe."

[19] *Ibid.*, pp. xiii–xiv.

like Rabelais, Etienne Dolet, Bonaventure Des Périers, whom one later would call atheists or libertines, and at the same time she was equally enthusiastic over the pious lessons of Roussel, Calvin, LeFèvre......."[20]

The life of Marguerite illustrates the creative character of the times. It was an epoch of beginnings. The excitement attending such new developments is one of their most attractive features. To appreciate the zeal of young Calvin to excel in letters one must see him as the gifted student he was in the midst of the French awakening of the first four decades of the Sixteenth Century. It is hard to conceive that there had been a mighty current of cultural life in the then French kingdom without the patronage of the King and his sister. So significant were the lives of these two royal persons that without them there had perhaps not only been the distinctive French culture of the 16th to the 18th Centuries, but there had been no Calvinism as we know it from the writings of John Calvin and his spiritual heirs.

[NOTE—The literature on Francis I and Marguerite is large. We present the following in addition to the works already cited: LAVISSE-RAMBEAUD, *Histoire Générale* ...., IV, 136ff, 225f., 228; *Catalogue des actes de Francois Ier*, publié par l'Académie des Sciences morales et politiques, 1887-1908, 10 vol.; *Ordonnances des rois de France; règne de Francois Ier;* publiée par id.; *Journal d'un bourgeois de Paris sous la règne de Francois Ier*, 1536, Ed. Bourilly; Bacon, J., *The Life and Times of Francis the First, King of France*, London, 1830; Heubi, W., *Francois I et le mouvement intellectuel en*

---

20) *Ibid.*, p. xv. Cf. also the excellent estimate of Marguerite in ABEL LEFRANC'S *Les dernières poésies de Marguerite de Navarre, publiés pour première fois avec une introduction et des notes*, (Paris, 1896), [Introduction, pp. i–lxxvii]. "Quand on songe que la meme personne, qui a dicté ces considerants empreints d'une tendresse si eclairée a l'egard de l'enfance, a aussi composé l'Heptaméron et les Chansons spirituelles, défendu Rabelais, Marot, Des Périers, LeFèvre, d'Etaples, Dolet, Calvin et les Vaudois, deviné un Amyot ou un Jean Ango, compris une Renée de France et une Vittoria Colonna, gouté un Cellini, un Serlio et un Clouet, protégé les premiers lecteurs en grec et en hebreu, sans parler de tant de hardis imprimeurs et de doux poètes; quand on songe qu'elle a, durant trente ans, pris une part aussi active que salutaire à la politique exterieure d'un des plus grands royaumes de la Chrétienté, suggéré plusieurs des réformes administratives les plus fécondes de règne de François Ier, soutenu et conseillé son frère au fond des prisons de Madrid, et enfin ramené la prosperité economique et une strict justice dans son propre royaume, on comprend qu 'il soit permis d' affirmer qu'il n'y a pas dans toute la Renaissance de figue plus admirable ni de plus digne d'être aimée, et qu'il n' en est aucune qui ait personifié d'une façon complète les aspirations multiples de cette grand époque." (pp. xix–xx.)

*France*, 1913; Saint-Armand, Imbert de, *Women of the Valois Court* (translated from the French by Gilbert Martin), N. Y., 1893, pp. 1-119; Lefranc, A., *Marguerite de Navarre et le platonisme de la renaissance*, in Bibliothèque de l'école des Chartes, 1897, T. LVIII; Genin, F., *Lettres inédites de la Reine de Navarre, Marguerite d'Angoulême*, 1841; Marc-Monnier, *La Renassance de Dante à Luther* (Histoire Général de la littérature moderne), Paris, 1864, p. 451, for the relation of Francis to art, especially Italian, and for Marguerite's dependence on Boccacio.]

## Section 3.  Decadence of the Church

Of significance for the development of Calvin's humanism was the decadence of the church.  Once the nurse of enlightenment in Europe, the church was now too involved in worldly affairs to give attention to the expansion of the mind.  Her attitude, generally speaking, became one of hostility, so that there came to be recognized a party of progressives on the one hand, and a party of backward men on the other.  Thus we have the Reuchlinists over against the theological faculty of Cologne in Germany, and the Fabrian-Budean group over against the Sorbonne (Montaigu particularly) in France.  There was no sharp line between Roman Catholics as such, but there was a definite alienation of the progressive mind from the political-economic mindedness of the hierarchy ruling the church.  The Christian humanist could not help discovering many things in the Scriptures and the fathers to disconcert the clergy.  It was impossible to avoid clashes.  LeFèvre's treatise on the three Marys is a case in point.

Had Calvin not been converted to radical Protestantism he would doubtless have been for life a Roman Catholic of the type of Budé, as LeFèvre, or Erasmus, only less so.  There would have been for him no deep, abundant joy in being loyal to the papal church.  He would have become more and more a humanist.  His religion would all but have perished.  Only the name would have clung like a shadow.  It was in this direction he was heading when he wrote the Commentaries on the *De Clementia*.  The classics, and a scientific study of the fathers were a delightful means of escape from the issue.

Add that such enlightened political Catholics as the Pope

and Francis I had constantly been negotiating about bene-
fices and annates, instead of the moral and spiritual welfare
of the church and realm.[21]   It was very common for the
lower clergy to be involved in moral lapses.   The irresponsi-
bility of bishops to their diocese was notorious, living as
they did in Paris instead of in their parishes.   Even the
monastic discipline had been broken down after notable
reforms by Standonck.

The church presented no fitting career for a man of
Calvin's moral sense and intellectual attainments.   For
example, Loyola had strong moral sense, and remained in
the church to become one of the leading factors in the
Counter-reformation, but he lacked Calvin's training of the
mind.   Critical humanism was not in his armory.   Loyola
would find a place for every pursuit under the roof of the
church, true to the Catholic tradition.   Calvin had learned
that the classics could be studied without appeal to the
church.   In the Commentaries on Seneca he quotes some of
the fathers and pagan authors in the same breath, and he
omits the title of "saint" when speaking of Augustine and
other fathers not only, but also when he refers to the Apostle
Peter.   He voices the desire of the moral humanists of the
century by exhibiting the consolations of a pruned and refined Stoicism for the turbulence of the times. Young Calvin
found truth far beyond the confines of the church, a fact
which lay at the heart of his work as a reformer.

---

[21] RENAUDET, *op. cit.*, p. 577 ff.

# CHAPTER II

## CALVIN AT THE UNIVERSITY OF PARIS

CALVIN spent five years, 1523-1528, at the University of Paris. The purpose was to prepare himself for the priesthood. But never had a lad gone to school with such an aim at a more unpropitious time. The third decade of the Sixteenth Century found the new spirit of humanism making such triumphs in Paris that the old University with its out-dated methods of teaching and its prejudices against real scholarship had become the laughing-stock of the learned world. The students were among the first to appreciate the situation. To be a priest was losing its glamor for them. It was so much more interesting to read Erasmus, Louis de Berquin, and Luther than the scholastics. The name of Guillaume Budé was more potent than a dozen fanatics like Béda. A study of Calvin's first period in Paris will reveal that for a brilliant mind like his humanism had (at least for a time) everything to offer, while a career in the church would appear positively repulsive.

### Section 1.  The Childhood of Calvin

Before taking up Calvin's period at the University of Paris, we must orient ourselves as to his earlier years, for it happens to have been of some importance that he was the son of Gérard Calvin, that he formed connections with certain families of the nobility, that he early received financial aid for study from a chaplaincy, to mention no more.

He was born July 10, 1509, at Noyon in Picardy. The town was very old; an episcopal see since 531, made famous by the coronation there of Charlemagne as joint king of the Franks in 768, and most likely, by the crowning of Hugh, the first of the Capetians, in 987. Ever since the beginning of the Twelfth Century it had been an important ecclesiastical center, dominated by the somber cathedral which had been built in the middle of the Twelfth Century. The town's most important resident was undoubtedly the bishop who was also one of the twelve peers of France by virtue of his position. A certain Charles de Hangest held this office from 1501-25. The de Hangest family was of significance for Calvin, for under them he held ecclesiastical positions which enabled him to attend college. To one of them, Claude, he dedicated his Commentaries on Seneca's *De Clementia,* to pay, as he said, an old debt of gratitude.[1] Three de Hangest boys accompanied him to the University of Paris in 1523. His friendship with this family was a favorable reflection on his character, just as it was of help to him in financing his studies. The fact that his closest friends from boyhood had been related to the bishop of a powerful diocese tended to confirm for a long time his loyalty to the Roman Church. It conditioned his desire to belong rather to the gentleman-ly reform party than to the violent, if more vital, party of reform by Lutheran methods.

Calvin was a true Picard.

> Eager, controversial even to fanaticism, enthusiastic, dogmatic, and persistent, they have fought on all sides of the controversies by which France had been divided; but they have never been lukewarm or indifferent. They are capable of producing men of leadership, and ready to carry principles to logical consequences. A territory that has given birth to Peter the Hermit, the philoso-phers Roscellin and Ramus, and the Revolutionists Desmoulins and Baboeuf, to mention no others, was a land where reformatory ideas of the early 16th century could not fail to find response; and Picardy contributed significant names, besides that of Calvin, to the list of French religious reformers. Le Fèvre, Olivètan, Roussel, and Vatable were among its sons......[2]

Geography cannot account for everything, but certain traits in Calvin were perhaps conditioned by his Picard blood: sensitiveness, pride, directness, logicity, and so forth. His genius certainly cannot be accounted for by it, however. If John Calvin was a genius, his brother Antoine was a very commonplace man. If Calvin became a radical reformer, Le Fèvre, Roussel, and Vatable were mediating types.

John Calvin's father was a respected member of his community. A citizen of Noyon before 1481, he was engaged in professional employment rather than manual

---

[1] Cf. *Opera* V, 6, 7, Preface to Comm.
[2] WALKER, *op. cit.,* p. 21. Cf also LEFRANC, A., *Jeunesse de Calvin,* p. 23 ff.

labor. In this he distinguished himself from his father and brothers. He was skilled in legal and administrative business. By "1481 he had won the position of one of the registrars of the city. To this he added duties of 'solicitor' in the ecclesiastical court, fiscal agent of the country, secretary to the bishop, and attorney of the cathedral chapter, (and) was . . . . by 1497 . . . . . admitted (as) member to the somewhat exclusive bourgeoisie. . . . . ."[3] His mother was reputed to have been a considerable beauty, though her influence on her second eldest son could not have been significant, since she died while he was still young. Altogether substantial people, these Cauvins (Cauvin was the family name), what of father Gérard's rise in the world, his intimacy with the de Hangest family, and so on. The ambitious spirit of Gérard was undoubtedly passed on to his second son Jean. The determination to succeed in whatever he took up was present in the son. And when the first great project, the publication of the Commentaries on the *De Clementia,* failed to make the success he had pictured for it, it was, I believe, a deep wound to his spirit, a spirit long accustomed to success. It may have been one of the factors conditioning his conversion to radical Protestantism.

That his family were of the parvenues, the rising middle class type that were playing for contacts with the great of the land, had its influence on John. His father did not work with his hands. John certainly never did. Contact with the soil and handling of commodities from whose touch a living was to be wrested were unknown to him. If women were to attract him we do not know of it. His marriage was as much a result of having been counselled thereto by Bucer as romanticizings of his own (though it was not an unhappy union). It has been said that such a man could not live as elementally and tensely as most of us do at times. This estimate is absolutely wrong. It is true, of course, that he did not live on planes so common to many, but his plane is that of men whose minds are highly-sensitized mechanisms for dealing with cultural problems. Browning notwithstanding, he found in the Grecian urn not ashes but fire. And if it be objected that he was cold to real life as he met it in his own day, the reply is obvious. For after all he allied

---

[3] WALKER, *op. cit.,* p. 23.

himself with the one vital religious movement of the day at high tide in Germany, a thing to him so vibrant with energy that it revolutionized his life. Calvin was a man in whom culture and religion *could* clash. Most men are too dull for it.

All of which does not imply that he had nothing to do with money. For as a student he made his living somehow. It is well to study this. For one feels that one knows a man better for knowing how he made his living. Father Cauvin did not hesitate to use his "pull" to obtain for his sons such ecclesiastical positions as could be held "in absentia," thus providing the means for study. In fact, young John was given a chaplaincy attached to the altar of La Gésine two months before he attained the proper age of twelve. Of course, a mere child could not discharge the actual duties of office; these were observed by the regular clerics. The office was purely nominal, but it drew for the holder a neat sum, the tax on grain, payable by the farmers of Voienne and Espeville. The officiating clergy received a percentage of this. It was possible to hold more than one such position at the same time. Young Calvin for the space of two years held the chaplaincy of La Gésine along with another, a curacy at St. Martin de Martheville (1527-29). All the fine points of the matter do not interest us at this place. He gave up the chaplaincy on April 30, 1529, to resume it again as late as February 26, 1531. Only after his final break with Rome did he relinquish it forever.

One naturally expects more of a reformer than of an ordinary man. It is not fair, however, to blame Calvin too much for having held these "sinecures" which paid him money. They were used as a form of scholarship aid to students in many cases. For our present purpose it interests us only to note what bearing emoluments of this sort had on his studies. In passing it may be remarked that in addition to the patrimony he inherited he must have saved enough of the money thus received to finance his publication of the *De Clementia* Commentaries. It gave him a certain economic security. I believe that in Calvin's life it was one of the reasons for his plunging so desperately into a study of the classics, after certain contacts with Olivètan and others had inclined him toward the German reform movement. The contention of some writers (Doumergue, Goguel, et al.) is that he was a Protestant already when in 1531 he was writing the Commentaries on Seneca. This has led them to say that this volume is a great Protestant document, even though they admit that it was a sort of under-cover apologetic of the movement against Rome. It is sufficient to answer this by referring them to the fact of Calvin's resumption of the chaplaincy on February 26, 1531, when he certainly had already contemplated the commentaries. Gross dishonesty was not among the vices of this young man. That he was under powerful Protestant influences I believe. However, the solution for this is not so difficult, if we consider that it is altogether human for the greatest of men to suppress forcibly certain feelings, which, though growing upon them with irresistible progression, are distasteful in the extreme. The Protestant religion was distasteful to him, for it was associated with violations of security, and the good breeding which he found in classical pursuits. Protestant meant for him the loss of security not only, nor merely a violation of taste, but also the abandonment of hope of making a name for himself among European humanists among whom Budé and Erasmus were his models. It is about this time, 1530, that he gets his personal touch with Budé, a fact I deduce from his intimacy with the family of Dr. Cop who was very intimate, in turn, with Budé. The latter was bitter in his condemnation of the German religious reformers and those in France who followed them. He called them madmen. He hated above all else their tendency to repudiate the culture of humanism. Under such auspices Calvin lived for some time. What young man with humanistic ability as great as his could resist such an atmosphere! The result is that the Commentaries on Seneca are produced. They are to an extent his gesture of repressing whatever sentiments of teutonic reform were surging in his breast.

Very early Gérard Cauvin gave close attention to the education of his boys. He sent them, we know, to an endowed school popularly known as that of the Capettes. The only significance of this episode for Calvin is that there he fraternized with the young men of the de Hangest, Montmor, and Genlis families. Of far more importance is the fact that at fourteen he was sent to the University of

Paris. Thenceforth, though getting his financial support from his chaplaincy, he would seldom see Noyon. His life interests would be bound up with the schools of Paris, Orléans, and Bourges. Being at Paris meant that he would begin his formal education in the higher studies at the very heart of European orthodoxy. But the ecclesiastical loyalty of the faculty was from the start so belligerent that very early Calvin must have sensed a good deal of stupidity in their opposition to the growing humanistic movement in France. To him it must have seemed the height of sense-lessness to oppose a movement that stood for better latinity, and cultivation of the Greek language. The severe discipline the students were subjected to was calculated also to discourage revolt. Nevertheless it made real students of those who could endure it. The tremendous erudition of his first publication was made possible by habits of unflagging application and concentration.

### Section 2.  At the Collège de la Marche: Cordier

That Calvin's Latin and his French are praised by competent men as pure and vivid must be credited largely to his teacher, Mathurin Cordier. He studied under this man only a few months at best, but the friendly relation set up between master and pupil was to last till death. That he studied under Cordier at all was by sheer good fortune, since for some unknown reason he was transferred from studying under a tutor in his uncle's home to the Collège de la Marche. (In the Dedication to Cordier of his Commentary on I Thessalonians, Calvin speaks of an "inept" preceptor who likely instructed him in his uncle's home in Paris. It is conjectured that his father therefore had him transferred to the Collège de la Marche.[4])

Besides,

> The very year that Calvin entered the Collège de la Marche, M. Cordier did a thing that reveals his character. He had till then taught rhetoric with distinction in the first class. This function would place him in line for the rectorate, but seeing his pupils "formed only for show and swollen with wind, without any solid foundation," he experienced "such an insuperable ennui"

---

4) Cf. LaFranc, *op. cit.*, p. 59.

that he descended "to the fourth class so as not to have always to instruct the pupils over again from bottom to top." Now the fourth class was the one that came immediately after that of the a-b-c's, where one learned to read and write in Latin and French. It is to this unusual devotion that Calvin, entering the fourth class, owes the good fortune of meeting Cordier.[5]

Quicherat calls him "the ideal teacher."[6] He was not only one of the first pedagogues of his time, but the founder of modern pedagogy.[7] Born in 1477 in the Perche, he studied for the priesthood, in which profession he was engaged briefly, however, for he loved better to teach children. Having taught at Rheims, Sainte-Barbe, Lisieux, Navarre, we now find him at the Collège de la Marche. It was said among the grammarians of his time, "Wherever M. Cordier teaches fine letters flourish." Quoting further from Doumergue, "To know what his teaching was, it suffices to hear Cordier in the Preface to the book he published: 'It is often asked, he says, why strangers arriving at the University can so easily converse with the savants, since our young men speak such bad Latin. Among themselves they always prattle in French (Gallice semper garriunt). It is the fault of the masters, of their negligence......'[8] Cordier deplores also the lack of the Masters' interest in the spiritual welfare of the child. He says that at best "they prefer a lettered child who writes well to an upright child who lives well. What gymnasiarch places charity before gain?" Again, he protests against the excessive punishments inflicted on the pupils. "These daily and assiduous flagellations turn honest young people so much from their studies that they hate the schools more than the bite of a dog or serpent, and they think they live in a galley or a prison."

Calvin studied under a man of such culture for three months. It was not only the general influence of Cordier's spirit that affected the young man, however; he also received from him in large measure something that was to be one of his greatest assets, his style.

---

[5] DOUMERGUE, op. cit., p. 59.
[6] Histoire de Sainte-Barbe (1860), I, p. 152.
[7] DOUMERGUE, op. cit., p. 59.
[8] Ibid., p. 60.

It is this way: Language was passing through a terrible crisis. Latin became more and more a dead language, and the scholars treated it with a growing scorn. But the French freed itself with difficulty. To a bad Latin corresponded a French that was not very good. Olivètan..... has said that 'for the most part the French is drawn from Latin, and often a corrupted Latin at that.' He added 'the French language is a barbarity......' And it was not only the language of the kitchen; everywhere the most detestable macaronic style was enthroned. To cap it all, those who fled ridicule for this evil fell into another. Under the pretext of using only French words they used only Frenchized Latin words...... Such was the state of the French language when Calvin studied at the Collège de la Marche. The great reform of Cordier was to separate the French from the Latin...... And naturally this reform was very useful to the French,—the more so as Cordier managed this language like a master, with a penetrating charm.[9]

That Calvin learned this well is seen in the fact that he was both an excellent latinist and a writer of an elegant and constantly improving French. That he never forgot Cordier we know not only from the life-long friendship between them, but also from the hearty appreciation he expresses for his old master's instruction in Paris, recorded when he published his Commentary on I Thessalonians, the Epistle Dedicatory of which is addressed to Mathurin Cordier.[10]

### Section 3.  At the Collège de Montaigu: Standonck, Béda

After about three months of study under the delightful Mathurin Cordier, Calvin was transferred to the Collège de Montaigu. Just why this had to be can only be conjectured. Perhaps his chaplaincy of the Altar of La Gésine in Noyon

---

9) DOUMERGUE, *op. cit.*, pp. 65, 66.

10) q. v. Calvin remembers Cordier's moving from the first to the fourth class. "And this (my appreciation) I was so desirous to testify to posterity, that if any advantage shall accrue to them from my writings, they shall know that it has in some degree originated with you"; cf. also LAUNOY, *Regii Navarrae gymnasii Parisiensis historia*, who lists the works of Cordier; LEFRANC, A., *op. cit.*, p. 59 ff., 60 and note; *Cyclopedia of Education*, (Editor, Paul Monroe, New York, 1915) "Maturinus Corderius," which says that Cordier's Colloquies were as popular as the Colloquies of Erasmus; QUICHERAT, *Histoire de Ste. Barbe*, I, 76, 152, 201 f.; *Bulletin* XXIV, 565, for list of his works, and for numerous references to him see General Index of *Bulletin*.

had something to do with it. Receiving financial support therefrom, the Cathedral officials may have ordered him to attend a college of more strictly ecclesiastical character.[11] Had they scoured the whole world they had not been able to find one quite so strict as the Collège de Montaigu. It was notoriously disagreeable. The somber picture Rabelais has drawn of it in the *Gargantua* is verified by historical documents. "Collège de pouillerie," he called it, adding, "If I were king of Paris, the devil take me if I should not set fire to it, and burn the principal and regents who endure such inhumanity before their very eyes."[12]

The head of this college was Noel Beda, one of those men who should never have been entrusted with so important a position. Ambition in him was matched by a sincere narrowness of mind. The persecutor of Lefèvre, he had already proved himself the first heresy-hunter of the time. Reactionary of the most obnoxious kind, he at one time, however, had collaborated with Standonck, a reformer of stern character but also of considerable idealism and saintliness.

To know the Collège de Montaigu one must have an acquaintance with John Standonck.[13] He was born in the middle of the Fifteenth Century at Malines of poor and pious parents, and brought up in a "milieu sacerdotal et monastique." At an early age he repaired to Gouda where the Brethren of the Common Life had offered him a scholarship. There he came completely under the influence of the Brethren, the first of whom Gerard Groote had gathered about him in 1376. They practiced a simple and hearty piety, and shunned scholasticism and theology, opposing the thomistic realism. (Groote had studied at Paris under disciples of Occam.) This attitude was reflected in the *Imitation of Christ* which made famous the name of Thomas à Kempis. Abandoning the abstract intellectualism of the scholastics they turned to the Bible (chiefly the New Testament), and to Augustine and Bernard as their favorite

---

11) LEFRANC, *op. cit.*, p. 64 f.

12) Cf. RENAUDET, A., Jean Standonck, un réformateur Catholique avant la Réforme," *Bulletin* LVII, 80; also FAIRBAIRN, A. M., Calvin and the Reformed Church," *Cambridge Modern History*, II, xi, 250 f.

13) The briefest and best account is found in RENAUDET, A., *Bulletin*, LVII, pp. 5–81.

fathers. They almost devoured the mystics, particularly the German. From the first they opened schools, inviting poor children to an education. They loved books. They read Virgil, Ovid, Horace, Cicero, Seneca. But Medieval methods of instruction prevailed; e. g. logic was taught to children barely out of their infancy. A cloistral discipline was imposed on the pupils, even the smallest being forbidden to run and jump, and abundant corporal punishment was administered. (The rules laid on Montaigu had a precedent.) Standouck soon rose to eminence as a grammarian at Gouda. He wrote a rude Latin, remained ignorant of Greek, and was unmoved by the ancient poets. But he read the Bible, the fathers, and the mystics (especially à Kempis). The work of John Busch, a monastic reformer (1428 *seq.*) made a deep impression on him. The seeds for effecting a general reform, beginning with the monasteries, and by imposing a monastic rule on the schools, had fallen in a ready heart.

Calvin certainly did not get his enthusiasm for the classics from the Standonian tradition. If the Brethren of the Common Life read Virgil, Seneca, et al., Standonck was not interested in promoting their popularity at Montaigu. His stay at Paris was to make of him a reactionary. After all he was the teacher of Béda, though the latter lacked every mark of his master's greatness. When he came to Paris in 1471, he found there Guillaume Fichet,[14] an enthusiastic platonist and humanist, who got permission from the Sorbonne to place on its grounds the first German press. He was succeeded in 1472 by Robert Gaguin.[15] Reuchlin (1473) found pupils of Gregorio de Città di Castellio to instruct him in the elements of Greek. Pagan culture and letters were coming into favor in Paris. Confidence in the human spirit grew. Nominalism was popular. All this did not affect Standonck. When in 1474 the Bishop of Avranches got a commission to effect an order that only Thomas, Albertus Magnus, et al., were to be taught, Standonck acquiesced. He threw himself into preaching against lay and clerical corruption. His appointment as regent of the Collège de Montaigu in 1483 did not abate his zeal. He

[14] TILLEY, A., *The Dawn of the French Renaissance*, p. 86 f.
[15] *Ibid.*, pp. 185–211.

acquired a fluent use of the French. Despite his long association with the Brethren of the Common Life in the Netherlands, he became a rigorist in doctrine. When Jean Laillier, a student at the University, publicly defended certain theses of Wycliffe, and when the Sorbonne condemned him, Standonck sided with them. He developed a fanaticism later reflected in Béda. This gives us reason to think that Calvin owed none of his classical fire to Standonck.

Still, the memory of Standonck, the saint, died hard. His close association with François de Paule (1493) left an indelible impression on him. It effected an entire dedication to asceticism in his life. More than anything else did this prove to give to Montaigu its standing with the masses. And Béda's intimacy with Standonck, the saint, gave him an almost boundless popular authority.

In 1493 Standonck presented his famous Articles on the reformation of the church. Through Admiral de Gravèl Charles VIII had been interested in reform, and at Tours there was held a great convention of clergy with representatives of the Court. The proposals were radical, but fell short of a general Catholic counsel on the plan of Basel (which plan was not displeasing to the Sorbonne, and had frequently been suggested and pressed during the Fifteenth Century). But Standonck was no theorist. He set about to reform the education of the clergy, and he began with Montaigu. First, he imposed a most rigorous discipline, including the merciless beatings he had observed at Gouda, though it must be observed that he acquired considerable more room to house the poor students. Next, he called from Holland certain teachers from among the Brethren. Then he undertook to spread his reform to the oldest monastery in Paris, that of St. Victor. This ended in failure, despite the fact that so enlightened a man as Corneille Girard, a friend of Erasmus, was one of the "missionaries." At this time Erasmus spent the fall and winter at Montaigu, but left in disgust with its rigors.

In 1499 came Standonck's exile. Charles VIII had died, and was succeeded by Louis XII, a man less favorable to reform. The contest with Briçonnet and the royal divorce occasioned the banishment. In exile he succeeded in getting funds to found four colleges on the plan of Montaigu:

Cambrai, Malines, Louvain, and Valenciennes. In 1500 he
was recalled to Paris by order of the king.

He now received permission to advocate his reforms
generally. He pressed on with his program at Montaigu.
Not forgetting entirely his training under the Brethren, he
furnished the students with all the books they needed,
especially those of the mystics. It is almost certain that
Calvin got an early acquaintance with à Kempis, for the
fundamental ideas of the Brethren of the Common Life are
not strange to the Calvinism expressed already in 1535.[16]
Certainly his favorite fathers are Augustine and Bernard.
While therefore, in short, the Collège de Montaigu under
Pierre Tempête and Noel Béda was a horrible place to spend
five years as a student, there were sweetening influences, a
subtler Standonian spirit, which would tend to produce in
him a religious power and enlightenment, once his classical
fever of reaction against a senseless regimen had passed.[17]

The death of Standonck in 1504 left Montaigu leaderless
in more than an official sense. It was difficult to choose a
successor. Of all possible candidates Béda appeared to be
the most likely to be worthy of the great master.

Noel Béda became "Père des Pauvres et Principal de
Montaigu" February 10, 1504. The trustees confirmed his
appointment with some distaste. But his close association
with Standonck had won him general esteem. Besides, the
well-known de Graville chose him for confessor and continued to endow the school, as many others did.[18] The
college grew in numbers. In 1510 there were about five
hundred twenty-five students and teachers. Some of the
professors were famous, for example, John Mair, David
Cranston, Guillaume Chéron, an unnamed Spanish professor of logic, and Antonio Coronel.[19] Into this group Béda
injected an apostolic zeal for regenerating the church. But

---

[16] HYMA, A., *Devotio Moderna, or The Chritsian Renaissance*, Chapter VII.

[17] The humanists have not been kind to Standonck, in a way deserv-
edly so. Cf. *Erasmi Opera*, I, 806: Ἰχθυοφαγία; RABELAIS, *La Vie de
Gargantua et de Pantagruel*, I, 38. For good accounts of Standonck cf.
besides RENAUDET, *op. cit.*, RENAUDET, A., *Préréforme et Humanisme à
Paris*, pp. 172–183; GODET, M., *La Congregation de Montaigu*, chaps.
I–IV; HYMA, A., *op. cit.*, chap. VII.

[18] GODET, M., *op. cit.*, p. 60 f.

[19] *Ibid.*, p. 60.

it was impossible to achieve the desired results. For the school was getting so rich as to become corrupted. The regimen of piety was there, but the spiritual power was lacking.[20] Decadence was now rapid. By 1509 Béda had dissolved the superiority of Montaigu over the "subaltern" houses. Again, the too strict asceticism broke the students' bodies as well as their minds and spirits. Add to this the general disrepute into which the school fell. It was bad enough to feed on rotten eggs, spoiled vegetables, bad cider ("gasté et pourry"), to see some of the students "perish with despair" and fall ill or die under blows, but the boys also found themselves ridiculed heartily by the humanists of the age.[21]

Pierre Tempête succeeds Béda in 1514 as Père of the college, a man whom Rabelais called "horrida tempestas," and immortalized in the *Pantagruel* as that "grand fouetteur d'enfants."[22] It was during this man's reign that Calvin studied there, and he resigned the very year Calvin left for Orléans (1528). Béda was all the while connected with the college, but loosely, for he was involved as Syndic of the University in the theological controversies coming to the fore. He was harrassing Lefèvre, Erasmus, de Berquin.[23]

The humanistic ridicule of his Alma Mater must have exercised an influence on Calvin that the records by their silence do not acknowledge. It was one of those subtle things that may be ignored for a time, but never escaped in the long run. True, the *Gargantua* did not appear till the early thirties, but there had been the *Colloquies* of Erasmus, and Erasmus must have been known to every Parisian in this decade. But more insidious than literature is conversation. The enlightened men with whom more and more Calvin contacted held the Collège de Montaigu in light esteem. It is therefore profitable for us to call the roll of his friends during these first five years in Paris.

---

[20] *Ibid.*, p. 62.

[21] See above for literature; also GODET, M., Le Collège de Montaigu," in *Revue des Études Rabelaissiennes*, VII.

[22] RABELAIS, *op. cit.*, chap. iv; GODET, M., *La Congregation* . . . , p. 66 f.

[23] DOUEN, O., "La Réforme Française: est-elle la fille de la réforme allemande? *Bulletin*, XLI, 57–92, esp. 72 ff.

## Section 4.  Contacts at Paris 1523–28

The records yield very little information about Calvin's contacts while at the Collège de Montaigu. Only one of his teachers is referred to, the unnamed Spanish professor of logic. It is said that he afterwards attained some reputation in medicine, and while at Montaigu was drawn to Calvin to such an extent as to accept him as a personal friend. This man must have counteracted the disagreeableness of the school for Calvin, and must have been one of the factors in the opening of his mind.

The circumstance that the University of Paris encouraged students to associate with the men from their own nation or province brought about intimate contact for Calvin with the "nation of Picardy." By this means Lefèvre had met and befriended Gérard Roussel, Vatable, and others. So we know that Calvin associated with the Montmor boys, Joachim, Yves, and Claude. But there was also his cousin Pierre Robert, better known as Olivétan, who was to exert on him a major influence in favor of Protestantism. A man of enlightened mind, he was also to be one of the molders of modern French through his translation of the Scriptures into the vernacular. He had not a little to do with the reformation that took place in Noyon before Calvin's conversion, a movement of which the conflict of Charles Cauvin (John's brother) and perhaps that of his father with the church were symptoms. It is not the place here to discuss his influence on the conversion of Calvin. Their meeting in Paris at this time interests us only as one of the causes contributing to Calvin's escape from the dogmatic slumbers and the anti-cultural spirit of Montaigu, and perhaps had something to do with the formation of his literary taste. An inventory of Olivétan's library, made by M. Reuss, shows that his taste in literary matters was most varied. Rabelais and Alain Chartier figure among his favorite authors, besides Homer, Hesiod, and Chrysostom.[24]

Another man from Noyon was Fourcy de Cambrai, doctor in theology, vicar general of the diocese, who had at first been regent of philosophy at the Collège de Sainte-Barbe, then rector of the University of Paris in 1510—a man of

---

[24] LEFRANC, *op. cit.*, 102, n. 1.

great influence in the faculty. He certainly introduced his young compatriot to his friends. Even as late as 1530, after the rupture of the Cauvins with the church had begun, he was on intimate terms with the family, and at the trial of Charles Cauvin he was called as "commissaire délégué."[25]

There was inscribed as student at the University a young man called Nicholas Durand, better known as Villegagnon, who later became a famous Protestant, a man with an unusually adventurous spirit. At this time he studied at the expense of his uncle, a canon of Noyon.[26] He was to be a figure in the Reformation in France not only, but the first to found a Protestant group in Algeria.[27] In 1555 he served under Coligny and founded in Brazil a colony of Protestants, a venture he discussed with Calvin. He later slew the Protestant members of the expedition, and returned to Catholicism.[28]

There was also Pierre Billory, and the famous Antoine de Monchy who is better known as Démocharès. It is worth giving Lefranc's note on this man in full:

> Born at Ressons-sur Metz, in the diocese of Noyon, 1514, he studied at Saint-Barbe, under Gélida. Rector of the University of Paris in 1539, he became doctor of theology the following year. It is largely due to him that the Catholics triumphed at Noyon over the Protestant clan. Before having become so thoroughly orthodox, he had set himself up as an irreconcilable adversary of scholasticism. He called the professors of the old school "fellows who retail smoke at a farthing and a half a portion, worshippers of silliness and error, opinionated adepts of the Spanish strategy, who cease not to conspire against progress, who appear to have devoted themselves to the infernal gods, etc." One may see that before taking the well-known rôle he played at Trente, Démocharès changed his opinions. But when Calvin knew him in the years now occupying our attention he still defended the cause of liberty.[29]

Besides, there was the family of Dr. Guillaume Cop, first physician of King Francis I, and professor of medicine at

---

25) LEFRANC, *op. cit.*, p. 69 f.
26) LEFRANC, *op. cit.*, p. 68.
27) PANNIER, J., "Les Protestants françaises et l'Algerie," *Bulletin* LXXIX, 146 ff.
28) LEFRANC, *op. cit.*, p. 68, n. 1.
29) *Op. cit.*, p. 69, n. 1.

the University. Called to this position from Basel by the king himself, he occupied a place of unusual importance. Young Calvin was definitely affected by this man and his family. First of all because Cop had three sons with whom Calvin was very intimate, particularly with Nicholas whose rectoral address, 1533, he was to write or revise (as the case may be). Through his close friendship with the sons he must frequently have met the father, and must often have been a guest in the Cop home. Now Dr. Cop was not only famous as a physician, but almost as much so for his interest in letters. As a result he was in close contact with the great literary lights of the day. He was a personal friend of Guillaume Budé who was soon to be one of the model humanists in Calvin's eyes, a man whose name must have been a household word in the Cop family, and whose person must often have been present there. It is almost unthinkable that Calvin should not have met him face to face. It was in this home also that the name of Erasmus was frequently mentioned. Cop was designated to correspond with him concerning his proposed coming to Paris to help found the Lecteurs Royaux, and this hoped-for institution of which Calvin was to be one of the early students was one of the daily subjects of conversation in this household.

Through the Cop family he must have known the botanist Ruel of Soissons, and his own compatriot Jean Fernel of Montdidier, who came to Paris the same year Calvin did, 1523.

> Of universal spirit, embracing at the same time astronomy, mathematics, and medicine, he was able to make discoveries and make innovations in these three branches of science. So besides having been one of the first to measure a degree of the meridian, he also merited being called "the creator of pathology." His career was very rapid: a bachelor in 1526, he began to teach already when Calvin left Paris (1528).[30]

Nicholas Bérault was also well-known as a scholar, and in this epoch was associated with Budé's circle of humanists. In 1521 he had published a Greek and Latin dictionary, in 1528 *Oratio de pace*, and in 1532 *De jurisprudentia vetere a*

---

[30] LEFRANC, *op cit.*, p. 68.

*novitia,* besides *Metaphrasin in Oeconomicon Aristotelis.*[31]

It is worthy of remark that among the men with whom Calvin formed social connections there appears to be none that can at this time be called a reactionary. They are of the progressive type. They are scientists and men of letters. The humanist in him had every early advantage.

### Section 5.   La Farce des Théolgastres

Contacts with men only do not account for the development of Calvin during these five formative years at the University of Paris. As has been intimated, Béda and the Sorbonne were in hot pursuit of the new religious ideas and the men promoting them. It has been observed by several that the connection between Humanism and Protestantism was very close. There is reason to suppose that Reformation and Humanism were more closely associated in France than Germany where the reform was certainly more popular, and far less restricted to the educated class as was the case in France. The *Bibliotheca Lindesiana*[32] presents the names of at least seventy-five printers in Germany in the 1520's who were printing Protestant tracts and books. By the end of 1523 Luther alone had no less than three hundred thirty works in print. Ten years later he had over five hundred on the market. It was said that "every sermon or speech he made was immediately printed."[33]   Besides, most of these were in the vernacular. Contrast this with the situation in France. Lefèvre, the father of the French Reformation, appealed after all to a limited circle of readers. His Commentaries (Psalms, 1509; Epistles of Paul, 1512; and the Gospels, 1522) were heavy folios written in Latin, intended for savants. We know only of his translation of the New Testament and the Psalms (1523-25) and his Epistles and Gospels for the fifty-two weeks of the year (1525), or familiar explanations of the ecclesiastical peri-

---

31) DE BUDÉ, *Vie de Budé,* p. 220; DELARUELLE, L., "Études sur l' humanisme française: Nicole Bérault.   Notes biographiques suivies d' un appendice sur plusiers de ses publications" in *Museé Belge,* Tome XIII (1909) 253–311.

32) *Bibl. Lind.*—Collection and Notes.   No. 7: Catalogue of a Collection of 1500 Tracts by Martin Luther and his Contemporaries, 1511–1598.

33) *Ibid.,* Introduction.

copes which had been able to attract the public that knew only French.[34]

Thus it is that the Latin writings of Luther were known first of all to the learned in France. Luther notes that his treatises please Paris and are read by the Sorbonne.[35] And Tschudi writes that "the writings of Luther are received with open arms by the entire army of savants, even by those who relish the least praiseworthy."[36] No books were bought with greater eagerness. We know that Budé praised Luther until 1521, and Erasmus, even after his rupture with Luther (1525) is said to have loved the *Tesseradecae Consolatoria pro Laborantibus et Oneratis* (written 1521).[37]

The growing rift between Erasmus and Budé and between the Protestant reformers could not take away that they had more in common than they had with the Sorbonne and its like. Young Calvin must have felt this as time went on. Surely, he did not wish to acknowledge it until his conversion. He wanted no break with the status quo till then. In the meantime the course of events could work its own lessons into his spirit. Leaving aside all that happened before he arrived in Paris (1523), omitting the fascinating story of Briçonnet and his wonderful group of reforming spirits in his diocese of Meaux, passing by even the persecution of Lefèvre (which must have come to Calvin's astonished attention very early), leaving out also at this point all but a mere mention of Marguerite d'Angoulême whose protection of Lefèvre, de Berquin, and others, was well-known, and whose *Dialogue en forme de vision nocturne* appeared in 1524,[38] I shall note only the fortunes of that dramatic propagandist of Lutheranism, Louis de Berquin, whose

[34] WEISS, N., "Notes sur les traités de Luther traduits en français et imprimés en France entre 1525 et 1534: La Littérature de la Réforme française," Art. I, *Bulletin* XXXVI, 664 ff.; also PANNIER, J., "Les Origines françaises du Protestantisme français," *Bulletin* (July–Sept., 1928), pp. 209 ff.; PIPER, OTTO, Vom französischen Protestantismus, *Zeitwende* (März, 1930), pp. 251 f.

[35] HERMINJARD, *Correspondance des Réformateurs* . . . , I, 48.

[36] *Ibid.*, p. 47.

[37] *Bulletin*, XXXVI, 670 f.

[38] Cf. LEFRANC, A., "Idées religieuses de Marguerite de Navarre," *Bulletin* XLVI, 7 ff., 72 ff., 137 ff., 295 ff., 418 ff.; XLVII, 69 ff., 115 ff.; PANNIER, J., "Recherches sur la formation intellectuelle de Calvin," *Revue d'Histoire et de Philosophie Religieuse* (May–June, 1930), 264 ff.

activities are at their peak in the very years that Calvin spent in Paris.

It is the year 1523. Young Calvin had just arrived from Noyon. De Berquin had translated something of Luther into the French. Thoroughly ill at ease the Sorbonne had accused him before the Parlement. His books and papers[39] had been seized, examined, condemned. He was locked up in the Square Tour of the Palace. At the moment when the sentence of death is expected, the Court intervenes. He is freed August 8, 1523.

The University students, elated over this, and more zealous than prudent, celebrate the occasion. They do so by staging "La Farce des théologastres."[40] The story of the play is evidence of the fact that by 1523 the name of Luther was generally known in Paris, and that it was associated with the progressive group over against the Nachtschule of the Sorbonne. Now since the Thirteenth Century the so-called morality plays had been presented on the stage. Out of twenty-one collected by M. Picot only one was found to have been written by an out and out loyal Catholic. The "Farce des théologastres" was one in line with the tradition of *l'ancien théâtre français* therefore. It was written by a friend of de Berquin. The title speaks for itself. The play itself heckles the reactionary spirit of the Sorbonne and the Collège de Montaigu. There are six characters: Théologastres, Fratrez, Foy, Raison, Le Texte de Saincte Escripture, Le Mercure d'Allemagne. Louis de Berquin is identified with the last, the messenger from Germany.

After lamentations about the "mal Sorbonique" it is suggested that Raison be summoned to provide a remedy. But the theologizers do not know where Reason is to be found, and ask:

"Ou est ce?   En la grande Bretaigne?"

To which Foy replies:

"Nennin, non.   C'est en Allemagne (Germany),
  Ou elle fait sa residence."

---

39) For a full account of these cf. Longueval, Fontenay, Brunooy et Berthier, *Histoire de l'Église Gallicane*, Tome XXII, (4th Ed., 1827), 129 ff.

40) *Bulletin* XXXVI, 169 ff., 225 ff., 337 ff. Series on "Les Moralistés polemiques ou la controvers religieuse dans l'ancien théâtre français," by Émile Picot.

The Théologastres and the Fratrez understand the reference to Luther and recoil with fright. They do not see what can be done. Then Foy suggests calling La Texte de Saincte Escripture. The latter appears on the stage, bruised and bloody, bewailing the times and praising the zeal of the Interpreter from Germany. Who is this Interpreter?

"Le seigneur de Berquin..... !"

De Berquin enters as Mercure d'Allemagne. He announces:

"Je suis Berquin."

The Fratrez ask:

"Lutherien?"

Berquin:

"Nennin, non, je suis Chrestien,
Je ne suis point (ung) Sorboniste,
Halcotiste, ni Bricotiste....."

Théologastres:

"Erasme et toy,
Fabri (Lefèvre), Luther, en bonne foy,
N'estes que garçons heretiques."

Mercure (Berquin) rejects the word and does not wish to equivocate:

"Ne cuydés point icy jeugler
Comme Béda, qui proposoit
Que ung lure condamné avoit
Lequel jamais il n'avait vue."

Certainly this "farce" is evidence of the drift of opinion among the students, and in a way of the people of Paris. Calvin could not escape the pressure of such mass opinion in the direction of liberty.[41]

### Section 6. What Did Calvin Read in Paris?

The question of what young Calvin read in these years is very important. Omniverous reader, gifted with a prodigious memory and with a keen sense of what was worthwhile, he must have been mightily affected by the things he read.

It is understood that he applied himself to the formal studies of the college. But these interest us little compared

---

[41] Cf. also PANNIER, J., *op. cit.*, 279 ff., 283.

with the literature he devoured on the side. His likely contact with the writings of the Brethren of the Common Life has been touched on already.

There can be no doubt that he continued to keep touch with Mathurin Cordier, his first great master, who was capable of being an excellent adviser in the matter of reading. Again, by his fortunate associations with the family of Dr. Cop and with the members of the Picard nation, he must have read things of a scientific and literary character. There is no trace of likelihood that he applied himself to inferior literature.

A discussion of the literary influences he underwent in this epoch were entirely inadequate if we should neglect to point to the fact that the subject of books was given more attention just now than ever before in the history of Paris. The city was book-minded. It began in earnest when, two years before Calvin's arrival, the Sobronne had been given absolute authority to censure all printed works and to forbid the printing of all that had not received their approval. This faculty had ever since engaged in a hot campaign against proscribed books.

The most frequently discussed group of progressive men was that which Bishop Briçonnet had gathered about him at Meaux, very near Paris. Desiring to reform his diocese, and loving the company of men of letters and learned in languages, he invited from the University of Paris a number of such men and gave them positions of influence. So there were Lefèvre, Farel, Gérard Roussel, and François Vatable. Lefèvre and Vatable were particularly important as humanists. While the latter came into no conflict with the authorities, Calvin's choosing him as a teacher when the Lecteurs Royaux were established may indicate an earlier acquaintance. Lefèvre must have been known to him through his writings. There is no direct evidence of this, but the fame he had got from the Sorbonne's persecution for his writing on the three women of the Gospels[42] would have led any

---

[42] In 1517 Lefèvre published a work in which he showed that Mary Magdalene, Mary the sister of Lazarus, and the sinner of John vii were three persons. It is strange, by the way, that the last work caused him to be persecuted, while the more profound heresies of the work on the Pauline letters (1512) were not noticed till later. Cf. Weiss, N., "Paris et la réforme sous François Ier," *Bulletin* XLIII, 245 ff.; also Doumergue, *op cit.*, 91 f.

live student to peruse his works. He was certainly proficient enough by 1525 to handle Lefèvre's Latin as well as his French. The books of Luther were cherished by this group, that is, after 1521 at least.[43] This reform of Briçonnet threatened in the space of two short years to Protestantize the whole diocese. Hence in March, 1523, a Council of the Diocese held in Paris, condemned certain books there found: Two books against clerical celibacy (one of them by Carlstadt of Wittenberg), all the books not approved by the Sorbonne,—which were ordered taken out of the libraries and brought to the officials by whom they were burned. Among these were books by Luther and Melanchton. They had been avidly read and circulated. This was shortly before Calvin arrived. Forbidden fruit, they found appetites whetted the more. When Calvin came to the city he heard everybody talking about the men from Briçonnet's diocese and the confiscated books.

In October of 1523 more books were confiscated. This time that fine young humanist collaborating with Luther in Germany, namely, Melanchton, got the spotlight alone. If Calvin had perhaps not paid particular attention to him before, now this spirit, so congenial to his own in later years, was to hold his attention no doubt. Of course, Calvin was but a lad of fourteen years, but he was an unusual one. The following books of Melanchton were declared contraband: Loci Communes, Commentaries on Romans and I and II Corinthians, Brief Declarations Concerning the Doctrines of St. Paul, The Invectives against the Decrees of the Theologians of Paris, and the Letter of the Dispute at Leipzig. It was generally agreed that Melanchton's works were more dangerous than Luther's because their style was more fascinating and persuasive.[44]

Let us return to de Berquin once more. Immediately after the Council of Paris certain officers made their rounds of inspection of the libraries, during which they were informed of a certain gentleman by the name of Berquin (of Artois) who had suspected books in his private library. Accordingly these were confiscated and on May 13th ordered to be sent to the Paris Faculty for examination. It was found that he

---

[43] *Hist. de l'Eglise Gall.*, **XXII**, 121–26.
[44] *Ibid.*, p. 127–129.

had three classes of books: First, books by de Berquin himself on diverse matters of religion. They were discovered to contain several dangerous propositions favorable to Lutheranism. Secondly, translations of Latin works which were judged scandalous and schismatic: There were translations of writings relating the reasons why Luther had burned the Decretals and the Canon Law, books entitled "La Tyrade Romaque," "La Paradise du Pape Julius," and "La Catholique du pape et de Moïse." Thirdly, there were copies of the Babylonian Captivity, Concerning the Abolition of the Mass, Concerning the Refutation of the King of England, Concerning the Exposition of the Lord's Prayer, the Loci Communes, the Expositions of Luther, of Melanchton, and of Carlstadt. The whole library contained only two "harmless books."[45]

Unlikely as it is that Calvin should not have read some of these writings, it is beyond doubt that, if he had not, the discussions revolving about them must have surrounded him daily. The names of Luther and Melanchton were not the only ones heard. Erasmus and Reuchlin were praised by the German reformers, and they were all associated with each other in the mind of people generally. It will be recalled that Luther, Erasmus, and Lefèvre were coupled in the "Farce des théologatres." Calvin entered Paris under auspices which gave the intensest publicity to progressive thought.

That same year Noel Béda indicted Jaques Merlin, a famous cleric and scholar who wrote a book explaining Origen and setting him in a favorable light. Again, the charges brought by the Faculty against one of its own doctors, Arnould de Barnosse, for holding quasi Lutheran opinions, were an event. Add that the king's mother requested the Sorbonne to check the heresy, which she claimed was even invading the Court. The reply, presented two weeks later, this same year, took the form of a censure of a large number of propositions against Lutheranism.[46]

The next year some anonymous writers published a satire: Judgment of the Faculty of Theology of Paris on

---

45) *Ibid.,* 129–33.
46) *Ibid.,* 137–41.

Certain Propositions. The Faculty replied with 35 counter propositions.[47]

Again, in 1524, the famous Josse Clichtowe published his Anti-Luther, a work which betrays the large influence of Luther in France. The first of the book's three parts is directed against Luther's "pretended" Christian and evangelical liberty, showing that his tract on this subject had been at work in the country.

The same year another significant book was put forth. It was written by none less than Marguerite of Navarre, sister of Francis I. She called it *Dialogue en forme de vision nocturne*,[48] a poem revealing that the author was in the van of the most progressive religious thought of her country. Marguerite had been a prominent defender of the Briçonnet circle, and though she was never to leave the Catholic fold, she would always remain a protagonist of enlightenment (as her part in the establishment of the Lecteurs Royaux proved.). Written in French the *Dialogue* was accessible to young Calvin. It is unlikely that he had not seen it at an early date. Progressive ideas thus got standing to his mind, not only by the royal protection of Lefèvre and de Berquin, but by literature emanating from high places in the Court.

Again do we meet with Louis de Berquin. It is the year 1526, and once more is his library rifled. Incorrigible, he had collected a new stock of books, and on March 7th they are condemned by the Sorbonne. It is interesting to learn how de Berquin worked. The censurable opinions which he had written he did not, as a rule, collect in a single volume over his own name. They were set down as notes in the margin or at the foot of the pages of certain works of Luther or even of Catholic authors. Therefore even Catholic works in his library were ordered destroyed. The Faculty, furthermore, attacked the other works of this author, to-wit: a letter to a friend in which he justified his position (i. e., his Lutheran sentiments); a translation of the letter of St. Jerome against Vigilantius (it contained a censurable pas-

---

[47] *Ibid.*, p. 151.
[48] Cf. PANNIER, J., *op. cit.*, p. 264 ff. Pannier discusses the *Dialogue* as one of the factors in the intellectual formation of Calvin. LEFRANC, A., "Idées religieuses de Marguerite de Navarre," *Bulletin* XLVI, XLVII, containing a number of articles presenting in detail the significance of all Marguerite's poetry.

sage); and a translation of some of Erasmus' writings. There were also works whose titles were sufficient to condemn them. These were: a collection of passages of Scripture, chosen and put together in the form of a concordance; a commentary of François Lambert d'Avignon on the rule of the Friars Minor; a compilation of the sentiments of Luther, Carlstadt, and Melanchton added to a book in defense of the seven sacraments against Luther(!); a book of prayers and meditations containing Luther's Christian Liberty (!); another of Luther which does not name the author; a packet entitled "La Passion de Luther"; one which was called "Les Travaux de Luther sur les Paumes"; another, "Des Grands Actions de Luther"; and last, not least, a copy of "Defender of the Peace" by Marsilius of Padua![49]

A marvelous collection, the most representative Luther library in France no doubt. Once more the Sorbonne invited the attention of students and citizens to Luther. Again the Faculty caused Erasmus, this time by de Berquin's translations, to step into the lime-light. People were, it appears, not permitted to forget. And let it be remembered: in this confiscated library was the *Defensor Pacis* of Marsilius of Padua! It was one of those condemned by the Sorbonne, this arresting volume, a precious forbidden book that invited perusal anew! Strange irony, the very faculty

---

49) *Hist. de l'Eglise Gall.*, XXII, 250 ff.; cf. also D'Argentré (Carolus du Plessis)—*Collectio Judiciorum de novis erroribus qui ab initio duodecim seculi . . . usque ad 1632 in ecclesia proscripti sunt et notati . . .*, I, ii, 42. Determinatio Facultatis super quibusdam libris Erasmi e Latino in Linguam vulgarem traductio . . . "Queremonia Pacis"—"1525 (1526 in our reckoning)—Decanus et Facultas theologiae Parisiensis sapientissimis Judicibus in Causis Fidei e sede apostolici a per Regnum Franciae constitutis Salutem: Cum paucis ante diebus super libris et codicillis Ludovici de Berquin ad nos vestro nomine transmissis nostrum judicum tulissemus; et inter illos invenirentur nonnulli libri Erasmo Roterodamo ascripti, videlicet, Enconium matrimonii, Symbolum Apostolicum, Queremonia Pacis & Brevis Admonito de modo orandi e Latino in linguam Gallicam per praefatum Ludivicum de Berquim translati, & a nobis nuper damnati, in favorem Fidei requisistis, ut excerptas in illis propositiones propter quas illos damnaveramus vobis una cum nostra censura communicaremus: quod aequium esse et pium attendentes secimus. Matura itaque praevia discussione super illis, ut sequitur, censuimus." Cee JOURDAIN, CAR., *Index Chronologicus Chartarum pertinentium ad historiam Universitatis Parisiensis . . .*, 1862, pp. 322, 326, 327, 329, 331, 332, 333, 337 for a succinct account of all the acts of literary censureship by the Theological Faculty from the Reuchlin controversy to that concerning Marguerite of Navarre's "Miroir . . . "; also CREVIER, M., *Histoire de l'Université de Paris depuis son origine jusqu' en l'année 1600.* (Paris, 1761), V, pp. 133, 137 f., 205, 207 ff., 271 ff.

that had favored the conciliar principle now condemns the author who had been its most eloquent exponent. It was not accidental that de Berquin, one of the French Reformers before Calvin, and a precursor of Calvin, should have harbored conciliar views, and it is significant that he should have possessed a copy of the one famous book defending these views. It was fortunate for Calvin to have the faculty advertise, in spite of themselves, that the book was still available.[50]

As we know, the king freed de Berquin a second time.

It strikes me as a matter of utter significance that the Sorbonne condemned the works of Erasmus in 1526.[51] This judgment, delivered by the most august body of theologians in Europe, the only body to whose opinion even Luther had deferred (1519-1521),[52] concerning the acknowledged dean of European letters, was a step that was bound to awaken interest in the breast of so independent a youth of seventeen as John Calvin. It will be recalled that Erasmus had just the previous year broken with Luther in the open. The Sorbonne's action must have been pronounced an absolutely retrogressive step in the circles in which Calvin moved. Think of Dr. Cop and his friends, who, by the way, in four brief years would establish the Royal Readers as an open competitor of the University!

It would have been quite useless for one to differentiate sharply in the 1520's between humanism and the Protestant revolt in France. It was impossible for the humanist to side with the Sorbonne. He could not help discovering numerous things in his researches on which the Faculty would take issue with him. The note of human liberty struck by the Reformers could not but encourage the free investigation of all things, which humanism championed. Budé and Erasmus might repudiate Luther as much as they pleased, yet it remains true that Budé set up the Lecteurs Royaux over against the Sorbonne, and himself moved steadily towards at least a greater inner emancipation from the Catholicism of the day. And Erasmus pronounced an

---

[50] In 1535 it was translated for Henry VIII into English.

[51] Cf. *Hist. de l'Eglise Gall.*, pp. 253–311, for the full list.

[52] WEISS, N., "Paris et la réforme sous François Ier," *Bulletin* XLIII, 24 f.

excellent word of praise over the martyred de Berquin from his retreat beyond the scene of the stake,[53] and himself died without clerical unction and was buried in the Protestant Cathedral of Basel.[54]

One could not expect young Calvin to differentiate at this time between Protestantism and humanism, as Budé and Erasmus did for reasons of their own. Calvin would do this for a year or so only, while writing the Commentaries on Seneca. At the present time, 1526, he must have seen but one great progressive movement condemned by the Faculty —a movement in which de Berquin, Luther, Erasmus, Lefèvre, Budé, were alike involved.

It is said that Calvin read one of the more violent tracts of Zwingli against the church at this time, and that he was disgusted with it. This would be symptomatic of the drift of his opinion. He was still Catholic, loyally so. To Sadolet he would some day write of his one time "reverentia ecclesiae." Attacks on the fundamentals of the institution were distasteful to him. At the same time we cannot discover the least evidence of a feeling against the reformers as such. The silence, even in the 1530 correspondence, on this whole matter is significant. He seems to pass the whole movement by. He would do so by looking at it objectively, coldly scientifically. He would do so by engaging in purely classical pursuits. Eschewing any attempt to bring freedom to the masses, a business that was bringing exile to Farel, Lefèvre, and death to de Berquin, he would enter the liberty reserved for scholars.

Though cowardice was not one of Calvin's failings, he was by nature a timid man. How bold timid men may become would be shown in his later career. A study of the growth of persecution in France during the 1520's, and of the Roman church's girding herself for determined opposition against Lutheranism, is interesting to the student of Calvin. Two years after the condemnation of Erasmus' books the

[53] A Letter to Charles Utenhove, July 1, 1529, HERMINJARD, op. cit., II, 183–193, relating the circumstances of the trial and execution of de Berquin The details had been collected by him from witnesses and friends, and there is an account of his personal relations with the martyr.

[54] Budé tried to save de Berquin, pledging himself to take steps to "have him come to himself and retract." Hist. de l'Eglise Gall., pp. 349–51.

country is flooded with ecclesiastical councils. First the famous Council of Sens which consolidated all Catholic forces against the heresy. In the same year the Council of Lyons, Bourges, Tours, Rheims, Rouen, in every one of which Lutheranism was condemned.[55] Just as the church is tightening her reins, Calvin quits the study of theology to take up law. This was at the order of his father who himself is in trouble with the church in Noyon. We are told that Calvin did not like to begin the study of law; still we may be sure that he was not sorry to leave theology as taught in Paris, ultra-reactionary as the hierarchy had become.

Whatever desire he ever may have had to align himself with the party of reform would have been effectively suppressed by the events of 1528. Surely, they would be absolutely choked by the time of the burning of de Berquin, April 22, 1529. After a year under Pierre Taisan de l'Estoile at Orléans he went to Bourges to sit under the new and renowned interpreter of law, Andrea Alciati. Though considerably influenced by the latter who certainly was an enlightened Catholic, he subscribes to Duchemin's *Antapologia* in defense of the ultra-conservative de l'Estoile (and writes the preface for the same). Then, 1531, after his father's death, he returns to Paris and joins the student band at the Lecteurs Royaux, and commits himself to classical letters.[56] In 1532 the *Seneca Commentaries* appear. In these he rises to eloquence in his praises of Budé and Erasmus, his models. He would be like them—a humanist, but decidedly not a Protestant; a progressive in the study-room but not in the religious forum, a champion of free investigation of all things except ecclesiastical.

An ill-balanced life this—as bad as a Protestant who desires freedom in worship but not in the sciences. Humanism and Reformation could not forever remain separate to Calvin. His conversion settled that. The conversion of Calvin may be interpreted as the liberation of his religious

---

55) *Ibid.*, 311–40.

56) BEZA and COLLADON say that Calvin *abandoned* the study of law after his father's death, *Opera*, XXI, 55. For a refutation of this cf. G. BEYERHAUS, *Staatsanschauung Calvins*, p. 41f. Though he did abandon the study of law at a school of law, his *Seneca Commentaries* show that his interest in jurisprudence is still profound.

nature so that the man in him might be truly free; that is, free in the sense that he had no apologies to make to his deeper, inner self.

#### APPENDIX TO SECTION 6—*Louis de Berquin*

*Le Journal d'un Bourgeois de Paris sous le règne de François I (1515-1536)* (éd. par V.-L. Bourilly, Paris, 1910), contains descriptions of the fortunes of de Berquin which impart a contemporary atmosphere.

> p. 142. Audict an mil cinq cens vingt et trois, le samedy huictiesme aoust, furent bruslez plusiers livres, par l'authorité de la cour de Parlement, devant la grande eglise Nostre Dame de Paris, qu'avoit faict un gentilhomme, nommé Loys Barquin, seigneur dudict lieu, en Picardie, qui qui estoit grand clerc, mais il estoit lutherien; lequel avoit esté prisonnier à la Conciergerie du Palais, à Paris, et depuis rendu à l'evesque de Paris, comme clerc. Et fut ce faict pour lesditz livres estans heretiques et maulvais contre Dieu et sa glorieuse mere. Depuis fut prisonnier quelque témps à la cour d'eglise, neantmoins il en fut mis hors, de par le Roy, qui estoit près de Meleun et s'en alloit delà les montz, lequel il envoia querir par son cappitaine Frederic et des archers de sa garde; et fit de ce le Roy pour luy saulver la vie, car aultrment il eût esté en grand danger de sa personne d'estre mis à mort par justice, car il l'avoit bien gaigné.

The journalist[57] relates the capture of de Berquin in January, 1526, "à cause qu'il estoit lutherien, et avoit autre-fois esté reprins par ladicte cour de ce qu'il tenoit la doctrine de Luther." The emphasis given to the fact that he was known as Lutheran is significant. Having been freed by

> ledict Grand Conseil sans en avoir esté aulcunement absoulz, et s'en retourna depuis en son païs de Picardie, ou il persevera encore en son propos. Dont à ceste cause, ladicte cour l'envoia querir comme dit est devant, et environ huict jours après son arrivement à Paris, ledict Mailly, huissier, fut renvoié audict lieu d'Abbeville et ès environs, de par ladicte cour, pour informer de la vie de dudict Berquin, pour y pourvoir par justice. Et depuis ladicte cour fist son procez, tellement qu'il fut bruit qu'il estoit conclud à mourir, après que les com-missaires qui estoient deleguez le rendirent à la justice laye, en le declarent heretique; mais madame la

---

[57] p. 324.

Regente manda à ladicte cour que l'on surceast l'execution jusques à la venue du Roy. Et depuis, le Roy arrivé
manda à ladicte cour qu'on ne le fist mourir et qu'on le
gardast tant qu'il fut en France.

On Friday, April 26, 1529, the sentence of death was for
the last time pronounced on de Berquin, "parce qu'il estoit
lutherien, et n'estoit marié."[58] Then the history of the case
is reviewed. In 1526 he had been freed not only by the king,
but also on instance of "madame d'Allançon, royne de
Navarre."[59] The entire record covers five pages, showing
how large this affair loomed in the Parisian mind. At the
end[60] we read: "Ledict Barquin avoit environ cinquante ans
et portoit ordinairement robbes de veloux, satin et damas et
chesnes d'or, et estoit de noble lignée et moult grand clerc,
expert en science et subtil; mais neantmoins il faillit en son
sens; toutesfois il mourut repentant.[61]

[58] p. 317.
[59] p. 318.
[60] p. 321 f.
[61] Cf. also pp. 423–27.

# CHAPTER III

## CALVIN'S STUDY OF JURISPRUDENCE AND THE CLASSICS

### Section 1.  At the University of Orléans

AFTER five memorable years at the University of Paris, Calvin at the age of eighteen goes to the University of Orléans. He abandons theology for law. It has already been stated that his father ordered him to take this step, the reason being that law was the most certain way to wealth and honors.[1] The Court was indeed favoring men with legal training for high offices, rather than churchmen. The shrewd father knew what would promote the fortunes of his son. But ambitious as he was, he had perhaps not made this decision with respect to John, had he himself not been involved in difficulties with the Chapter at Noyon.[2] The rift between his own family and the church could not have

---

[1] Cf. CALVIN'S *Preface to the Commentaries on the Psalms*, Opera XXXI, 22. "Dés que i' estye ieune enfant, mon pere n'avoit destiné à la théologie: mais puis apres, d' autant qu'il consideroit que la science des loix communément enrichit ceux qui la suyvent, ceste esperance luy fait incontinent changer d' avis. Ainsi cela fut cause qu'on me retira de l'estude de philosophie, et que ie fus mis à apprendre les loix: ausquelles combien que ie m' efforçasse de m'employer fidelement, pour obeir à mon pere, Dieu toutefois par sa providence secrete me fait finalement tourner bride d'un autre costé." BEZA'S *Vie de Calvin*, Opera XXI, 29, has this account: " . . . tellement que son coeur tendoit entirement à la theologie qui fut aussi qu'on le pourvent d'un benefice en l'eglise cathedrale de Noyon. Toutefois son pere se resolut de la faire estudier aux loix ami nommé maistre Pierre Robert, autrement Olievetanus, qui depuis traduit la Bible d'Hebrieu en François imprimee à Neufchatel, gousté quelque chose de la pure religion, commençoit à se distraire des superstitions Papales: qui fut cause pu' outre la singuliere reverence qu' il portoit à son pere il l' accorda d'aller à Orleans pour cest effect, là ou lisoit pour lors un excelent homme nommé Pierre dle 'Estoile, depuis President en la cour de parlement de Paris . . . " That he "commençoit à se distraire des superstitions papales" and had "gousté quelque chose de la pure religion" under the influence of Olivètan, his cousin, did not take away what Calvin himself says of his spiritual condition before his "conversion subite." For in the Preface to the Psalms he says: " . . . comme ainsi soit que ie fusse si obstinément addonné aux superstitions de la Papauté . . " Note the word "obstinément." It would be interesting to know just what Olivètan talked about to Calvin. It is, in our opinion, not hard to guess, for the air of Paris was full of Lefèvre, Luther, Erasmus, de Berquin, etc., as has been indicated.

[2] Cf. LEFRANC, A., *La Jeunesse de Calvin*, p. 15 ff., p. 196 ff., for a fair account.

left him unmoved. It did not cause an alienation from the church on his own part, however. He was "obstinément" loyal. Still the fact that it resulted in his abandoning theology was of tremendous meaning for his development as a humanist. For it signified that he was now forever free from the immediate influence of the reactionary University, and that he was to enter a secular field.

The University of Orléans could in a way thank the Faculty of Paris for its eminence in the study of law. For the latter had prevented the establishment of chairs of divinity there, fearing competition, so Orléans had bent all its efforts in the cultivation of the science of jurisprudence. As a result there were "eight doctors of the law of whom de l'Estoile was by far the most noted, being charged with its exposition."[3] He was "esteemed the keenest lawyer of all the doctors of France."[4] It was said that "Reuchlin, Aleander, Erasmus, have taught in this city, but de l'Estoile eclipsed all the suns."[5] Calvin was to boast of his "penetration of spirit, his address, his experience in the law, of which he remains in this epoch the prince, without a peer."[6] He alone would be considered a competitor of Alciati, internationally famous expositor of the law.[7]

The University of Orléans was a pleasanter place than the Collège de Montaigu. It enjoyed an international popularity.[8] The freedom permitted was a delightful change for Calvin undoubtedly, but he took little advantage of it. It appears that he did not take care of his physical well-being there. The regimen to which he subjected his body weakened his resistance considerably.[9] He developed his memory to an extraordinary degree. His brilliance gen-

---

3) WALKER, W., *John Calvin*, p. 47.
4) DE BEZE, THEO., *Histoire ecclesiastique*, I, 17.
5) DOUMERGUE, E., *op. cit.*, 127 f.
6) *Preface to the Antapologia of Duchemin.*
7) BEYERHAUS, G., *Staatsaanschauung Calvins*, contains a bibliography on de l'Estoile and a brief review of his principles, pp. 26–30; also STINZING, R., *Ulrich Zasius*, pp. 135 ff., 349. And of course we refer the reader to our Appendix to Section 2 on the Antapologia, which contains considerable more information about de l'Estoile.
8) LEFRANC, A., *Jeunesse*, 74 f.
9) *Ioannis Calvini Vita*, by BEZA, Opera XXI, 122, and *Vie de Calvin*, by BEZA and COLLADON, Opera XXI, 55, describe his system of protracted study far into the night, and beginning again early in the morning to review all that he had read before retiring. It was here that he contracted dyspepsia (ventriculi imbellicitatem contraxit).

erally attracted so much attention that he was regarded
more as one of the teachers than a student.[10]   This was
amazing for a young man who had been studying law for
only a year.   The astounding erudition of the Seneca Commentaries can in part be accounted for by his acquired
habits of concentration and economizing of time.[11]

There was at Orléans a man to whom Calvin was deeply
indebted as a classical scholar.   This was Melchior Wolmar,
born 1496 in Rothweil (allied with one of the Swiss cantons).
He was brought up in Berne, studied under Berthold Haller,
and went to the University of Paris in 1521.   There he
learned Greek under Glareanus and Nicholas Beroaldus,
and soon published some annotations on two chants of
Homer (1523).   His studies were crowned with brilliant
success: of one hundred candidates for the licentiate he
passed first.   For three years he taught at Paris, and was
procureur of the German "nation."   But the liberty with
which he expressed his opinions forced him to leave the
Capitol.   He was in effect a Lutheran.   So in 1527 he came
to the more congenial University of Orléans, where Calvin
made his acquaintance the next year.   In 1529 Marguerite
of Navarre invited him to the University of Bourges where
Calvin continued his contact with him.   Wolmar introduced
Calvin to the mysteries of the Greek language, and did it so
well that many years later the pupil acknowledged the
excellent work of the master for him, in the Dedication of
his Commentary on II Corinthians.[12]   The theory that
Wolmar led him to become a Protestant finds no support in
the Dedication, for Calvin does not mention a thing about
it.   Doumergue speculates on the fact that Wolmar read the
New Testament with him, and that this could not have been
without comments!   But the word of Beza and the silence
of Calvin fail to substantiate this conjecture.[13]   The influ-

---

10) BEZA, *Opera Calv.*, XXI, 29.

11) Calvin must have enjoyed the study of law, as his enthusiasm to
master it indicates.   But he must now already have been repelled by the
bad Latin and the casuistry of the medieval jurists.   Cf. LECOULTRE, H.,
"Calvin d'après son Commentaire sur le De Clementia de Senèque," p. 52,
*Rev. de Theol. et de Phil.*, 1891; RABELAIS, *Gargantua and Pantagruel*,
I, 2; BUDÉ, E., *Vie de G. Budé*, pp. 16–68.

12) Cf. *Opera* XXII, p. 364 f. (1546).

13) DOUMERGUE, E., *op. cit.*, 181 f.; BEZA, *Hist. Eccles.*, I, 18; HERMIN-
JARD, *op. cit.*, I, 281.

ence of Wolmar must be thought of as classical rather than religious, though the kindly nature of this master must have made his heresy appear unrepulsive.

Calvin was specially befriended by three men at Orléans: François Daniel, who was of a well-to-do family, which afforded Calvin no little social diversion. Later he will correspond with Daniel about the *Seneca Commentaries*.[14] There was also François de Connan, son of one of the Masters of the Chamber of Accounts, to whom he will address the Preface to the *Antanologia,* a man to whom he would submit his *Seneca Commentaries* for approval before publishing them. Finally, Nicholas Duchemin, some years his senior, in whose house he roomed for a while, and the man who wrote the *Antapologia.*

De l'Estoile was a conservative teacher, and it was perhaps well for Calvin to get his first taste of law from one who used the Accursian and Bartholian commentaries. It would give him the background for appreciating the critical work of Budé and even Alciati. The admiration he had for de l'Estoile would be reflected in his endorsing of Duchemin's *Antapologia.* As will be seen, his first contact with Alciati, the dramatic teacher of new ways of inter-

---

14) Henri Clouzot asks the interesting question whether François Daniel got his friend Calvin acquainted, in turn, with his friend Rabelais, and proceeds to build up a structure of probabilities that is plausible. He points to the fact that when about the end of 1533 Calvin writes a letter in which he speaks of the action of the Sorbonne against the Pantagruel, this letter is sent to François Daniel. Let me present the whole paragraph: "It is rather generally admitted today that the author of the Pantagruel and the author of the Institutes of the Chrisian Religion were not strangers to each other. They perhaps met in the class-rooms of the Collège de France, and in the Angoulême at Louis du Tillet's whom he (Rabelais) liked to visit." (Cf. also LEFRANC, A., *Hist. du Collège de France*, p. 134, and *Jeunesse de Calvin*, p. 118.) . . . We will then suppose that Rabelais entered into relations with Calvin in 1528 or 1531, when like his hero Pantagruel he attended the Universities of the realm. The numerous references to Orléans contained in the Second Book, and particularly the long passage in Chapter V prove, in our opinion, that Rabelais knew this city before 1533. (Cf. Bk. II, 5, 7, 15, 33, and Bk. III, 23, 24, 52.) . . . But we have a new argument wherewith to support the proposition that these two were in connection with each other, for in the unpublished notes of Bernier . . . one reads this singularly clear passage: "I have seen a manuscript letter of Calvin to Rebalais." Bernier was too good a Catholic to have forged for his favorite author so compromising a friendship. His testimony, then, yields a new and decisive fact for the history of the relation of Rabelais with the reformers." "Les amités de Rabelais en Orléans, et la Lettre au bailli du bailli des baillis, par Henri Couzot," in *Revue des Études Rabelaisiennes,* Tome III, pp. 174–75.

preting the law, was not when that teacher was at his best.
And even after Alciati had improved, the personal hostility
of Calvin for him would prevent a full appreciation of his
merit. His abandoning the old for the then modern method
was to be brought about by Budé's *Annotations on the
Pandects* (which was the first successful attempt to reform
the science of jurisprudence, and the work which undoubtedly had affected Alciati from the beginning.)

### Section 2. At the University of Bourges:  Alciati

In the spring of 1529 Calvin and his three friends went to
Bourges, having been attracted by the fame of Alciati, the
new professor of law.

This university was to figure importantly in the history of
legal reform.[15]   It was one of the three founded by Louis
XI. His brother Charles, Duke of Berry, desired a school in
Bourges, the city of his birth, and Louis at once acquiesced
(1463). It has been asked why he showed himself so eager,
and as history indicates, so insistent against the opposition
of Orléans and Paris, to establish this institution of
learning.[16]   Did he think that scientific progress and the
diffusion of knowledge would promote the stability of his
kingdom? Did he wish to propagate the teaching of the
Roman law with its doctrines of uniformity of administration and imperial omnipotence? Did he wish to diminish
the immense body of students from all countries crowding
the University of Paris? It appears to us that the object of
propagating the teaching of Roman law may well have been
present in the royal mind. The increasing absoluteness of
the French monarchy would commend this, as on the other
hand the scholastic Accursians and Bartholians discouraged
it with their obscurations of the royal prerogatives in favor
of others' claims, say, the papal.[17]

The rival universities of Orléans and Paris long contested

---

[15] Cf. *Histoire du Berry depuis les temps les plus anciens jusqu'en
1789*, par M. Louis Raynal, Bourges 1844, Tome III, 349–441.

[16] Raynal, *op. cit.*, p. 350 f.

[17] We know that Henry VIII established lectureships in law to vindicate his caesaro-papalist rule. Did Alciati's popularity with Francis I
have the same roots, and did the king interpret Budé's Annotations in the
same light?

the right of the new institution.[18] But it grew rapidly. Soon however a decline set in, due mainly to economic causes, and the school did not revive until Marguerite became Duchess of Berry. She donated money to it and furnished it with good teachers. The most famous of these was Andrea Alciati, whose stay of five years enriched him financially and in reputation, and made the university famous throughout Europe.

NOTE—On Alciati see:

1. *Andrea Alciati Emblematum Fontes Quattuor, namely, an Account of the Original Collection Made at Milan, 1522, and Photolith Fac-similes of the Editions, Augsburg 1531, Paris 1534, and Venice 1546.* Edited by Henry Green, M. A., with a Sketch of Alciati's Life and Bibliographical Observations respecting Early Reprints. 1870.

2. Grimaldi's (Alessandro) Funeral Oration, Jan. 19, **1550**, for Andrea Alciati. Translated for the Holbein Society by Henry Green, 1871. A photolith fac-simile is appended.

3. Andrea Alciati V. C. *Emblemata cum Claudii Minois Diuionensis ad eadem Commentariis, Quibus Emblematum omnium aperta origine, meus auctoris explicatur, et obscura omnia dubiaque illustrantur.* Editio quarta. 1591. About 750 pp.

4. *Andrea Alciati Jurisconsulti Clarissimi, De Singulari Certamine Liber,* 1548. Beginning with p. 80 we find a supplement: Consilium in materia Duelli exceptum ex honorem sum nisi armis tueri. Quo modo dignosci quis provocatur, quis item provocatus sit.

5. *Andrea Alciati Jurisconsulti Mediolanensis Tractatus Contra Vitam Monasticam* (Leiden 1740). Edited by Antonius Matthaeus.

6. Tiraboschi, *Cav. Abato Girolamo, Storia della Letteratura Italiana,* 1809, Tome VII Parte prima, Bk. I, V, par. XXVIII, pp. 258, 718ff.

7. Doumergue, E., *op. cit., I,* 141-49.

8. Raynal, L., *op. cit.,* III, 305, 368-82.

9. Beyerhaus, G., *op. cit.,* pp. 31ff., 45ff.

10. Costa, Emilio, *Andrea Alciato 'e Bonifacis Amerbach,* in Archivo storico italiano, 3 fasciule, 1905.

---

[18] From 1463–1474, RAYNAL, *op. cit.,* 352–358; perhaps also because it followed the Italian plan of Universitas studentium seu generale studium, *Ibid.,* p. 360.

11. Giardini, Ottavio, *Nuove indagini sulla vita e le condotto di Andrea Alciato*, in Archivo storico lombardo, t. xxx, 1903.

12. *Enciclopedia Italiana di Scienze Lettere ed Arti* (Institute Giovanni Tuccani, 1929) Article, "Alciato," with portrait.

13. *Grand Encyclopedie*, Article, "Alciat," Vol. II, 24.

14. Alciati, Andrea, by Mortet. *In Tres Posteriores Cod-Iustiniani libros annotatiunculae*, 1513.

It is significant that Alciati was the only Italian professor Calvin ever had. He brought with him the atmosphere of the trans-Alpine Renaissance. The fame of Italian learning and culture filled the land. What young Frenchman with a thirst for knowledge would not take advantage of Dr. Alciati's coming to Bourges! Hostile as he was to the person of the new professor, it is unthinkable that he was not fired by him with a new ambition, namely, to master the classics. Hitherto he had in his formal studies drunk from the fountains of scholasticism, save for the year with Wolmar (but that was elementary Greek), as his quarter under Cordier was to study the Latin primer. If he had read Erasmus, or distantly admired Budé, now he was to spend many months in the class-room of one of the most eloquent teachers of the century, whose lips dripped with the nectar of ancient Greece and Rome. Nectar to Calvin it must have been, who thus discovered a new world, a world that was beautiful. He was not cold to the esthetic appeal of the classics; his *Seneca Commentaries* are full of charming quotations. More than nectar were the words of Alciati to this young man. For they revealed that the ancients had a sense of ethical values that often exceeded the moralisms of his own age.[19] It is difficult to over-estimate the influence of all this on young Calvin. Undoubtedly Alciati opened to him the treasures of the Italian humanists. He must have felt that he was a missionary to the barbarians (not an unusual

---

[19] Calvin may or may not have been present when Francis I paid a formal visit to Alciati's class-room, upon which occasion the latter delivered a speech to the king, that contained the following sentences: "Agesilaüs, king of Sparta, was once asked what virtue he preferred, courage or justice. The answer was that there is no courage without justice. It was even said by Pompey to Phraates, king of the Parthians, that empires ought to be governed not by arms but by justice." RAYNAL, *op. cit.*, p. 378.

attitude of the Italians at this time), that he was bringing a real gospel to them, and it were the height of improbability that he should not have recommended enthusiastically the great names of Valla, Perotti, Politian, Pomponius Laetus, et al. (all of which are used as authorities in the Commentaries). Lefèvre, Budé, Erasmus, and others had gone to Italy in person to know the Italian Renaissance at first hand; in the case of Calvin and his friends it was brought to them by one of its best exponents.

Alciati was born May 1, 1492, at Alanzo or Alzato, near Milan. Very early he devoted himself to jurisprudence, and before he was fifteen he composed his Paradoxes of the Civil Law. He studied Greek under Janus Parrhasius at Milan; his teacher of law at Pavia was Jason Mainus; and his teacher of law at Bologna was Carlo Ricini. When only twenty-one he was accorded the Doctorate of Laws. Up to 1517 he practiced law at Milan from where he went to the University of Avignon where he taught with great acceptance. He had left his wife behind in Milan. In 1521 he returned thither. Then, in 1522 he composed, and perhaps printed (though the 1522 edition has nowhere been found) one hundred of his Emblems. Each Emblem has an appropriate device in woodcut. The subsequent editions were augmented by new Emblems each time they appeared. The last one contained two hundred eleven of them. They were translated into French, Spanish, and Italian, the original being Latin.[20]

Francis I and Marguerite seconded the attempts of the University of Bourges to get the services of Alciati with such liberality that the latter dedicated to the king his *De Singulari Certamine Liber* (March, 1529), and the same month he entered the city in solemn procession. On Monday, April 29th, at nine in the morning, he taught his first class.[21]

Since Calvin in all likelihood attended his classes almost from the beginning, it will interest us to know that Alciati began with the exposition of the third part of the *Digest* (Digestum Novum), and chose as the subject of his first lessons De Verborum Obligationibus.

---

[20] GREEN, H., Sketch of the Author's Life, in *Andr. Alciati Embl. Fontes Quattuor*, Introduction.

[21] RAYNAL, *op. cit.*, p. 370 f.

His fame had immediately attracted a crowd of students, most of whom were far advanced in the study of law.[22]

But during the first months, fearing that storms of envious protest might arise from the older members of the faculty who were faithful to the older traditions, Alciati departed very little from the accepted methods of the glossators. He made no use of his vast erudition, his profound knowledge of antiquity. At every instance he would quote Accursius and Bartholus.

Instead of speaking the elegant Latin of his books, he used a medieval barbarity of Latin. He continually lost himself in endless details. The students, who had come from afar to hear him were disillusioned and dropped off. When he asked why they left him, they presented their gravamen which is preserved to us by Alciati himself. They complain that they had come on the strength of his books with their fine Latin and their fresh presentation of matters, and now their money is as good as thrown to the wind. They ask him to substitute for his rustic language a more elegant one,[23]

for today in the midst of this mass of books and professors one must be a frank Boetian and a thick-headed spirit indeed to remain mediocre in the culture of letters. They desire that he spare them the incessant refutations.... and not to imitate the splitters of grains of cummin and the gormandizers of nothing and the gravers of cress..... We pray you to explain to us in each lesson the conclusions of twenty laws at least..... Instead of exegeting, as they (the other teachers) do, four to six laws, interpret to us a hundred or so and explain to us as many complete books of the Digest..... What can we say to those doctors who tarry three months over one title except that which was replied by the Lacedemonians to the deputation of the Samians: O Samians, your discourse was so verbose that we have forgotten the first part, from which results that we do not understand the second.

It is generally suspected that Alciati deliberately provoked this gravamen to get an expression from the students of what they demanded. After resisting for some time still, he at last became himself. With the popular demand behind him he no longer feared what his rivals in the Faculty might

---

22) *Ibid.*, p. 372.
23) DOUMERGUE, E., *op. cit.*, p. 141 ff.; RAYNAL, *op. cit.*, p. 373.

do or say. Raynal describes him as Calvin must have heard him when he was at his best:[24]

> Since then he adopted a greater, more literary method, free from fastidious repetitions quite disengaged from the fatuities of the glossators: he defined the texts, analyzed them, and explained them complete, ly, but rapidly. He devoted one hour to giving thorough explications of the subject of the lesson; another hour was used for dictation; but, as he remarked, the students took his words down so inaccurately, and these in turn were further denatured by successive copies, that as soon as possible he had the dictations printed. With such instruction they made remarkable progress, and the teacher's reputation traveled far, in spite of the accusations and reproaches of the old school.

Two of the known critics of Alciati were Duchemin and Calvin. An examination of Duchemin's *Antapologia* does not warrant the idea that their criticism grew out of the situation resulting in the students' gravamen against Alciati. For a discussion of the *Antapologia* see Appendix of this section. At this place we shall continue the story proper.

Francis I was evidently proud of his professor of law.

---

[24] RAYNAL, *op. cit.*, p. 374. Alciati's *De Singulari Certamine Liber* gives a fair idea of his text-books. Some of the chapter headings are: 1. Duellum unde Dictum. 3. An duellum Iure concessum sit, et quibus casibus. 9. Quid si provocantis querela iusta sit, quemadmodum provocatus respondeat. 10. An ex nova causa, vetere omissa pugnari possit. 15. Quid si provocatus latitet, vel nolet responder. 16. Quibus exceptionibus detractare quis certamen possit. 20. Quid si provocator semel victus fuerit (num iterum poterunt admitti?) 26. Quid in filiofamilias, si pater prohibeat, quid si consanguinei. Throughout illustrations are taken from the classics, from Homer down through the Greeks, and with great erudition from Roman customs and codes.

A paragraph in Grimaldi's *Funeral Oration* illustrates the vividness of his teaching. The author appears to have been one of Alciati's former students. At least he had heard him lecture: " . . . But the noble science of war . . . he so understood, that you would have said that he had been accustomed to do nothing except take up a station for a camp, to surround the same with a rampart, to beat off the enemy, and draw up an army in array."

Cf. also Tiraboschi, *Storia della Litteratura Italiana*, Tome VII, p. 258, describes his distinction "in both severe legal studies and the charms of literature, besides having put many things in the four books of the History of Milan, made a most complete collection of inscriptions conserved in his fatherland, and which we now have in the Vatican and Ambrosian collections. . . " Tome VII, Bk. II, chap. IV, deals with his in "giurisprudenza civile ed ecclesiastica" which before him was "un amaso disordinato di citazioni . . . un frequente abuso di scholastische speculationi." But "Il grande Alciati fu il primo a rischiarar quelle tenebre colle fiaccola della critica e della erudizione, e a dar l'esempio ai legisti di scrivere con ordine e con precisione."

During a sojourn in Bourges, the date of which is so uncertain that it may lie anywhere between 1529 and 1533, the king and his nobles wished to attend one of his lectures, "hommage intelligent rendu par la royauté à la science,"[25] and it is said that the king "lowered the royal insignia to the majesty of the law."[26]   On this occasion Alciati delivered a speech to the king in which the Roman Law is praised. Among other things he says:

> Agapetos, who later became chief pontiff, having visited the Emperor Justinian, addressed him (so the authors say) with these words in Greek: "Kingdoms and empires are given by the 'sort,' and those who possess them owe more to God than other men; for they have received from him more since he has clothed them with more eminent dignities. Let them therefore show themselves grateful, by governing their subjects after the image of the heavenly kingdom. . . ." Now, when we see that you appreciate the study of such great things, who would not believe that we are living in a new Golden Age, where the philosophers reign and the kings are philosophers?  For the first part of philosophy concerns itself with morals; and although Aristotle and Plato have written more than forty books on this subject, it is evident that they cannot be compared with our jurisconsults; for no one ever governed his country according to the rules of their politics, while the law of the Romans has been carefully preserved by even those peoples who overturned their empire, the Goths, the Franks, the Herules, the Germans, the Lombards.  [The tacit endorsement of the principle of absolute monarchy must have been sweet to the ears of Francis.][27]

The Emblems of Alciati, which were enjoying several editions, must have been known to young Calvin.  Incidentally we can learn from them how the Sixteenth Century amused and sometimes instructed itself.  Their appeal was to the leisure class.[28]

> One of his contemporaries, Wolfgang Hungerus, regarded his Emblems as the light reading which may occupy our inclination at the breakfast-table or during supper-time.  And in all probability the greater part of them were composed in the sunny or festive hours of

---

25) RAYNAL, *op. cit.*, p. 377.
26) GREEN, *op. cit.*, Introd.
27) RAYNAL, *op. cit.*, p. 378 f.
28) GREEN, *op. cit.*, Introd.

life, when literature, like love in idleness, cannot over-
come the habit of indulging its natural propensity. The
Preface of the Introduction to his friend Peutinger
manifests that in this way Alciati himself regarded
them,—as the slight skirmishes of wit rather than
serious warfare; for thus he addresses the learned
society:

> "While boys with nuts beguile, and youth with dice,
> And sluggish men the figured board detains;
> For festive hours each emblem and device
> We forge, that artist's hand illustrious feigns."

Bagatelles then to play with, trifles to amuse, is the
light in which we should regard Alciati's Emblems. But
at the same time they are the trifles which none but a
scholar could gracefully sport with, and none but a man
with talent invent.

I have said that there are two hundred eleven Emblems.
There were originally two hundred twelve. Only two or
three editors have published editions containing the two
hundred twelfth. Very generally this has been condemned,
however, for the one omitted in all the standard editions
was "an intensely coarse-minded Emblem and Device."
That he was capable of doing anything of the sort may have
disgusted Calvin, assuming that he was cognizant of it, and
assuming that his published witticisms were of a higher
order than his campus talk. The great majority of the
Emblems are light bits of innocuous advice. A number of
the Devices portray nudes. It is amazing the use he makes
of the figure of Cupid. He loves to treat of the student in
love. If we should care to build a structure of probabilities
further to elucidate his character, and the probable reaction
on Calvin, we might ask why he once upon a time had left
his wife in Milan while he trekked to Avignon and stayed
there four years (and always making decent money.) Calvin may have regarded him as a frivolous Italian.

In considering the personal hostility of Calvin for Alciati
it is well to remember that a patriotic young man may well
have regarded the appointment of an Italian under such
generous auspices a slap at de l'Estoile as a Frenchman.
From our section on Budé it will appear how jealous French
scholarship was of its new-won independence and true
greatness. It may be pointed out in passing that Hotman,
the greatest exponent of Francogallism, was professor of

Bourges University later; it is possible that Alciati had left the soil seeded with Italogallism. Besides this, Alciati was a typical Italian hedonist. Not only did his Emblems witness to this, but his greed for gold and his habits of inordinate eating.[29] Add to this his intolerable vanity, and the case is clear why the personally ascetic Calvin should have disliked him.

### APPENDIX TO SECTION 2—Duchemin's *Antapologia*

In the Bibliothèque Nationale at Paris there is a volume entitled *Nicolai Chemyni Aureliani Antapologia Adversus Aurelii Albucii Defensionem Pro And. Alciato Contra D. Petrum Stellam Nuper Aeditam. Parisiis ex officina Gerardi Morrhii Campensis apud Collegium Sorbonae. M.D.XXXI.* Though it had been written already in July, 1529, it was not published till March, 1531. There is a photo-stat copy of it in the Library of the University of Chicago.

This book is particularly interesting because Calvin wrote the Preface for it, and it even appears that he had something to do with its composition (he calls it a joint venture in writing, "communemque scriptorum aleam experitur"). However small his actual contribution to its composition may have been, the volume certainly reflects his personal views. It therefore is a document of the highest value in estimating young Calvin as a student of law at Bourges in 1529, and since he saw it through the press at Paris in the spring of 1531 we may conclude that his sentiments had not changed in the course of these two years.

Our discussion of the *Antapologia* will take the form of an outline which sets in relief the principal points of interest.

P. 1b. "Nicolas Chemynus to the brothers Hardoynus and Anthony, now gone forth from the Academy of Orleans, sons of that most famous man D. Adam Fumaeus.....," to whom (Fumaeus) a panegyric of twenty lines is dedicated.

P. 2a-5a. "Epistola-Nuncupatoria. N. Chemynus to the most famous men and most worthy masters Claude de Hangest, Abbot of St. Eloi at Noyon, and Anthony de Lalaing

---

29) Cf. RAYNAL, *op. cit.*, p. 381; DOUMERGUE, *op. cit.*, p. 146; TIRA-BOSCHI, *op. cit.*, Tome VII, p. 722.

of Hoochstraten......" Duchemin begins with a plea not to think him over bold, and proceeds by exhibiting some of his difficulties:

> Ad quod praeter haec impulerat & illud me, quod ubi perficiendum certum quid mihi de medio sumptum, ac praefinitam aliquam suis cancellis materiam absolute mihi excutiendam praestitui, longe operi instantiorem interim me esse, atque studiosorem me praestare aliquo iam usu sim expertus, quam alias, *quam is mihi per totam Digestorum sylvam vaganti frequenter accidit, quod usu venire iis solet, qui in dubiis, quas vocant, coenis accumbentes, per copiam, ut ille inquit, inopes fiunt:* nempe ut ego tum reum avocatus multitudine, tum suspenso eligendi iudicio detentus, praeterquam quod magnam interim facio temporis iacturam, ad alia etiam ut divertam adduci facile possum (p. 3a).

Toward the end of the letter Archbishop Stephen Poncher among others receives a word of praise (p. 5a). This letter was evidently written just before publication of the book, "..... Aurelias Calend. Martiis."

Pp. 5b-6b. The letter of John Calvin to Francis Connan: "Epistola: Ioannes Calvinus Francisco Connano Iuris S(t)udiosissimo. S."

John Calvin to Francis Connan, most studious in the law:

> Here at last appears the Antapologia of our Chemin, and it proves to be a joint venture in writing, though it was not intended by him to be written that it might at any time be given to the public. But it is only fair that there be publication of these things of which that man (Alciati) made sport, thanks to his exciting and agitating temperament, lest de l'Estoile should be in want of defense, and Albucius, I know not who (that is), might have sung his pæans to him without blood and sweat. Now if anyone prefer Alciati to Albucius, I shall not be so bold as to affirm, nor do I desire to rebut; but certain wiser men have smelled out that Alciati by a mutation of names had wished to dissimulate, lest his flow of impatient language, toothed above normal, should be thought retaliatory. Neither must anyone think that de l'Estoile was destitute of defense, nor must his silence be interpreted as confession, by which he has thus far allowed the victory to be Albucius's. Let him know that a true man, occupied by one matter of business after another (seriis negotiis), supported also by this trust of

his in truth, has not wished to lose labor in things least of all necessary, for he has said that he had had enough of this affair. For the rest he also might have drawn forth the pen against a thousand Albuciuses, by which he (de l'Estoile) is gifted with a keenness of genius, what of his industry, his experience in the law, the pre-eminence in which he might obtain in our day, in one way or another, without controversy. Chemin was of this persuasion, and he had not been able to put the (necessary) spirit into the matter of publishing this little work, had he not been convinced by solid proofs that certain men held forth that his patience with de l'Estoile was (patience) with a fraudulent man. Thus certain brawlers had even contended that he (de l'Estoile) would not have refrained from this affair, had he been able to make a defense,—as he had already made a steady resistance to Zazius. Just so, led on by this necessity, our Cheminus changed his opinion, and desired by this work, now already suppressed for two years, to show the world that their calumnies ought to be crushed. He wished from the first, however, that this work should come into the hands of men uncor-rupted and unmutilated. Thus when he heard that I was setting out to adorn Paris (Itaque quum audiret me profectionem adornare Lutetiam), he demanded of me, in behalf of those things which befell between him and me by friendship and wont, that I should take diligent pains with this work, lest errors should creep in. I have gladly taken up this duty, providing, however, that I maintain no other guilt except carelessness. And Aciati should not take this with annoyance, while he will esteem himself to have been opposed first by right, so naturally he should take it soberly and shamefacedly (and the preface not having been overpassed as a debt of honor). To that extent, I think, he should have in mind the public good, to that extent he should defer to the truth, that he does not claim anything for himself on the pretext of his authority. Therefore, since he knows that the truth is sunk down, he should agree that it has been uprooted by disputations; let it (therefore) be merely discerned that the very truth that has been sought after may be lost by excessive altercation. Mean-while I want it said that I would vindicate this work to myself, to Alciati, and you (Connan), that I may not re-spect the zeal of a man in a hostile cause;—(a cause) to which you are more or less inclined; in fact, you draw this very thing into the charge, that I may not be hostile to the partisans of Alcati. I know indeed in what manner you are wont to speak of him, no doubt a most grateful disciple of the most excellent of teachers. But concerning de l'Estoile also, whom you have heard, you think rather well, and you did speak with respect about him, even recently in private conversation, and previously very often in your many letters, (from which) I know that I ought not to doubt that you have an unprejudiced opinion in this disputation, especially since you know very well him who has undertaken to defend this affair; you know him for his judgment, namely our Cheminus, a man whom you know as most patient in midnight studies, (a man) of clear-sighted genius, (a man) who from the first surpassed in a most exact judgment; who also might be accomplished in the art of fine letters to the finger-tips, but most fortunately has turned and for the longest time had done so already, to the study of the law. Be a judge now of books for the reading public, not, to be sure, for the common run of readers, but for those who will penetrate a bit deeper into the mysteries of the law, (and see) why he (Duchemin) comes to the present cause! Most learned Connan, be a judge, not however as one of the people, but as one apart from them by virtue of that numerous merit of interior learning. Indeed, as it is now, I think that this disputation is of such a sort that it is easily possible that both for your judgment, and for that of whatever reader's is deserving of merit, it ought to be won by us. Farewell.....[30]

Then comes the body of Duchemin's book.

Fo. 1a.  Nobody knows who Albucius is; Alciati is called a most erudite man; and he must not take the Antapologia ill.

Quando Albuci, quisquis es, prodiisti praeceptoris tui traditiones adversus excellentis Jurisconsulti D. Petri Stellas argumenta defensurus, non iniquum est, opinor, neque tibi non placere, neque Alciato ipsi viro eruditis-

---

[30]) Calvin's letter speaks for itself. As the book will show the facts appear to point, in the opinion of the authors, that Alciati had deliberately attacked de l'Estoile, and had concealed himself under an assumed name. At least nobody seems to know who Albucius is. Again the reason for this writing was not to attack the teachings of Alciati as such, but to defend de l'Estoile of Orléans. It was almost a patriotic duty. Moreover, Calvin was of a mind not to have Alciati make unsubstantiated claims "on the pretext of his authority." I point out also that Calvin speaks of "the common run of readers," which is worth observing. In the Seneca Commentaries he has no compliments for the unlearned. From his final sentence it is clear that his respect for "that numerous merit of interior learning" is great. And furthermore, if he was developing a distaste for law, it was a distaste for "la pratique du barreau," not for that knowledge of principles that results from penetrating "deeper into the mysteries of the law."

> simo videri indignum debebit, si & ipse ratione nequa-
> quam infirmiori motus, praeceptoris mei de me
> hactenus semper bene meritissimi causam non deferam,
> illumque etiam quantula possum industria, eo animo
> suscipiam tutandum.

One must guard against deferring uncritically to the
opinions of a teacher; not to have done so has brought woe
into the world of letters. May it not happen in our work.

> ..... Quo nobis esse duco circumspectius cavendum,
> ne praeceptorum nostrorum opinionibus impotenter
> addicti, obiici quicquam non nisi aegro animo audire
> possimus, quod ab iis ullo modo dissentiat, easdem ipsi
> quo iure, quoque iniuria numque non defendere para-
> tissimi. Tu enim vides, puto, quantum ea labes malum
> in orbem hodie invexerit. Quantumque perturbationis
> ex hac sua omnia quomodocumque tutandi pervicacia
> in literarum studia irrepserit. Quod eo diligentius pro-
> videndum est, ne hanc etiam nostram invadat disci-
> plinam.

After pointing to history, he proceeds in the same sentence
to inveigh against Accursius as the idol of men.

> Atteius Capito, Labeo et Antistius; Massurius Sabinus,
> et Nerva pater, caeterique porro eorum discipuli
> semper, ut Pomponius refert, cum successu adaugere
> perrexerint: quemadmodum ex recentioribus etiam
> istis Itali fere omnes privato hactenus studio quodam,
> ac stultis instincti affectibus, idωlum suum, ita enim
> vocant, Accursiam adversus quamlibet invicta Cisal-
> pinorum obiecta protegendum ut plurimum puta-
> verunt.[31]

Fo. 2a. Duchemin seconds the complaints of Alciati about
the low estate of jurisprudence, which in France is due to
the ignorance and negligence of her own doctors.

> Et laudabilis illa, amplectendaque etiam conscriben-
> darum in alios notarum consuetudo a verteribus quon-
> dam iuris auctoribus instituta, si a nostris etiamnum
> doctoribus bona fide observata fuisset, neque secura
> adeo ignavia, tamque oscitanti incuria in legum inter-
> pretatione fuissent versati omnes, onme genus quan-
> tumvis deploratae inscitae homines, dum acriorum
> iudicia interpretum, doctiorumque suorum aequalium
> censuras reformidassent: neque tantis hodie erroribus
> ius civile dehonestaretur.

---

31) For the history of these ancient controversies between the Roman
jurists cf. KARLOWA, O., *Römische Rechtsgeschichte* (1885), I, p. 664.

Fo. 2b. Albucius's book is commendable in as far as it brought out the above matter. But why should he presume that de l'Estoile oppose Alciati in this? Certainly de l'Estoile criticized Alciati. Why not? He even did so in the class-room, for he was thorough, and he was free to say what he felt. Besides there were at Orleans studious fellows who wanted to know the fine points about everything.

> Proinde, quod in ipso statim libelli tui exordio scire te ais non raro consuevisse Stellam, quum docentis personam pro suggestu sustinet, ab Alciato dissidere, arduasque plerumque controversias in sum dicendo excitare. Fateor quidem illum nonnumquam dissidere ab Alciato: Sed quidem mirum? homo ab homine: neque profecto tam mirandum est, quod auditoribus utile: et Stellae ipsi necessarium esse, si modo frugi ille, sedulique doctoris personam sustinere velit, nemo ignorat, cui, exploratum sit, quidam ab eo, qui publico docendi munere fungitur, praestari oporteat: nec ills unquam in Alciatum dicendi captavit occasionem, sed ipsam forte oblatum obiter ut plurimum non repudiat, lubenter alioqui omissurus, si non tam anxiae esset, ac laboriosae diligentiae, ut inter docendum nihil prae-termissum velit, quod ad loci alicuius praelegendi enarrationem pertinere ille, omneis omnium forulos excutiens, arbitretur: id quod si non accurate praesta-ret, vigilantiores studii discipulis, qui huic nostrae Academiae nunquam desunt, minime satisfactum esse existimaretur: et revera indignaturi essent illi, qui scholas numquam adeunt, nisi probe antea praemedita-tione, ac versata sollicite lectione instructi, illius ipsius hac in re consilio intentes.

The charges of Albucius against de l'Estoile are based on hearsay. The years spent as a student and friend of this master have proved that he is a most human person to everybody.

> Sed quod tam arduas ille, quod credivis, in Alciatum controversias excitet, mirum, nisi divines, quorum delatione id ad aures pervenerit tuas. Nam ipse cum integro plus minus sexennio assiduous illius auditor, domesticusque fuerim discipulus, nihil minus, quod tale quippiam in Stella animadverti viro, quum in omnes humanissimo, tum in hos etiam principatum hac aetate in iuris interpretatione secum tenentes.

Fo. 3a. De l'Estoile was never unfair; he was most courteous in his controversy with Zazius. "Imo tu vides

quantam ille in Zazium dicendi materiam habens, quanta
cum aequanimitate responderit......."

Whenever he refers to recent writers de l'Estoile makes
only honorable mention of them, as may be seen from his
writings. He has called Alciati "most diligent and most
expert in the theories and subtleties of the law."

> Quae se omnia satis ex illius scriptis produnt, in
> quibus quidem ipsis ut nullius unquam ex recentioribus
> nisi honorificam fecit mentionem, ita nec Alciato maius
> quicquam, quod ad iuris peritiam spectat, attribuere
> potuisset, quod ut diligentissimum sum, atque in iuria
> Theoriis & subtilitatibus valde exercitatum pronunci-
> asset.......

Fo. 3b-4a. Duchemin goes on to relate that de l'Estoile's
work was done in the open. He describes his large audiences
which numbered about a thousand, and his skill as a teacher.
In these audiences were august persons to discuss the issues.
Debates were frequently announced by means of posters in
the streets. The fame of de l'Estoile is compared with that
of Alciati, to the advantage of the former. Incidentally the
Apology of Albucius is described as a "Dialogue" (".... qui
ipse non tantum in tuo dialogo damnas"). The students
were highly appreciative of their master's work. Would
that Albucius had taken cognizance of all this!

De l'Estoile's capacity for work is enormous.

> At monini tot dignitatibus auctorato, tot munerum
> oneribus, ac negociis districto, ut vix respirare illi, sicut
> est in Proverbio, per infinitas alias aliis succedentes
> occupationes liceat, quomodo omneis tanto tempore
> dictatas praelectiones, ita de integro percurrere vacet,
> ut si quis est in rebus error, emendatur, et quae paucis
> ab eo verbis suggerendae tantum memoriae causa
> notata sunt, explicatiore, dilucidioreque oratione con-
> scribantur.

Fo. 4b. A fine tribute to de l'Estoile's modesty. "Equidem
Stellam ipsum, quae summa est eius modestia .... Quando-
quidem seduli ille fidelisque doctoris nomine contentus,
eloquentiae titulum non ambit."

Fo. 43. The study of the law has not been adorned by fine
art hitherto; but some are now "delitiis humanorum
literarum delibuti."

> Conquesti sunt, scio, antea permulti, et fortunam
> suam, simul et saeculorum infelicitatem deploraverunt,

> quibus bonas artes, hancque potissimum nostram disciplinam eloquentiae decore illustrari non licebat. Sed est et hodie, quod florescente dicendi venustate conqueramur quodam delitiis humanarum literarum delibutos......

Literary adornment is better than barrenness, but "recte Euripides simplicem veritatis esse orationem dixit," and from Venulius we learn that we should have regard "de rebus, non verbis." Nevertheless Horace counsels: "Omne tulit punctum, qui miscuit utile dulci," and the Apostle Paul spoke of "gratiarum divisiones," and Virgil said that "non omnia posse omnes." "Suum quisque talentum habet sibi a domino concessum." Then, Fo. 5a, follows some advice on making use of the "industria uniuscuiusque," but not so as to lose the power to judge concerning things as such.

Albucius had evidently argued that de l'Estoile was uneloquent. But de l'Estoile does not affect eloquence. "Quamquam non video, unde tu Stellam arguas ineloquentem, qui se praefatus est pauculas illas disputationes, non nisi scholastico conscriptes stylo, et ut e suggesto dictatae fuerant, invulgari permississe, illic minme, siquam habet, exercere affectans eloquentiam."

Concerning the eloquence of Alciati better men than I (Albucius) have judged. Erasmus has estimated it in the *Ciceronianus*. "De Alciati eloquentia meum non est, neque mei similum censere, sed hoc scio, de ea qualia sint doctissimorum quorundam hominum iudicia, quamque se magnifice de eadem sentire Erasmus in Ciceroniano declararit."[32]

Albucius engages in a vain attempt to free Alciati from certain "tacitae..... praevaricationis nota." There appears

---

[32] In the *Ciceronianus* Bulephorus asks: "Perhaps you will be more favorable to the younger men. What do you think of Alciati?" To which Nosoponus answers: "I will give you the opinion of scholars who knew the man better than I. The virtues which Cicero divided between Quintus Scaevola and Marcus Crassus, the one of whom he called the most legal minded of orators and the other the most eloquent of lawyers, both in this one man are said to meet. His power of eloquence we have seen in the preface of Cornelius Tacitus. For in the Annotations he meant to teach, not to speak as an orator." Scott, *Controversies over the Imitation of Cicero*, I, Pt. II, p. 99. Duchemin apparently accepts the opinion of Erasmus, and unquestionably Calvin did. It is worth noting that the *Ciceronianus* was being read by the students of that day. They were following the famous Ciceronian controversy, and from what is here found both Calvin and his friend sided with Erasmus.

to have been some difference of opinion between de l'Estoile and Budé on the meaning of "libellus" and "supplicatio," Alciati taking sides with Budé (Fo. 5b). So also they differ on the meaning of "decretum," and Duchemin defends de l'Estoile by saying that he taught what always had been held on this subject. Then he charges Alciati with plagiarism and insufficient erudition.

> Quid habet, quod non acceperit? Quod enim ille de decreto scribit, ex doctorum omnium commentariis transscripsit: Quod dixit de libello, Budaeo debet: et in universum quicquid hic sibi ascribere conatus est, Fulgosio acceptum referre oportuit.... quod Alciatinae huic interpretationi fenestra aperire. Atqui si Fulgosii commentarium tum minime habebat Alciatus, unde desumere illud potuisset: Iason id refert, quem haud est verisimile, non hic esse ab Alciato perlectum.[33]

But Duchemin does not want to cast aspersions on Alciati as much as to clear the name of de l'Estoile. He wishes Alciati well.

Fo. 6b. The date of Albucius's Apology was May, 1529, and the place was Lyons. ".....Huic ubi Maiis Calendis per Academiae huius Bibliopolas Lugduno allatus est tuus libellus......"

Now as soon as the Apology of Albucius was out a copy of it came into the hands of de l'Estoile. The students were reading it "in concessum." De l'Estoile entered the room, took it from them and read especially such parts as appeared to refer to him. He did not think it worth answering. But Duchemin determines at once to do this for him.

Once more the suggestion is made that Albucius is none other than Alciati himself.

The rest of the book (Fo. 7a ff.) is an inquiry into the meaning of "bonorum possessio decretalis ac edictalis."

The closing sentence (Fo. 24b) is a plea for toleration. ".....Ut enim dissidere ab altero humanum, et ex se malum non est reprehendere, ita cuiquam male velle, est a Christiana professione alienissimum."

In closing the date (Aureliae, 1529, Idibus Julii) and a table of Errata are given.

---

33) These sentences indicate the author's acquaintance with Fulgosius and Jason.

## Section 3.   At the Royal College (Lecteurs Royaux)

During his Bourges period Calvin made some trips to Paris. It was on one of these (March, 1531) that he published the *Antapologia* for his friend Duchemin. Scarcely had he returned when the sickness of his father recalled him to Noyon. The latter's death, we know, caused a change in his plan of studies. He decided to give himself to literary and philological labors. So he established residence once more in Paris in the summer of 1531. Before settling finally in Paris he went to Orléans, surely to visit Francis Daniel. On his return he is known to have walked the entire distance back to Paris.[34]

Upon his arrival a certain Coiffartus offered him lodging, but he declined his hospitality since his house was too far from the "school of Danès."[35] It is apparent, therefore, that he designed to take advantage at once of the King's new foundation of the Royal Readers.

It is not necessary to conclude that his new studies signify a radical break with the study of the law. The *Seneca Commentaries* indicate a live interest in legal questions of a fundamental sort. Rather must he be thought of as wanting to be a thoroughly equipped humanist who was interested in the Justinian *Pandects* not only but also in the classics generally. He was a philologian first. Valla had been the first to point out forcefully the dignified Latinity of the *Pandects,* and thenceforth they were part of the library of the finished humanist. If Calvin manifested a deeper interest in the *Pandects* than Valla did, it was because the French humanism made its appearance when

---

[34] LEFRANC, A., *La Jeunnesse de Calvin,* p. 87. "Like most men of his time he appears to have been a great walker. These indefatigable travellers did not shrink from physical activity. They undertook journeys on foot or bodily exercises as regularly as they passed long hours in study. All these men of the 16th century travelled much. It was the secret of that balance of mind and body that surprises us. Contrary to the prejudices that obtain on their account, they cannot be accused of leading the solitary life of a hermited savant always buried in books. They were people whose company was most agreeable. . . . Seeing much of the world, surrounded by numerous friends, they did not know isolation. Calvin is a most striking example of this. In Paris as in Orléans, in Bourges as in Noyon, he lives in a most lively circle. . . . His correspondence shows him in these years of study as a young man of agreeable manners, very expansive, loved and sought after, entrancing all he met."

[35] Cf. *Opera* X (Pars II), 10.

jurisprudence was more studied. Plain it is, however, that Calvin was not of a mind to give himself to the law as a profession. The reason is that he was averse to the routine of the courts, certainly not because of an aversion to penetrating deeply into the mysteries of the law. And so he passes from Bourges to Paris. He will study the classical literature as a whole.

The institution of the Royal Readers merits description.[36] Under the influence of Budé, Cop, and others King Francis I had for some time contemplated the establishment of lectureships in Latin, Greek, and Hebrew. This was one of the progressive things to do in that age. The old universities were so backward in cultivating these three languages that the humanists cried for institutions of their own. So in Louvain since 1515 there had been an institution where these languages were taught. Founded by a merchant, Busleiden, who bequeathed to his city the sum of 20,000 livres for that purpose, it was established and at first directed by none less than Erasmus. Also in Rome the College of the Young Greeks, founded by Leo X, had begun to attract the savants of Europe in general, and Budé in particular.[37]

The king made promises, but delayed fulfilment of them. There appears to have been considerable negotiation with Erasmus for the purpose of getting him to establish the school. Erasmus, however, did not desire to reside in Paris, and made his excuses.

At last Budé calls the affair to his king's attention by means of his Greek Preface to his *Commentary on the Greek Language,* a most famous work. He reminds his sovereign of all his promises, and impresses on him the

---

[36] The last and most learned historian of the Collège de France, outgrowth of the Lecteurs Royaux or Royal Readers, is Abel Lefranc who has given us his fulsome study in *Histoire du Collège de France, depuis ses origines jusqu' à la fin du première empire* (1893). Cf.also DE BEZÉ, THEO., *Histoire ecclesiastique,* I, 6 f.; DOUMERGUE, E., *op. cit.,* p. 201 ff.; HERMINJARD, A. L., *ap. cit.,* I, 27 f.; DE BUDÉ, E, *Vie de Guillaume de Budé, fondateur du Collège de France (1467–1540),* 1884; CREVIER, M., *Histoire de l'Université de Paris de puis son origine jusqu' à l'année 1600"* (1761), p. 245 ff.; LAVISSE–RAMBEAUD, *Histoire Générale . . . ,* IV, p. 178 f.

[37] DE BUDÉ, E., *Vie de Budé,* p. 26 ff.; cf. also Latomus (JACQUES MASSON), *De trium linguarum et studii theologici ratione,* which appeared in 1518 (Anvers). Through Budé Latomus later obtained a chair in the Royal College. In 1537 he became rector of Louvain.

utter need of the lectureships. Among those who second the appeals of Budé is Marguerite of Navarre.[38]

In March, 1530, the new institution was finally opened. Beza wrote later that for this one deed Francis had merited the title of "the Great."[39] It was a revolutionary act. The new teaching broke flatly with the current habits and methods of teaching. It substituted liberty for routine, the spirit for the letter. No obligatory grades, no tuition, elective courses. "It was all a revolution of which nobody perhaps, not even those who called it forth, could measure the results.[40] At first there was no separate building, that is, no school in the proper sense of the word, nor even fixed chairs, only courses. So at the start there were two courses in Greek by Pierre Danès and Jaques Toussain, two courses in Hebrew by François Vatable and Agathias Guidacerius, and one in mathematics by Oroncius Finé. In 1531 a third professor of Hebrew was added, Paul Paradis.[41]

It is natural that Calvin should have been drawn to Danès. Without official prerogatives, he appeared from the beginning as chief of all the Readers. The fame of his teaching was one of the principal causes for the success of the institution. He was of a lordly presence. He was credited with a vast knowledge, and his mind embraced an encyclopedic culture. He was one of the most powerful spirits of the Renaissance. Latin, Greek, Hebrew, mathematics, medicine, theology, were like play to him. Politically influential, in favor at the court, he was besides internationally famous as a scholar. Amyot, Barnabas, Brisson, Gagnaeus, were his disciples. Some of his contemporaries rated him higher than Budé. An enthusiastic listener said of him:

Magnus Budaeus, major Danesius ille,
Argivos norat, iste etiam reliquos.[42]

To praise Danès above Budé is extravagant, however. Comparing the two one must concede that the latter made a more solid contribution to learning than the former.

The question of where Calvin got his knowledge of Hebrew was apparently not raised until Baumgartner

---

[38] Preface to the Commentary; DE BUDÉ, op. cit., p. 38 ff.
[39] Op. cit., I, p. 7.
[40] LEFRANC, A., op. cit., p. 107.
[41] DOUMERGUE, E., op. cit., p. 204.
[42] LEFRANC, A., op. cit., p. 172.

brought it up.[43]    Even Lefranc had supposed that he had
learned it from Wolmar in Orléans and Bourges,[44] though
it cannot be proved that Wolmar knew Hebrew very well.[45]
Lefrance scarcely pays attention to Vatable in connection
with Calvin's days at the Lecteurs Royaux. Yet this man
was on very intimate terms with him. Vatable was "rich in
an immense erudition which he knew how to communicate
to his students. He attracted large audiences among whom
were found even Jews."[46] Vatable left no writings; students
published some of his class-notes.[47]

What impelled Calvin to study Hebrew? As far as we
can determine he was not yet deeply interested in the Scriptures. His cousin Olivétan was already well-versed in the
Hebrew, and he may have had something to do with it. We
must be on our guard, however, to think that Calvin studied
Hebrew in the year 1531-32 with the same zeal that he did
Greek and Latin. Tradition has it that he began with
Hebrew in Basel and Strassburg.[48] Vatable as a teacher
of Hebrew is never connected with Calvin, not even by Beza.
Compared with his interest in the classical languages his
interest in Hebrew seems to have been that of a dillettant.
His mind was set on Greek and Latin philology, and the
result was the *Seneca Commentaries,* replete with Latin
and Greek, but containing only one loose reference to the
Old Testament Scriptures.

Hebrew attracted him in a general way only. It was
something the younger progressive humanists were expected
to take up. Knowledge of it, even the most general, would
open the door of acquaintance with another set of scholars.
There was the great Reuchlin, of course, whose Hebrew
Grammar had appeared in 1506; Böchenstein and Wolfgang
Capito who published theirs in 1518; there were the books

---

43) BAUMGARTNER, A. J., *Calvin Hébraisant et interprète de l'Ancien
Testament,* (Paris, 1889).

44) *Jeunesse de Calvin,* p. 81.

45) BAUMGARTNER, *op. cit.,* p. 14.

46) BAUMGARTNER, *op. cit.,* p. 15; DE BEZE, Tœ., *Les Vrais Pourtraits,*
p. 139. En quel rang te tiendrons-nous, Vatable, tant admiré en ta profession par les Juifs mesmes, qui as tant aprins à grand nombre de
chrestiens: vue que tu as tenu si peu de compte du thrésor des saínctes
escritures, dont tu faisois part aux autres, que meme tu l'as rejetté?"

47) DOUMERGUE, E., *op. cit.,* p. 205, n. 4.

48) BAUMGARTNER, *op cit.,* p. 8.

of Elias Levita (1517-18); Moses Kimchi's *Rudimenta hebraica* (1520); and the grammar of Matthew Aurogallus.[49] The conflict, moreover, of Reuchlin with the Cologne Faculty had lent luster to the study of Hebrew in the eyes of the youth. The suspicion that it was a dangerous thing to study this language gave it a tang that made it tasteful.[50] Even the enlightened Erasmus feared that the study of Hebrew would perhaps cause a revival of Judaism, just as the study of the classical languages had issued in much paganism.[51] Small wonder that the Sorbonne should seek to interdict the study of Hebrew as well as Greek, as it did in 1533. Both Danès and Vatable were ordered to appear before the Parlement on charges of heresy.[52]

I take it that it was a mixture of curiosity and a sense of humanistic superiority that led Calvin to study Hebrew under Vatable. Just so the Egyptologist and Sumerian scholar rate higher academically than the average minister with only a Hebrew training. The fact that Calvin became a very great reformer should not blind us to the fact that he may have been happy to be numbered among the most progressive radicals of the day. Neither must we suppose that he did nothing except for the most weighty reasons. In the meantime he little supposed, I dare say, what a vast use he would some day make of the Hebrew.

We next hear of John Calvin in the spring of 1532. On April 4 of that year,[53] his Commentaries on Seneca's *De Clementia* are published. He had spent two or three months in Noyon, after his father's death in 1531, so that it could not have been earlier than August or September that he began to attend the lectures of Danès and Vatable. In the

---

[49] BAUMGARTNER, *op. cit.*, p. 17.

[50] HERMINJARD, *op. cit.*, I, p. 9 f. Letter of Reuchlin to Lefèvre, August 31, 1512.

[51] HERMINJARD, *op. cit.*, I, p. 29 f. Letter of Erasmus to Capito, February 26, 1517. " . . . Unus adhuc scrupulus habet animum meum, ne sub obtentu priscae literaturae renascentis caput erigere conetur Paganismus: ut sunt et inter Christianos, qui titulo pene duntaxat Christum agnoscunt, caeterum intus Gentilitatem spirant, aut ne, renascentibus Hebraeorum literis, Judaismus meditetur per occasionem reviviscere. . . . Optarim frigidos istas argutias, aut amputari prorsus, aut certe solis . . . . Theologis, et Christum illum via fieri posse existimo, si linguarum adminiculis adjuti, in ipsis fontibus philosophemur."

[52] BAUMGARTNER, *op. cit.*, p. 15.

[53] Cf. HERMINJARD, *op. cit.*, II, p. 413, n. 7, for critical remarks on this date.

space of seven or eight months thereafter he had his volume on the press. This was an amazing achievement, even if we look upon it as a sort of doctor's thesis (which it was not of course). Certainly he must have economized his time. His refusal to lodge at Coiffart's house because it was too far from the school of Danès indicates this. Again, he took no special work in Latin, as there was no Latin chair as yet. Besides, his aim was to master the Greek above all. The Commentaries testify to this hard work on the Greek authors.

The decision to publish this book must have been made before attending the Lecteurs Royaux. The months in Noyon, in the summer of 1531, must have been devoted mainly to outlining his course for the year.

Behind his decision to write on Seneca's *De Clementia* there lay a background an examination of which will reveal much that is of the highest interest in young Calvin.

## CHAPTER IV.

## THE BACKGROUND OF THE SENECA COMMENTARIES

THE Commentaries on Seneca were in a way the culmination of Calvin's youthful humanism. In them he has
gathered up the results of his early training and thought, in
so far as the contents of Seneca's treatise on Clemency permit. An investigation into the reasons for Calvin's writing
this work is not only necessary but pleasurable, for it lays
bare several things about his mind and heart in these early
years. Again, these Commentaries form a link with his
work as a reformer, for though the *Institutes* breathe a
different spirit and set forth a different system of thought,
they betray sympathies that had not been there were it not
for the author's one time indulgence in the Stoic philosophy.

### Section 1.  The Revival of Stoicism

The author of the essay on Clemency was the most famous
of the Roman Stoics. Calvin's electing to study this author
is of unusual significance because it offers us the opportunity
for investigating the sources of the alleged Stoical elements
in his theology. But there is another reason, namely, that
Calvin's Commentaries on Seneca are only one volume on
Stoic thought among several in the Fifteenth and Sixteenth
Centuries. There was in those days a very diligent study of
Seneca in particular and of Stoicism in general. Léontine
Zanta has accordingly called her admirable study of this
phenomenon "The Renaissance of Stoicism in the Sixteenth
Century."[1]

Stoicism was first of all looked upon by the learned as a
useful philosophy of consolation for disturbed times. As
such it found a situation quite ready for its services. The
crumbling of the empire in 1250 and the transference of the
papacy to France at the end of 1306 had delivered Italy up
to anarchy. Civil wars, local tyrannies, the glorification of
physical power, the reduction of morality to a justification
of means being sanctioned by ends,—all this brought pres-

---

[1] *La Renaissance du Stoicisme au XVIe siècle* (Paris, 1914).

tige to what was called "effort." It produced a radical individualism. It brought an era of great personalities, e. g.,
Cosmo de Medici, Niccolo Niccoli, thanks to whose interest
and generosity all doors were opened to artists, erudites,
humanists, who brought back the classical culture newly
discovered.[2] Intellectual culture opened the way to honors
for its devotees. The rise of Eneas Silvius Piccolomini illustrates the church's zeal to recognize the new spirit. A species
of heartless egotism develops, however, exhibited in the
terrible war of pamphlets of the Poggios, the Filelfos, the
Vallas. The fierce struggle for princely or ducal or papal
favor, on which depended the productivity of the scholar or
artist, is vividly pictured in Benvenuto Cellini's *Memoirs*.

The boundless individualism of these two and a half
centuries, the Fourteenth, Fifteenth, and the first half of
the Sixteenth, was in itself quite unlike Stoicism, but was
nevertheless the only condition for its development. For if
the hand of every man was lifted up against his rival's, the
only possible condition of survival was to appeal to a higher
law. Conscience got a new meaning. Cellini's constant
reminding the reader that he is merely an honest man, and
that therefore all was well with him, is significant. Virtue
and happiness became almost identical in meaning. The
incorruptible Cato's life became a sermon. The future
life tended to become less and less of a consideration in the
determination of conduct.

Another factor in the popularization of Stoicism was
found in the danger of Epicureanism. Valla[3] and Antonio
Beccadelli Panormita were its apologists. But the average
man cannot endure the liberty of the hedonist. Leonardo
da Vincis are rare. Whither to turn for a defense against
this doctrine? The church was too corrupt itself politically,
and where she was pure she was too austere, too wanting in
art. But men still clung to the old church. People had no
mind to become heretical seceders. So to save the situation
it was recognized that Christianity had to have a new spirit,
—that of the humanistic Christian. Though Petrarch attacked the reigning scholasticism he remained profoundly

---

[2] ZANTA, L., *op cit.*, p. 3 f.
[3] *De Voluptate*, Opera, pp. 896–999.

Christian.[4]  He warns constantly that the Christian must always survive the humanist. Less and less timid did humanism become, till with Sadoleto one "is convinced that to make Christians, it is first of all necessary to make men." He preached a mild Stoicism, more like that of Horace than Epictetus.[5]  Of course, when Caraffa had become Pope Paul IV, the Sadoleto type of Roman Catholic was passé. (Calvin's regard for Sadoleto is well known.)  The softening of conventions by appealing to higher moral laws, and the strengthening of minds and hearts against the allurements of hedonism by preaching the laws of duty constituted the two-fold service of Stoicism.  Thus it became the refuge of the noble souls of the times, as in ancient times it had been for Cicero, Seneca, Marcus Aurelius.  And for the enlightened it was the more welcome since in their eyes there was no major difficulty in reconciling an acceptance of Stoicism with their remaining loyal sons of the church.

The general esteem of Stoicism is reflected in the literature of the day.  Politian (who is cited in the *Seneca Commentaries*) published a translation of Epictetus's Manual in 1498.  Poggio wrote his *Historiae de varietate fortunae*, Tristano Caracciolo his *De varietate fortunae*. Again, Aenèas Sylvius wrote *Epistolae de fortuna*, and Pontano an essay which he called *De fortitudine*.  These works are representative, though they do not exhaust the list.  Besides works whose titles suggest Stoicism there are scores which contain whole chapters, sections, paragraphs on the subject.  It was the most popular philosophy.  Only the counter-Reformation checked it effectively in the Roman Church, and Protestant scholasticism in the Reformed churches.  Thenceforth philosophers do their thinking outside the fold.

The revival of Stoicism was also a factor in preparing the 16th century Reformation.  It will therefore be enlightening to study this phase of it, in as much as Calvin passed through so marked a Stoic period.

The neo-Stoicism promised to be more than a philosophy of consolation for the educated man.  Like the ancient Stoicism it sought to fill a deep need of the spirit.  When

---

[4]) ZANTA, L., *op. cit.*, p. 7; DE NOLHAC, P., *Pétrarque et l'humanisme*, nouv. éd., Paris, 1907, 6f.

[5]) ZANTA, *op. cit.*, p. 8.

the polis, the Greek City-State, fell, when Rome passed through the purgatory of the Second Punic War, it was Stoicism largely that stiffened the nerve and strengthened the hearts of men. Likewise the old state religions of Greece and Rome having petrified, having become mere machines for maintaining contractual relations with the supernatural powers, men sought for spiritual satisfaction elsewhere. Individuality was born. "With individuality came personality, and with personality, conscience—a word which the Stoics coined and popularized."[6] In contrast with the huge state machinery of mediation between God and man, Stoicism "made a vigorous attempt to attain a unified view of the world by eliminating the conflict between the natural and the supernatural."[7]

All this forms a striking parallel with the age of the Renaissance. There was the collapse of the Holy Roman Empire and the rise of nationalism; the passing of Medieval collectivism and the nascence of individualism; the petrifaction of the Roman Church (now little more than an instrument for contracting with God for the salvation of man) and the amazing growth of the opinion that its mediation is nonessential. In the midst of all the resulting confusion the neo-Stoicism contributed in a three-fold way to the restoration of order.

In the first place it began the spiritual renaissance of the West by an appreciation of man as man. Therefore it is rightly called humanism.[8] Apart from extravagances like that of Pomponius Laetus and his followers, the revival of respect for the human being was healthy. Nothing human is foreign to me, was a favorite quotation. Men felt a kinship with the noble pagans, and this new sentiment extended to noble contemporaries. In the person of Luther Christianity was beginning to recognize excommunicates like Huss and the Greek Orthodox Church. Over against the exclusiveness of the Roman communion there was developed the idea of

---

6) Angus, S., *The Mystery-Religions and Christianity: A Study in the the Religious Background of Early Christianity*, (New York, 1925), p. 207 f.

7) Case, S. J., *Experience with the Supernatural in Early Christian Times* (New York and London, 1929), p. 14.

8) Schevill, F., "The Society of the Italian Renaissance," in *The Civilization of the Renaissance*, by J. W. Thompson, G. Rowley, F. Schevill, G. Sarton (Chicago, University of Chicago Press, 1929), p. 60 ff.

differentiating between the visible and the invisible church. The Reformation churches would in the course of time become clannish themselves, of course, but their first protest was against this sort of thing, which Calvin and others proved by their unitive efforts.[9]

The neo-Stoicism was a mighty factor in the breakdown of Roman sectarianism and in the establishment of a new plane of communion, just as the old Stoicism had been in disturbing the authority of the mystery-religions. The latter had their sacraments, initiates, etc., much as the Roman Church had, while Stoicism stood for the equality of all men alike before God and the world-order, apart from initiation into the "mysteries." On this new universalism Christianity reared itself. When on the eve of the Reformation Christianity itself, in turn, had degenerated into merely another "mystery-religion," it was the task of the revived Stoicism to prepare the way for the much-needed Reformation. Nothing could stop the authority wherewith it demolished the artificial fences of the church. It was a thrilling sight to have the sons of the proud Western Church acknowledge the cultural superiority of their Eastern brothers who had opened to them the treasures of the real Plato and Aristotle. The logic of the situation demanded that religious thought should be affected to its foundations.

In the second place, the new Stoicism promoted free investigation, the scientific spirit. The modern natural sciences had not yet been born, but there were other fields. The passion for exploration and discovery was boundless. In scholarship this was shown by the new interest in philology. Restoring the received classical texts to their original purity was the reigning ambition. Just as the ancient Stoicism had inherited the scientific spirit of classical Greece, so the neo-Stoicism endeavored to unfold its possibilities in the Renaissance. The Stoic requirement that men are responsible to the moral world-order, and that therefore truth is of primary concern to everybody, the conviction that the church had by no means defined all of truth, despite the encyclopedism of Acquinas, Albertus, et al.; the discovery of the Byzantium treasures;—all this had to issue

---

[9] Mc NEILL, J. T., *Unitive Protestantism*, Chicago, 1930, presents a well-documented discussion of Protestant unitive efforts.

in scientific freedom. Lorenzo Valla's critical work had destroyed forever the faith of the Renaissance man in the Donation of Constantine, and with its fall one of the central props for the Roman ecclesiastical edifice crumbled. Worse still were his critical notes on the New Testament, destroying the infallibility of the Vulgate. His passion for investigating all things led him to a mockery of the jurists and their commentaries, and his laughter did not die until the reforms of Budé and Alciati were inaugurated. The Reformation, particularly the Calvinistic, was to be deeply indebted to this new scientific spirit. Leaving aside the horrible facts of Calvin's part in the burning of Servetus, and of opposition to Castellio because of the latter's interpretation of the Song of Solomon, his work proves how thoroughly the new spirit had affected him in three directions: First, in his freedom in the matter of church history. He does not accept the approved authorities, the official narratives and interpretations. Secondly, in his life-long endeavor to establish the true text of Scripture. He continued the work of Valla's textual criticism, and approved the more elaborate technique developed for it by Erasmus. Thirdly, he was one of the first famous critics of the principle of absolute monarchy. Hotman too was after all a Calvinist.

Thirdly, for the magic of ecclesiastical mediation between God and man the new spirit substituted the satisfactions gained from the simple discharge of duty, from being answerable to conscience only. The case of Cicero is a good illustration of this phase of ancient Stoicism. Cicero was an augur, but was at the same time committed to the ethical idealism of Stoicism, and shows its influence by his "frequent humorous mode" of treating the subject of divination.[10] Again, in Seneca, as in Virgil, there is present a strong sense of sin, with an accompanying practice of self-examination and sensitiveness to conscience.[11] In the Reformers conscience was largely personalized, as it were, at least they spoke of God rather than conscience, meaning to an extent the same thing. At all events, they sought for the cause of salvation in the direct relation of God to man,

---

[10] TEUFFEL, *History of Roman Literature*, I, 290, 298, 300; ANGUS, S., *op. cit.*, p. 33; CASE, S. J., *op. cit.*, p. 13.

[11] ANGUS, S., *op. cit.*, pp. 206–214.

not in the institution of the church. For that reason Gott-
schalk in the 9th century was already persecuted for heresy
because of his belief in predestination of the high Augustin-
ian sort. So Wycliffe affirmed predestination, and held
correspondingly subversive views with respect to the Roman
hierarchy. There had been the Brethren of the Common
Life who held the same view, but with a mystical emphasis.
That Luther and Calvin were both predestinarians was quite
logical; it was their final argument against the Roman
instrumentalism in effecting salvation. Moreover, it was a
monk's experience of the sense of sin that no official cere-
mony could appease. The Theses of October 31, 1517, were
not so much heretical in content as presumptious in that a
mere monk had an opinion at all.[12] The popularity of
Seneca in the Renaissance and early Reformation is well-
attested. His criticism of the old Stoic not withstanding,
Erasmus twice edited his works, and Zwingli called him the
"husbandman of souls." Calvin in the *Seneca Commentaries*
takes note of a paragraph in which Seneca is eloquent on
the subject of conscience, and quotes Cicero's "Magna est
vis conscientiae," adding that he has observed like utter-
ances frequently in Seneca.[13]

We have the evidence, therefore, that the revival of the
classics, and with it of Stoicism, was one of the factors
conditioning the Reformation. None of the greater minds
of the Reformation accepted a simon-pure Stoicism. They
drew their major premises from the profounder and broader positions of the New Testament and the fathers. Yet not
even the New Testament was without its historical prepara-
tion in Stoicism. Paul quotes the Stoic Aratus. The friend-
liness of Christianity to many of the Stoic conceptions could
not but be felt by the serious humanist. That this philosophy was inadequate for saving men who after all had 1500
years of church history behind them is apparent. But it
presaged great things for both the First and the Sixteenth
Centuries respectively that in each so wonderful a literature
as the Stoic was eagerly being read.

---

12) JANSSEN, R., "Principles of the Evangelical Reformers," in *Onze
Toekomst*, April 1, 1931, Vol. 34, No. 13, Section 2.
13) *Comm.*, pp. 102, 112, 142. It must be admitted that magical rites
were early used in the church, borrowed from the Mystery religions, but
these did not belong to the genius of the new religion. Cf. SCOTT, E. F.,
*The Beginnings of the Church*, p. 177 ff.

Just as Stoicism in ancient times had meant that the religions had to reform or perish, so the new Stoicism meant as much for the Sixteenth Century. It was one of the peculiarities of humanists that they wished indeed to be committed to the idealism of both Stoicism and primitive Christianity, but not to press unduly, to the point of jeopardizing their personal safety, the reforms implied. Their method of reform was the gentlemanly one of suggestion. Hence we have the *Seneca Commentaries* of Calvin.

### Section 2.   The Harmonistic Spirit

In this section we shall elaborate on the fact that Christians have generally seen points of resemblance, if not identity, between it and their own beliefs. We shall do so from the point of view that there has been a wide-spread desire to harmonize the teachings of the noble pagans with Christianity. While Calvin criticizes Stoicism[14] and never speaks of "our Stoicism," as he does of "our religion," there is obviously a thrust at bringing the two together. In fact, he is rather explicit about it in at least one notable place. In Book I, chapter I, pp. 17, 18, we find his comments on the beginning of that famous passage which Seneca puts in the mouth of Nero: "I of all mortals am accepted, and I am elected to function in the stead of the gods." Calvin remarks: "This speech is a mask behind which the emperor may cogitate. It is a fruit of conscience..... This speech hangs on the opinion of the Stoics, who attribute the procuring of things human to the gods, asserting providence, leaving nothing to the temerity of fortune....." Then he raises objection to the "dei otiosi" of the Epicureans. He approves Homer's speaking of Jove-nurtured kings, of his writing that Agamemnon was constituted king by Jupiter. He quotes an equally elegant passage from Pliny in the same vein. In Plutarch's reflections on princes he finds the teaching that princes are ministers of God, for the safety and protection of men. From Numa Pompilius he gets the expression that "regnum esse deorum ministerium." So the Artabani (in Plutarch) as kings are "simulacra dei omnia servantis." "Thus Plato, in the Gorgias, makes God a sort of emperor of the human race, assigning to each his place and station."

---

14) *Comm.*, pp. 154, 156, e. g.

This entire paragraph he closes with these words: *"That also is the confession of our religion,* namely, that there is no power except from God, and the powers that be are ordained by God, according to Romans XIII." (Est etiam illa confessio religionis nostrae, non est potestatem nisi a Deo, et quae sunt, a Deo ordinatas esse, ad Rom. XIII.) This is a most significant passage. It is the author's explicit statement of belief that the noble pagans agree on this important matter with his own religion. That God is the author of all royal authority is the basis for his belief that princes have no right to abuse their power. Compare with this his Epistle Dedicatory of the *Institutes*. This identity of "confession" is one of the bases of his theory of common grace. Christianity cannot help recognizing the good in man generally.

[NOTE.—Calvin perceived that the Christian ideal of virtue in some respects coincides with the Stoic. Cf. *Comm.*, p. 15f. where he comments on Seneca's words "Quamvis enim recte factorum verus fructus est......" He quotes Augustine, *De civitate Dei*, lib. viii, on virtue as the ultimate end, "virtutem scilicet esse ultimum finem, quem omnes actus, omnia vitae humanae opera et consilia respiciunt. *In quam sententiam accipiendus est hic locus."* Again, speaking of filial piety, the opinions of Cicero and Seneca are endorsed by Augustine, "Verum quoniam parentes nobis quasi deorum vice sunt, ad eos derivatur: quod innuit Augustinus libro x de Civitate. Pietas proprie Dei cultus intelligi solet, quam Graeci ευσεβείαν vocant....." (*Ibid.* p. 102). Yet the indifference of Seneca and Cicero to reputation, and their being satisfied with the mere approval of conscience is not approved by "our religion": "Haec apud philosophos valeant, nobis vero longe aliud praescribit nostra religio. Nam, ut ait Augustinus de communi vita clericorum: Duae res sunt conscientia, et fama: conscientia necessaria est tibi, fama proximo tuo. Qui confidens conscientiae negligit famam, crudelis est." Furthermore, *Ibid.* p. 154, "Pro misericordia contra Stoicos lege Augustinum libro ix et xiv de Civit." Cf. also *Ibid.* pp. 136, 142, 157. Calvin's references to other sources of Christian opinions can be found, *Ibid.* p. 37f. (Gregory), p. 123 (Jerome), pp. 124, 133 (Cyprian).]

In connection with our discussion of the harmonistic spirit of Calvin it is well to show that he was not at all revolutionary in this respect. For Stoicism in particular had always been more or less in favor with Christians. Never

had it been entirely assimilated, of course. For example,
Clement of Alexandria repudiated what he called the Stoic
materialization of God, but explicitly states that its morality
is worthy of the highest praise.[15]   So Lactantius places over
against the Stoic repression of the passions the Christian
doctrine of directing them.[16]   He refutes the Stoic doctrine
of the passionless God.[17]   But in general Lactantius
speaks favorably of Seneca.   As a satirist inveighing against
pagan idolatry, against philosophers who preach virtue but
do not practice it, or against Epicureans, Seneca wins his
warm approval.  He also finds in him many things that are
in direct accord with his own Christianity, e. g., in his
religious spirit with respect to the majesty of God, his
creative power, his exalted and untrammeled liberty.   He
endorses Seneca's noble maxims on virtue which alone can
lead man to happiness, on the true worship which consists
in justice and in purity of heart, and on conscience that is
always open to the view of God.[18]

The Middle Ages had lost that vivid contact with the pagan
philosophers which the early fathers had enjoyed, so there
is little use in tracing the thin stream of their appreciation
in these centuries.  It will be useful to describe the attachment of Zwingli, Calvin's elder contemporary and one of
the three great names in Reformation history, to the Stoic
philosophy.   Zwingli had been trained in the classics,
especially in Plato, the Stoics, and neo-Platonism, under
Bünzli in Basel, Heinrich Wölflin in Bern, in Vienna under
Conrad Celtis, and throughout by the reading of Erasmus.[19]
His debt to Seneca is as great as that to Plato, and both conditioned his attitude to the Scriptures.   "This was especially
apparent from his anthropology.   Although he is convinced
that one should permit oneself to be led only by the Word of
God, he nevertheless has taught what he had learned from

15) DE FAYE, E., Clément d'Alexandrie, Étude sur les rapports du
Christianisme et de la philosophie grecque au IIe siècle, Paris, 1898,
p. 157 f.

16) PICHON, R., Lactante, Étude sur le mouvement philosophique et
religieux sous le règne de Constantin, Paris, 1901, p. 148 ff.

17) Ibid., p. 167 ff.

18) Ibid., p. 233 ff.  On the Stoic influence in St. Ambrose cf. DE LA-
BRIOLLE, P., The Life and Times of St. Ambrose, transl. from the French
by Herbert Wilson, London, 1928, pp. 139, 145 f., 191 ff.

19) OORTHUYS, G., De Anthropologie van Zwingli, Leiden, 1905, p. 6 ff.

Plato and Seneca on this subject, and he has not been able to forget the influence of their doctrine. The Scriptural views never vanquish his pagan anthropology."[20]    The incisive influence of this philosophy on a man like Zwingli illustrates the debt of Reformed theology to the classics. His description of Seneca as "Ille animarum unicus ex gentibus agricola"[21] has been referred to. He quotes with approval a paragraph of Seneca, condemning the body as an enemy of the soul.[22]    Again, Seneca is called a saintly man, and referred to as an authority in the same breath with Moses and Paul, as having drawn knowledge from the same fount,[23] and finally he is called a believer.[24]    Calvin never permitted himself such extravagant language, but essentially his view, in 1532, is the same.[25]

### Section 3.    The Influence of Erasmus

Besides the fact that Stoicism and the "harmonistic spirit" were in the air, there was another reason why Calvin's attention would be drawn to Seneca. This was the appeal of Erasmus to the young scholars to re-edit the old philosopher's works. In his Preface to the 1529 edition of Seneca Erasmus had written that it was his desire that "some man more learned, more fortunate, less occupied than we, should add to this edition as much as we have added to the preceding, so that Seneca might be read without weariness and with profit. We have wished that this writer be provided with scholiums which may put an end to the temerities of the corruptors of the text."[26]    Undoubtedly it was this

---

20) *Ibid.*, p. 10.
21) *Ibid.*, p. 36.
22) *Ibid.*, p. 35 f.
23) *Ibid.*, p. 102 f.
24) *Ibid.*, p. 109 .
25) Cf. also GAGUIN, R., *Epistolae et orationes*, Edition Thuasme, 1903, who says that in the ancients one can find isolated thoughts that illustrate the Christian truths, that even certain of them professed doctrines which it is easy to reconcile with the dogmas of the faith.    Mention is made of Plato and the Stoics; BUDÉ, G., *De transitu hellenismi ad Christianismum*, Paris, 1535, a work very much in vogue in the 16th century, as also his translation of St. Basil's famous letter, *De vita per solitudinem transigenda*, Paris, 1502, maintains that profane culture, far from being an obstacle to theology, is in a way its natural prologue.
26) LECOULTRE, H., "Calvin d'après son Commentaire sur la De Clementia de Senècque," in *Revue de Théologie et de Philosophie*, 1891, p. 54 f.

edition that Calvin used in the main, and it is reasonably certain that he also had read Erasmus's exhortation to give the public a more readable edition of Seneca. But he had also read Erasmus's 1515 edition of Seneca. "In 1515 already there had appeared an edition of Seneca bearing the name of Erasmus; but Erasmus had declared it very faulty and had disavowed it in the Preface of his 1529 edition, affirming that he had furnished for the same only the Preface, and that for the rest it was the work of a friend in whom he had placed too much confidence."[27] This disavowal did not prevent Calvin from attributing the work of 1515 to Erasmus. "Twice did Erasmus sweat in this arena," he says in the Preface of the *Seneca Commentaries*. This was the sort of higher criticism he indulged in at this time, as both he and Duchemin had done previously in regard to the authorship of the Apology of Albucius. If Erasmus ever read the *Seneca Commentaries* of young Calvin, this imputation of error, to put it mildly, on his part would not be calculated to win his favor.

Nevertheless, the influence of Erasmus on Calvin could not have been slight. What young and ambitious humanist could escape his spell? Unchallenged master in his profession, it had been inexplicable had Calvin not deferred to him. Only Budé to his mind ranks with the great Hollander, and that the former was his country-man had perhaps something to do with that. The great work of Erasmus had already been done. There were the *Praise of Folly,* the *Adages,* the *Colloquies.* Surely, Calvin must have read them all. We are certain that he had also read the *Ciceronianus,* perhaps the most erudite satire that had ever flowed from his pen. His critical editions of the classics he knew well.

Not only had he absorbed much information about the classics from Erasmus, but also much of the old humanist's thought. As late as November, 1533, a document was given to the world, in the composition of which Calvin had been interested. It was the Rectoral Address of Nicholas Cop.[28] Whether or not Calvin had a part in its composition as such, it is certain that he was in perfect accord with his friend.

---

[27] *Ibid.,* p. 54.
[28] For a discussion of Calvin's part in its writing, cf. WALKER, W., *op. cit.,* pp. 68, 98–101.

The fact that part of the manuscript has been preserved in his own hand-writing at least indicates his desire to preserve it.[29] Now this address opens with an apostrophe to "Christian philosophy": "Magna quaedam res est ac longe praestantior, quam dici aut animo et cogitatione comprehendi possit, Christiana philosophia."[30] The expression "Christian philosophy" is characteristically Erasmian, though it had long been used by the Florentine Academy.[31] There is an evident dependence on the Preface to Erasmus's third edition of his Greek New Testament (1524).[32] Consonant with the spirit of Erasmus, there is no indication of wanting to break with the church. The Introduction of the address concludes with a salutation to the Virgin.[33] This proves that Nicholas Cop, and also Calvin, still shared the sentiment of the prevailing reform movement in Paris, though they were certainly too radical for the Sorbonne.

The spiritual authority of Erasmus lent weight to his position in letters. The evidence present is conclusive that Calvin was one of his followers. The elegant words of praise he gives the old humanist in the Commentaries were no extravagance. After his conversion to Protestantism he would withhold such encomiums as "Erasmus is the chief ornament of letters, none having greater charm."[34] Calvin's work on Seneca may to an extent be thought of as his contribution to reform in the spirit of Erasmus. It is true that he nowhere speaks of this in so many words. But the moral purpose running through the Commentaries is plain.

The influence of Budé towards writing the *Seneca Commentaries* will be touched on in our section on Guillaume Budé (Chapter IV, Section 3).

---

[29] LANG, A., *Die älteste theologischen Arbeiten Calvins*, p. 28; MULLER, *Calvins Bekehrung*, p. 231 ff.; WALKER, *op. cit.*, p. 101.

[30] *Concio Academica nomine rectoris universitatis Parisiensis Nicolai Copi scripta et recitata*, Cal. Nov. 1533. Opera Calvini IX, 873 ff., X, Pars II, 30 ff.

[31] Cf. TILLEY, A., *The Dawn of the French Renaissance*, p. 38.

[32] WALKER, W., *op. cit.*, p. 102.

[33] "Quod nos consequuturos spero si beatissinam virigem solemno illo praeconio longe omnium pulcherrimo salutaverimus (ave gratia plena)."

[34] *Comm.*, p. 35.

## Section 4.   A Muzzle for Machiavellianism

The question must be asked why Calvin wrote on the *De Clementia* in particular. Doumergue has offered the opinion that it was intended as a protest against religious persecution and an appeal to the royal clemency for the Protestants,[35] and that as such it is a "magnifique manifeste du Libéralisme, tel qu'il pouvait exister à cette époque." Just as Seneca's treatise was meant for the Emperor Nero's reflection, so the Commentaries were calculated to engage the attention of Francis I, and that with a view to effecting a milder treatment for the Protestants. This view contains an element of truth, perhaps, but it is far from adequately stated. Calvin was too little interested in the Protestant movement at this time to champion their cause. He was at the time of writing sunning himself in the favor of the scholars who were very close to the court,—Budé, Cop, Danès, and others, while from the Commentaries it is evident that he is aware of a gulf between himself and the masses.[36] At the same time, it is significant that he wrote on the *De Clementia*, and not on the *De Ira*, or the *De Beneficiis* of Seneca. The *De Clementia* is itself a very practical tract. It deals explicitly with the unreasonable hardness of tyrants. We may conclude that Calvin, too, had been offended by the universality of mercilessness. The moralist had awakened early in him. Stoicism, while a philosophy of consolation for times of transition and duress,

---

35) *Op. cit.,* p. 211 ff.

36) *Comm.,* p. 16 f.   Calvin dilates at length on the nature of the masses. It is in connection with Seneca's exhortation to Nero "to cast his eyes on this immense multitude, discordem, seditiosam, impotentem, in pernicem alienam suamque pariter exsultaturam, si hoc iugum fregerit." He remarks that seditiousness, inharmoniousness, and weakness are "perpetua epitheta multinudinis," which are applied to them with good reason. "Proponamus nobis historias, quantos tumultus excitarunt apud Romanos plebis seditiones: quoties reipublicae summam in discrimen adduxerunt: ut iam illud in proverbium venerit, Turba turbalenta. . . . The meaning of "discors" is "tot sensus, quot capita. . . . Non enim est consilium in vulgo, inquit Cicero pro Plancio, non ratio non discrimen.   Unde belua multorum capitum Platoni et Horatio. . . . Haec natura multitudinis est (says Livy), aut servit humiliter, aut superbe dominatur: libertatem, quae media est, nec spernere modice, nec habere sciunt."   These sentences are quoted without criticism.   They reflect the young humanist's attitude towards crowds which go about disturbing the peace.  Who were these crowds?  The class that answers the description, in the view of the court and of men like Budé, are the Protestants.

furnished excellent sermonic material for preachers of personal and social virtue. Philologist though Calvin wanted to be, the preacher in him lay deeper and would go farther. The most forceful passage in the whole book is quite homiletic, a quotation from Cicero against hypocrisy: "..... Vendant ut volent, populo tristes sanctimonias, erit aliquando ut fumo pereat, qui fumum vendiderit."[37]

Of deeper concern than Protestant persecution to the mind of Calvin would be the state-craft of Machiavelli. Let it be admitted that we have no mention of this famous Florentine in the Commentaries, and that we have no record of his work being discussed in Calvin's circle of friends. On the other hand no Frenchman could be ignorant of him, if he had any acquaintance at all with the Italian campaigns from Charles VIII on. Besides, Alciati and for that matter any professor of law who had the slightest idea of what was being written about politics would have brought the subject up for discussion, either from his own volition or in connection with the questions of the students. Machiavelli's *The Prince* was the outstanding book on state-craft. How could it have been ignored! Moreover, the author had died in 1527, one year before Calvin migrated to Orléans. The bruit of this was bound to awaken interest even where it had perhaps subsided.

Even granting the wild supposition that Calvin had never heard of Machiavelli or of *The Prince,* it must be borne in mind that the principles of this book are but the orderly and clear statement of the state-craft in vogue in Italy. We shall quote from A. J. Symonds who has summarized the contents in his article on Machiavelli:[38]

> "Up to the date of Machiavelli, modern political philosophy had always presupposed an ideal. Medieval speculation took the church and empire for granted, as divinely appointed institutions, under which the nations of the earth must flourish for the space of man's probation on this planet. Thinkers differed only as Guelfs and Ghibellines, as leaning on the one side to papal on the other to imperial supremacy. In the revival of learning scholarship supplanted scholasticism, and the old ways of medieval thinking were forgotten. But no

[37] *Comm.,* p. 27.
[38] *Encyclopedia Britannica,* 1894.

substantial philosophy of any kind emerged from
humanism. The political lucubrations of the scholars
were, like their ethical treatises, for the most part
rhetorical. Still the humanists........created a new
medium for the speculative faculty.... Simultaneously
with the revival, Italy passed into that stage of her
existence which has been called the age of despots. The
yoke of the empire had been cast off. The church had
taken rank among Italian tyrannies. The peninsula
was, roughly speaking, divided into principalities and
sovereign cities, each of which claimed autocratic jurisdiction. These separate despotisms owned no common
social tie, were founded on no common *jus* or right,
but were connected in a network of conflicting interests
and changeful diplomatic combinations. A keen and
positive political intelligence emerged in the Italian
race..... At this moment Machiavelli intervenes. He
was conscious of the change which had come over Italy
and Europe...... He founded the science of politics
for the modern world, by concentrating thought upon
its fundamental principles...... We feel the want in
him of a thorough philosophical education..... We sur-
mise that had he studied Plato's *Republic,* or the first
chapters of Aristotle's *Politics* and *Ethics,* he might perhaps have avoided what has been the stumbling-block to
generous readers—his indifference to moral righteousness as indispensable to states no less than individuals.
..... But when we have made these deductions (such
as that the end justifies the means, etc.) there remains
the fact of his achievement. He began to study men,
not according to some preconception, but as he found
them,—men, not in the isolation of one century, but as
a whole in history. He drew his conclusions from the
nature of mankind itself, 'ascribing all things to natural
causes or to fortune.' In this way he restored the right
method of study, a method which had been neglected
since the days of Aristotle. He formed a conception of
the modern state, which marked the close of the Middle
Ages, and anticipated the next phase of European development. His prince..... prefigured the monarchs
of the 16th and 17th centuries, the monarchs whose
motto was *L'état c'est moi!* His doctrine of a national
militia foreshadowed the system which has given
strength in arms to France and Germany..... When we
have made allowance for his peculiar phrases like 'frodi
onorevoli' or 'scelleratezze gloriose,' nothing is left but
admiration for his mental attitude. That is the attitude
of the patriot...... He neglected religion, or regarded
it as a part of the state machinery. He was by no means

indifferent to private virtue, which indeed he judged
the basis of all healthy national existence; but in the
realm of politics he postponed morals to political
expediency. He held that the people as distinguished
from the nobles and the clergy, were the pith and fibre
of nations; yet this same people had to become wax in
the hands of the politician,—their commerce and their
comforts, the arts which give a dignity to life and the
pleasures which make life liveable, neglected—their
very liberty subordinated to the one tyrannical conception......This it is which makes us feel his world a
wilderness, devoid of atmosphere and vegetation."

The Realpolitik of Machiavelli appears so much more
horrible to us than it must have to Calvin in as far as we do
not share the 16th century belief in the divine-right of kings.
In the *Seneca Commentaries* we find Calvin's interpretation
of the expression "princeps legibus solutus est," taken from
the Ulpian Code.[39] Literally it means that the prince is
bound to the laws of the realm. But in the Justinian Codes
it is interpreted as meaning that the prince is himself the
laws, or that he who makes the laws can break them personally. This interpretation is adopted by Calvin. We
shall discuss it more at length in our section on the Revival
of the Roman Law. Alciati and Budé were of the same
opinion, the latter even strengthening it. Add to this that
the tendenz of the times was in the direction of monarchical
absolutism. What the emperors of the Holy Roman Empire
had once been, in theory mostly, the national monarchs were
now. The oil of anointing had as it were infused them with
a divine substance, so that they were no longer as other men
are. The loyal Roman Catholic can even today feel what
the 16th century man felt toward his sovereign, for the consecration of a priest is based on the same principle as the
anointing of a king. Men like young Calvin might have
their doubts as to the adequacy of the priests and kings for
the purpose they were supposed to serve, but the idea of the
apartness of the priest and king could not but die with pain.
It is for this reason that the prince is regarded as essentially
not bound by the laws. And this is not a very far cry from
the Machiavellian politics.

---

[39] *Corpus juris Civilis* . . . , Francofurti ad Moenum, 1688, Bk. I,
Title 3, locus 31.

But the difference between the absolutism of Machiavelli and Calvin is that the latter put a two-banded muzzle on it, while the former permitted it to do what it listed. If it was out of the question for Calvin simply to deny the absolutist principle, and thus dispose of it as a danger to the welfare of society, the only procedure open to him was to hold it in check. This, as I said, was twofold: In the first place by his doctrine that all power is derived from God. Although the prince is not subject to his own laws, he cannot escape responsibility to the laws of God. He is answerable to the moral world-order. This is as far from the Machiavellian politics as heaven is from earth. The second band of the muzzle is found in Calvin's reflections on the conception of tyranny.

"What is the difference between a tyrant and a king?" asks Seneca.[40] Calvin answers that there is nothing in the word as such to regard it with disfavor, for etymologically it simply means to hold sway. The definition must be established from how the word has been used in the past. So he presents as illustrations some of the famous tyrants. Then he gives his definition: "Iam vero usus obtinuit tyrannum dici, qui contra suorum voluntatem dominatur, aut intemperanter exercet potestatem, ut sit nomen vitii." Which means that a tyrant is a person who rules contrary to the will of his subjects, or also one who is immoderate in the exercise of his power. On p. 92 he comments on Seneca's question "Et L. Syllam appellari tyrannum quid prohibet?" by saying that "though Sylla was indeed a tyrant he never was called a tyrant. He kept the name of dictator which the free people applied to him as magistrate. Yet who denies that he ought to have been called a tyrant, seeing he ruled with such lack of restraint?" On the other hand a king is one who acquires his realm legitimately, and promotes the public good.[41] Now it has been observed[42] that Calvin's definition of tyrant is not clear; for one who acquires a kingdom against the will of the governed may be a good ruler, while one who has obtained it legitimately may be a

---

[40] *Comm.*, p. 90.

[41] *Comm.*, p. 89: Qui legitimum imperium obtinet et bono publico accomodat.

[42] BEYERHAUS, G., *op. cit.*, p. 8 ff.

bad one. Still, at the same time, John Calvin has expressed a striking principle. Even though his interpretation of the character of historical tyranny should be incorrect, it is the interpretation as such that is of significance. A tyrant is one who rules against the consent of the governed (qui contra suorum voluntatem dominatur) and granted that he has a clear title to the throne, if he abuses his power he also falls within that class. When the tyrant may be expelled, he does not say, but from the nature of the case expulsion must follow. Neither does he draw up a catalogue of tyrannical acts; it was enough for him to have expressed the principle. For many years Calvin would remain with the mere statement of broad principles on the question of the right of rebellion. The monarchy is still very sacred to him. We take it, however, that on the basis of the foregoing the state-craft of Machiavelli is forever impossible in true Calvinism. In fact, the principle of the consent of the governed implied parliaments, ballots, constitutions, and reciprocation of duties between ruled and ruler.

# CHAPTER V

## THE SUBSTANCE OF THE SENECA COMMENTARIES

### Section 1.  The Dedicatory Letter

THIS letter is an important document for our study of Calvin's humanism.  Before pointing out some of its features we shall present a translation of it, for by reading the whole of it one can get the flavor better than from the best discussion of it.

*John Calvin's Preface to the Most Holy and Most Wise Prelate, Claude de Hangest, Abbot of St. Eloï's at Noyon.*

Whoever in this day has been born with more than average ability, most excellent Prelate (Praesul), generally rushes out with it into the world, fired with the ambition of getting fame, so that posterity may venerate his memory with monuments to his genius.  Thus posterity often praises men without sufficient reason.  Hitherto there have been few who knew how to moderate their talents.  Hence the insane passion to write something, which forthwith is followed by regret.  They seek to rectify their depravity in the eyes of the public by appealing to the benevolence of the readers, whose benevolence is actually abused pretty badly.  Publishing inchoate books the writers often plead the inexperience of youth, or the wanton entreaties of their friends, and chatter I know not what trifles to escape the imputation of having committed a mistake.  As for me, I should want to bring forth no embryos at all if I could produce only premature ones; in fact, I should rather abandon them as abortions than bring them forth before their time.  My purpose is not so much to commend myself to the benevolent reader as to critical one, the more so since I come from the common class of people (unus de plebe homunicio), and even if I should be gifted in erudition to a moderate degree, I have nothing that could excite any hope of fame.  This consciousness of my obscurity hitherto caused me to keep from the public, in fact.  And I did not consider these notes of mine, of whatever quality they may be, as worthy of publishing.  Nevertheless I kept on with the strain of study just as if I were actually contemplating to put them them on the market, lest by playing leisurely and carelessly with a ludicrous affair I might be producing a ludicrous piece of work.  So, not yet having come half-way, I read it aloud to some tried and true friends, and they (having frankly weighed all things therein) infused some hope in me of their being of a sort that would not be entirely excluded from favor if published. The authority of my friend Connan was particularly valuable, a most prudent and learned man, by whose judgment I stand or fall.

Add to all this that I was engaged in interpreting an author (Seneca) who, although a writer of the first rank, has been regarded by many as pretty shabby, in fact, has been held in practically no esteem at all. The result is that for a long time I had looked for some outstanding champion to arise who would claim for him his proper dignity. If to any degree I have succeeded in understandig him, it seems to me I shall not have labored in vain. Certainly (nempe) several things have escaped the eyes of Erasmus (otherwise the adorner of letters and a man of peerless charm), even though he twice sweated in this arena (1515 and 1529. B.); which may be said without ill-will.

Concerning Seneca himself I will not say much, for I fear that by error I might diminish the high praises of his genius. Neither is it necessary to recount his merits to praise, lest it appear that he himself has produced too little that deserves commendation. I should have kept wholly silent, had not a certain warped opinion occupied the minds of many men, an opinion which now has become established (as final), namely, that Seneca has no worth in eloquence, that his rank and importance as a philosopher is trivial. But his worth is hidden among his defects. So they say that Quintillian purposely denuded him of every sort of eloquence, so that by indirection he might expugn him from the list of approved writers. Thus Gellius with hostile words, but with more tact, pronounces him a writer without usefulness. Indeed though I had hardly dared to refute Quintillian (a man of the clearest and keenest judgment), nevertheless I wish that men might understand that Quintillian as a man did not treat Seneca with enough good faith, and certainly made the most of his opportunities for abuse. For Seneca had not dealt respectfully enough with the Elder Quintillian in the Declamations, and so had damaged the reputation of this Quintillian.[1] Really there is no one who should

---

[1] The father of Quintillian had indeed been mentioned coldly by Seneca in the Declamations. But this was the work of Seneca the rhetorician! Calvin identified Seneca the father with Seneca the son. Everyone did so in those days. Cf. LE COULTRE, *op. cit.*, pp. 54, 57. See also Calvin's "Vita Senecae," *Comm.*, p. 12, where he says that Seneca reached the age of one hundred fifteen years.

not see with what impotent rage there is brought against him in this part a charge that is rather insulting than serious. Certainly, however Quintillian and Gellius may have felt, posterity, which is beyond those enemies of the truth, spite and envy, has been better able to judge and counts him among the foremost chiefs of latinity. It was an easy thing for Quintillian to wrestle with one who was dead and buried. For a dead man does not bite; to bawl at the living is quite another matter. However, not even Quintillian has robbed him of all praise, for somewhere he bestows on him a choice encomium: recalling the Latin orators from the earliest times, he celebrates the (literary) wealth of one Seneca.

But why waste words here? The thing is evident. As far as I am concerned, it will not be irksome to bring up for discussion what I feel, as I will not force upon the readers any dogmatic opinion.[2] Let who will stand by our judgment; others may take counsel with their own minds, or choose a judge from among the throng of more expert men. If I understand anything at all, I take Seneca to have been a man of the most extraordinary erudition and most remarkable command of language. What thorough knowledge of affairs has this happy genius not been able to attain? He knew to a hair the mysteries of nature which belong to that part of philosophy which the Greeks call *ten phusiken*. Whenever he was occupied *en tois ethikois*, there he reigned omnipotently, and ran as it were in his own field. Well equipped in dialectics, he was just as adequate in the cultivation of oratory. As for the ancient narratives, as often as they could serve his purpose his faithful memory had them ready for his use; though sometimes it failed him, in that on occasion he would stretch a story.[3] The pure and polished discourse of Seneca is, as you may know, redolent of his age; an elegant and flowery manner of speaking, an unlabored style, flowing without hesitation, as becomes a philosopher. Now and then he rises so that, if he had aspired to it, it appears that there would be no lack of a sublimer vein in him. Almost everybody finds fault with him for the luxuriousness of his words and for his biting wit. Of all this I confess there is too much. The things which Quintillian says Seneca abounds in I interpret as charming vices. I also miss an orderly arrangement, which is not the least among the ornaments

---

[2] "Religione," which I have translated "dogmatic opinion," is a baffling expression and, I take it, must not be taken too literally.

[3] Cf. *Comm.*, p. 70 f., "Videri posset lapsus memoria Seneca, ut aliquando solet."

of speech. But what if we weigh the vices with the virtues, how little they are! It will be helpful to add that no genius has been acceptable without receiving some indulgence.

Let me stop here. This should be said once for all: Our Seneca is the next after Cicero who is the crown of Roman philosophy and eloquence. For Brutus and his peers have been lost to us. They who spend a good time reading Seneca derive from it profit and delight at the same time. I pledge my reputation that it will repent no one for labor spent, provided one was not born when the Musus and the Graces were unfriendly.

Indeed, illustrious Claude, for you it has been no task to preach gloriously these gifts of the man; instead of needing a monitor you have a sense of taste in your own right. You have in yourself and from your training at home (intus ac domi), as they say, a vivid and liberal genius, a judgment sharp and deep-lying, a copious memory that is always awake,—to which must be added a thorough training in our studies. Relying, as I may say, on these counsellors, you can easily discern what the difference is between good money and lupines (stage-money), and how it is that a good part of the Latin language depends on Seneca. In no other way would you accept our Commentaries, which sue for your favor, not the first-fruits of our harvest which by right and merit are dedicated and addressed to you. Not only because I owe all that I am and have to you, but the more since as a boy I was educated in your house, initiated with you into the same studies, and so am indebted to your most noble family for my first training in life and letters. And now it shall certainly not be the particular purpose of this Preface to try to make my industry acceptable to you. (Your singular benevolence toward me has kindly understood this a long time already.) In whatever manner other readers will receive it (it will not get everybody's approval), I am nevertheless confident that I shall not have merited the worst disfavor in the eyes of (you) my justest critic. It were difficult, even bad, to want to indulge everybody among such a variety of temperaments, so it was left to me to accommodate myself only to the best. To what extent this work may prove to have been successful, others may see; for myself I should not dare to guarantee it in a more or less self-confident manner, lest I be guilty of a species of arrogance.

(Paris, Day before April 9, 1532.)

Our discussion of this Letter will have the purpose of illuminating some of the more significant features. I call attention first to the fact that it is dedicated to a Roman Catholic bishop, which may well be borne in mind by those who regard Calvin as an outspoken Protestant before and during the writing of the *Seneca Commentaries*. He might just as well have addressed his Dedication to Marguerite de Valois, to Budé, or any one of a number of friends in humanism. The fact that he was a boyhood friend of Claude de Hangst would have meant nothing to him, had he felt a profound hostility to the Roman hierarchy at this time. It is also worth remarking that he calls the bishop by the Latin name of "praesul" instead of "episcopus." It is the only case of Ciceronianism in Commentaries, as far as I have been able to determine.

Secondly, the author asks no indulgence from the reader. He appeals to the benevolence of no one, but seeks rather the opinion of the competent critic. He feels that he has risen from the ranks of the common people, and is ready to run the gauntlet. At the same time he is rather nervous in his hope, for he does not dare to predict what reception his book will have. He is sure, however, that a fair critic will pass a favorable judgment. His hopes were evidently not fulfilled, for as far as we have ascertained there was not the least stir created by the *Commentaries*. Men were disturbed by issues more pressing than the opinions of Seneca. The Protestant Reformation was shouting for attention. The gentlemanly efforts to reform men by suggestion were passé. Calvin might rightly expect the humanists nevertheless to respond favorably to his work, for it was in line with what they themselves had tried. Why the book received practically no notice is a question that is hard to answer. The matter will be discussed again in connection with Calvin's reflections on Erasmus. Whatever the case, it must have been a terrible disappointment to him. It is hard to escape the thought that it had something to do with his conversion. That is, he had had high hopes of attaining a name as a humanist, and the humanists did not receive him into their circles. Therefore he would in turn react against the humanists as a group. Furthermore, the only other vital group in Europe was the Protestant. In fact, the latter was far more vital, for the former were shrinking from applying their critical principles to the institution of the church, while it was obvious to every unprejudiced mind that a great deal of fundamental reformatory work had to be done there. The unwillingness of the humanists to say B after they had said A was rather terrible to a young man gifted with a sense of logic. It is therefore reasonable to suppose that he gravitated toward the Protestants more and more. Still he was not of a mind to break with the Roman church. In November of 1533 he collaborates with Nicholas Cop on an address that contains a salutation to the Virgin and speaks of the Gospel as Christian philosophy. This address indicates, however, the trend of his thought; the inner logic of his humanism was leading him to criticising the foundations of the papal church.

The greater part of the Dedicatory Letter is devoted to a defense of Seneca as a writer and philosopher. It is an excellent bit of literary criticism. After saying that Seneca had found practically no appreciation among certain classical students, and that it had become an established custom to hold him in light esteem, Calvin says that "for a long time" he had wished to see some one rise up to champion the old philosopher. "For a long time!" How long was that? We cannot say definitely. Before trying to answer this question we remark that his words certainly indicate an interest in Seneca that is of comparatively long standing. Since he defends him in this Letter as a philosopher in things pertaining to physical nature not only, but especially in the field of ethics, we may say that certain of the fundamental positions of Stoicism as presented by Seneca had long appeared sound to him. Now as to the question how far back this desire to have a champion for Seneca arise, we can safely determine the year 1529 as the terminus a quo. For in that year Erasmus published his second and great edition of Seneca, which contained a very harsh judgment of his work as a writer and philosopher. From the following resumé of Erasmus's criticism of Seneca it will appear that Calvin's defense was directed against the great Rotterdammer:

> Not only had he criticized the doctrines of the Latin philosopher and scored his pantheism, his doubts on Providence and immortality, the small part of religion in morality, but subscribing to the unfavorable judgments of Quintillian and Gellius, he attacked in Seneca the writer

as such.  He found him unjust and disparaging with respect to the writers above named; one moment affecting
the clown in his satire on the vices of humanity; sometimes descending to the obscene; declamatory when his
subject does not require it; without order in his ideas and
without a sense of composition;—all in all very inferior
to Cicero.[4]

Erasmus had also attacked his Stoic lack of sympathy with
suffering, in which Calvin agrees with him.  But Calvin takes
sharp issue with Erasmus when he says that Seneca is not a
writer or philosopher to reckon with.

Add to this that Erasmus had disowned the 1515 edition of
Seneca, and that Calvin in so many words attributes this edition to him.  "Twice has Erasmus sweated in this arena!"[5]
Moreover, it appears that Calvin had paid practically no attention to the request of Erasmus for young humanists to devote
themselves to the task of further emending the text of Seneca.
He does not mention a single codex by name.  It is true that
he sought here and there to correct an Erasmian reading, but
on the whole he accepts the work of Erasmus as sufficient.
His interest in codices is so slight that when he comments on
the reading of "quoscumque ob adulterium familiae suas,"
he says: "Quod hic Erasmus divinat legendum filiae, nullius
est momenti."  Nullius est momenti (It is of no moment)!
The work of Calvin is a commentary, not a critical edition of
De Clementia.  It is fair to suggest that for a young man
of twenty-two this appeared presumptuous in the eyes of the
leaders of humanism.  As such the book would therefore not
be recommended by them.  The argument of silence seems to
have some significance against this background.  The chief
reason therefore why the Seneca Commentaries did not
sell (I assume they did not sell well) is that there was no reading public for them.[6]

---

[4] Cf. Le Coultre, op. cit., p. 55.
[5] "Nempe quum in hac arena bis desudarit Erasmus."  "Nempe" is
a strong word.
[6] Calvin did his best to promote the sale of the book, as his correspondence shows.  To Francis Daniel he writes that he has paid the cost of
publication out of his own pocket, and that he requests his friends to help
him sell it.  He had asked some of the professors at Paris to use the
book as a text-book in their classes.  He expects a professor at Bourges
to do the same, and hopes that Daniel and his friends will not do
less.  He sends him a copy for his own use, and plans to send a hundred
more which he wants him to dispose of.  Calvin had written similarly
to other friends.  Cf. Herminjard, Correspondance des réformateurs, II,

No reading public was created because there was no famous humanist to sponsor it, as far as we can determine. Certainly as such it was not arresting encugh to create a reading public by its own merit. The time was soon to come, however, when Calvin would find a public that was interested in him. In 1534 he writes the *Psychopannychia* which is eagerly read. In 1535 he writes a Preface for Olivetan's *Bible,* and in 1536 the first edition of the *Institutes* appears. In fact, retiring as he was by nature, Calvin could not long live without recognition. Underlying all his literary efforts is the desire to do something vital, something that will find response in men's hearts. The movement of French humanism was already on the wane. It had accomplished its purpose. Sound as the *Seneca Commentaries* were as a product of French humanism, there was in the latter so little vitality left that it did not even rise to recognize it. Now let John Calvin begin commenting on another classic, the Bible! At once he catches fire. "Vitalizing" Seneca had interested no one; "vitalizing" the Scriptures made of Calvin an international figure.

### Section 2.  The Sources

The object of this section is to give the reader an impression of the extent of Calvin's erudition in the *Commentaries.* It were fruitless to discuss in detail every source he used. Our plan is to give the periods of Greek and Roman literature, and the authors belonging to them (that is, those which Calvin consulted). Thus one may learn whether or not his knowledge of the classics is balanced.

---

p. 417 f. In the next letter to Daniel Calvin informs him that he had with difficulty procured a Bible which his friend had asked him to buy for him, and that in exchange for this favor he expects his help to recover the money which he had invested in the *Commentaries.* He also asks Daniel to tell him how the book had been received. Again, he wants him to get Professors Landrinus and Agnetus to expound it to their classes. He is sending a copy for Daniel and five for certain friends in Bourges. He complains that Duchemin has not yet answered his letter (certainly about the *Commentaries*). *Ibid.,* p. 418 f. Soon after this Daniel writes to Calvin that he has not yet received the promised copy of the *Commentaries,* but that he has written to Agnetus and Regius. *Ibid.,* p. 420 f. That is the last we hear of the affair. There is not a straw to indicate that the book had any success. His very friends appear not to have used it as a text-bbook, perhaps not even as required reading. Why that inertia?

## Roman Literature

*Third and Second Centuries B. C.*—Plautus and Terence.

*From Andronicus to Sulla*—(None).

*The Golden Age, 83 B. C.-14 A. D.*—Varro, Cicero, Lucretius, Sallust, Brutus, Publius Mimographus, Virgil, Horace, Celsus, Propertius, Ovid, Titus Livy, Justinus, Festenella, Pomponius Festus, Rutillius Lupus, Vitruvius, Annaeus Seneca.

*First Century of the Silver Age, 14-117 A. D.*—Columella, Valerius Maximus, Asconius, Pomponius Mela, Persius, Lucan, Pliny the Elder, Statius, Martial, Quintillian, M. Florus, Juvenal, Tacitus, Pliny the Younger, Celsus (pater), Celsus Balbus, L. Annaeus Seneca.

*Second Century of the Silver Age, 117-211 A. D.*—Celsus (Epicurean), Gellius, Apuleius.

*Third Century, 211-305 A. D.*—Nonius Marcellinus, Mamertinus, Augustae Historiae Scriptores.

*Fourth Century*—Nazarius, Aelius Donatus, Latinus Pacatus, Ammianus Marcellinus, Priscian, Servius Maurus, Vegetius.

*Fourth and Fifth Centuries*—Claudian, Macrobius.[7]

## Greek Literature

*Epic Poetry*—Homer.

*Tragic Drama*—Sophocles.

*Comedy*—Aristophanes.

*Attic Philosophy*—Plato, Aristotle, Xenophon.

*Attic Oratory*—Aeschinus, Isocrates.

*Period of Erudition and Rhetoric after Alexander, 300-150 B. C.*—Euclid.

*From Augustus to Domitian*—Dionysius of Halicarnassus, Strabo.

*Period of the Hellenic Revival (Nerva to Diocletian)*—Plutarch, Arrian, Appion, Dio Cassius, Herodian the His-

---

[7] Cf. Teufel, W. S., *History of Roman Literature*, Vols. I and II for outline of Roman literature here used.

L. Annaeus Seneca, the author of *De Clementia*, is of course referred to very frequently. Calvin has read him thoroughly. A brief account of his life, works, and significance can be found in Sandys, J. E., *A Companion to Latin Studies*, pp. 631, 669 f.

torian, Diogenes Laërtius, Herodian the Grammarian, Porphyry, Alexander Aphrodisianus.

Phalaris is also referred to, the tyrant of Acragas, whose letters are recommended by Photius.

Calvin also mentions Suidas the Byzantine lexicographer of the Tenth Century.[8]

## THE FATHERS

Cyprian, Lactantius, Eusebius, Synesius, Jerome, Augustine, Gregory I. All the Fathers are quoted either once or twice, excepting Augustine who is quoted fifteen times. One quotation is taken from his *Communis vita clericorum,* one from *De spiritu et litera,* while thirteen are taken from the *Civitas Dei.*[9]

## THE HUMANISTS

For frequency of reference Erasmus heads the list of humanists in the *Commentaries.* Use has been made of the *Adagia,* the first and second editions of Seneca, and the *Queremonia pacis.* Next comes Budé who is referred to seven times, two works being named, namely, the *De asse* and the *Annotationes in Pandectas* (the former once, the latter thrice). Third stands Valla who is referred to four times.[10] Then two references to Politian's *Herodian,* and two to Alciati.[11]

---

8) The outline is taken from CROISET, A. and M., *An Abridged History of Greek Literatue;* cf. SANDYS, J. E., *A History of Classical Scholarship,* for Alexander Aphrodisianus (p. 340), and Phalaris (p. 401), and Suidas (p. 407 f.).

9) *Comm.,* pp. 15, 23, 45, 90, 95, 102, 120, 142, 154, 156, 157.

10) Cf. Chapter VI, Section 2, "Lorenzo Valla."

11) For Alciati cf. *Comm.,* pp. 81, 146 f. The contest of Calvin with Alciati had apparently not ended with the publication of Duchemin's *Antapologia.* The question at issue, *Comm.,* p. 146 f., is a minor one, concerning the rank of the "magister equitum." Calvin is still bitter. Among others the following sentences occur: "Hic bisterque lapsus est Alciatus," and "Ad haec respondeat quae volet Alciatus, modo ne sub Albutii persona scurriliter ludat." The second sentence is particularly interesting, for it shows that Calvin still believes that Alciati was the real author of the *Apologia* of Albucius. This attack on his former teacher is the only place where he loses his temper in the entire volume. On the "Magister equitum" see *Dictionnaire des antiquités grecques et romaines,* "Magister peditum, equitum, militiae." PAULY, A., etc., *Real-Encyclopaedie 'der classischen Alterthumswissenschaft,* "Magister . . . equitum."

The following are named once: Beroaldus, Coelius Rho-
dignius, Perotti, Fenestella (Andrea Fiocco), Pomponius
Laetus, Egnatius, Zazius.[12]

## THE BIBLE

The *Commentaries* contain three quotations from Scripture, namely, from Romans, Proverbs, and I Peter. The last
is interestingly called "sua canonica," that is, Peter says something in his canonical letter. Was II Peter not canonical in
Calvin's opinion? [13]

### Section 3.   The Method

Calvin's model for commenting on the text of Seneca was
Budé's *Annotations in Pandectas,* in the opinion of Beyer-
haus who at the same time presents an adequate resumé of
Calvin's manner of interpreting the text.

His point of departure is determined by the interpretation of words and ideas, which he expounds by means of
etymology, or by picturing the evolution of their meaning, or by comparing them with similar or contrasting
phenomena of speech, according as the occasion de-
mands.[14]   Standing on the firm ground of philological
interpretation, Calvin seeks to understand the gram-
matical and logical connection of the sentences and their
place in the general context.   The wealth of rhetorical
figures with which Seneca's style abounds, gives Calvin
an opportunity to display his knowledge of rhetoric.[15]
Besides giving the meaning of the text, the author tries
to picture the life of antiquity, as far as the *De Clementia* permits it.   The word "muraena" offers him the
opportunity to give some details as to the popularity of
this fish.[16]   The meaning of "toga" and the social rank
of the gladiators are fereted out thoroughly.[17]

---

12) Cf. VOIGT, G., *Die Wiederbelehbung des classischen Alterthums,* in
loc.; BURCKHARDT, J., *The Civilization of the Renaissance in Italy,* esp.
pp. 279–81 for Pomponius Laetus; GRESSWELL, W. P., *Memoirs of Angelus
Politanus,* etc.; See Bibliography for the works of Politian (two editions
in Paris before 1530), Perotti and Beroaldus. Cf. also our Section on
"The Revival of Latin and Greek."
13) *Comm.,* pp. 18, 21, 53.
14) Cf. esp. his interpretation of "tyrannus," *Comm.,* p. 90 f.
15) Cf. *Ibid.,* p. 156 (prolepsis), p. 144 (paradiastole), p. 137 (meta-
basis), p. 43 (hyperbole), p. 17 f. (prosopoeia).
16) *Ibid.,* p. 120 f.
17) *Ibid.,* pp. 94, 159.   For the above and futher illustrations of
method, cf. BEYERHAUS, G., *Studien zur Staatsanschauung Calvins,* p.
35 f.   It is interesting to know that "toga" is one of the most thoroughly
discussed words in BUDE'S *Annotations.*

Further elucidation of Calvin's method may be made by presenting a translation of his comments on six or seven sentences of Seneca's text. We have selected the following from
the speech which Seneca puts in the mouth of Nero:

> Ego vitae necisque gentibus arbiter. Qualem quisque
> sortem statumque habeat, in manu mea positum est.
> Quid cuique mortalium fortuna datum velit, meo ore
> pronunciat. Ex nostro responso laetitiae causas populi
> urbesque concipiunt. Nulla pars usquam nisi volente
> propitioque me floret. Haec tot millia gladiorum, quae
> pax mea comprimit ad nutum meum stringentur. Quas
> nationes funditus excindi, quas transportari . . . mea
> iurisdictio est.[18]

Calvin makes his comments in the following manner:

> *Vitae necisque arbiter.*—On the same subject (as
> above). Curtius, Bk. IV: "Since you shall remain on
> the royal throne as lord of life and death of all citizens,
> beware lest you forget the responsibility which you as-
> sumed when you became king." And Seneca, in Thyestis:
>> 'You whom the master of sea and land
>> Over life and death gave high command.'
>
> What Seneca calls dominion in one place, high command
> in another, he here calls arbitrium, that is, full and free
> power from which there is no appeal. So also Pompeius
> Festus.
>
> *In manu mea positum 'est.*—Thus Coelius to Cicero,
> Bk. VIII, Epist. "It is in your hand how you wish to
> oblige him." What this locution may signify is beauti-
> fully shown in Cicero, Offic. I, as it were by epexegesis.
> It means what is before one, though to say that it is
> given in hand is more agreeable. We therefore express
> it more elegantly by "placed in hand," as if it were
> comprehended by the hand. One may also say "in the
> hands," "to the hands," "before the hands," "under the
> hand," and "between the hands." The last two are
> more rare, so I shall submit examples. Seneca to
> Lucilius: "Council ought to be brought forth in the
> day; this is too slow: under the hand, they say, is
> counsel brought forth." And Tranquillus, in Augustus:
> "In order that it may be more rapid, and that it may be
> announced and known under the hand what may have
> transpired in each province, you shall come in at the
> first convenient interval by the military ways. The
> vehicles have been made ready by him." So in Virgil,
> Aeneid XI . . . . Therefore Nero says that it is as easy

---

[18] *Comm.*, p. 13.

for one to be enriched as to be robbed by fortune. We can interpret "hand" also as government or judgment, as was said with the same meaning by Tranquillus, "He has done all things that had to be done, but the issue is in the hand of fortune. The sense is the same.

*Quid cuique mortalium fortuna.*—Here it becomes plain that the prince is nothing but the organ of fortune, by whose hand and ministry she establishes and over-turns all things. He uses the name of fortune for that of God, from usage rather than propriety. For to those who subject all things to necessity there is nothing fortuitous.[19] He appositely uses a verb of pronouncing, for it signifies that he who has jurisdiction ordains and judges.

*Et ("ex" in the text at head) nostro responso laetitiae causas populi.*—This refers to the legates of the nations, the mediators and interpreters of a community con-joined with the Roman people. For great was that Roman Empire, in fact, a great robber band,[20] which depended for their wages on peoples subjugated by war, and who preferred to make covenants, or would often buy off that ambitious society, not far from serf-dom (the Roman people).

*Haec tot millia.*—What Plautus says with respect to another matter can with propriety be predicated of the Roman Emperor: "That he is no doubt some earthly Jove who with his nod makes East and West tremble." For as Ovid says (Fastorum II):

"By this leader both sides of the sun are Roman."

And elsewhere:

"The extent of the city of Rome and the world is the same."

The order must be observed. First it arrogates to itself rights with respect to the private affairs of all men, thereupon in states and peoples; now he comes down to enumerating particular things, in what manner peoples and cities may have cause for happiness from his words.[21]

*Ad nutum meum stringentur.*—For emphasis has he used the expression "at the nod," since it had been

---

[19] Occasionally Calvin permits himself a philosophical reflection of this sort. Incidentally the substance of this passage agrees very well with his later doctrine of Providence.

[20] "Magnum latrocinium," an expression borrowed from St. Augustine.

[21] Calvin has attempted an analysis of the imperial psychology here: after pointing out that it begins with the arrogation of the rights in men's private affairs, it passes on to the affairs of other peoples. "Sibi arrogavit" certainly indicates that he disapproves.

sufficient to speak of an order.  But this is more telling; the prince does draw everything to him with a nod, and by a nod agitates them.  Virgil:

> "He nodded, and by a nod made high Olympus tremble."

Curtius, Bk. III,

> "The Macedonian army was attentive to the signal of the general not only, but even to his nod."

So Cicero . . . . . . . . .

*Quas transportari.*—It was an ancient custom to transport elsewhere peoples that had been subdued in war, that is, such peoples who by the advantage of their position could raise new revolts.  In the Panegyricus of Maximian and Constantine: "You have captured, received, and transported the most ferocious peoples of Mauretania from the inaccessible heights of the mountains, and the bold ones from their natural fortifications."  So Livy, Bk. VIII, . . . . .  Elsewhere he (Livy) said "traducere": "We are considering to lead every Alban to Rome. . . . . ."

So much for details on the substance of the *Seneca Commentaries.*  Other things pertaining to it are spread throughout our volume.

# CHAPTER VI

## THE FRENCH RENAISSANCE

### Section 1. Introduction

THE third decade of the Sixteenth Century was remarkably fertile in developing young writers in France. Not only Calvin, but Rabelais, Marot, Dolet were being formed for literary creativity. Amyot (born 1513) was a boy. Marguerite had only written her *Miroir de l'ame pecheresse* (1523). Despériers was still a young man.[1]

The Middle Ages had been generous to French letters, but a sharp decline is witnessed toward the end of the Fifteenth Century. There is now "a literature that is poor in ideas, of vulgar and cynical sentiment, careless and light in form, without grandeur,—to which the erudites of the feudal courts opposed a literature that was stripped of content, complicated in form, capable only of producing the feeling of immense effort which vanished in the failure to produce results, failed even to impress as to its intentions."[2]

Then France discovered Italy, the hearth of the Renaissance. Since the campaign of 1494 "a new conception of life awakes in them, and they began to transport homeward all that had delighted them so much there. They now wanted to have the palaces, the gardens, the tableaux, the statues, the clothes, the jewels, the perfumes, books, poets, savants, the rare animals, the science, the spirit, like the Medicis, the dukes of Urbino and Ferrara; when they reentered France the whole Renaissance entered with them."[3]

In the space of a single generation France had been conquered by the Italian culture. But it is amazing to see how the French genius succeeded to interpret it in accordance with the French nature. Less artistic than the Italian, its tendencies were practical and positive, which turned to the discovery of scientific or moral truth. It found support in this respect from the northern races,—England, Flanders,

---

[1] LANSON, G., "Histoire de la littérature française," Paris, 1895, in loc.
[2] *Ibid.*, p. 218.
[3] *Ibid.*, p. 221.

Germany, where the Renaissance took the form of philological erudition and religious reform. There were young men,
born in the last years of Louis XI, whom the scholastic
education had left dissatisfied, who eagerly read the great
Latin works whose deeper meaning and fine form the
Middle Ages had not appreciated. They read them with the
spirit of the Poggios, the Vallas, the Guarinos. Budé had
avoided the monastery, as Rabelais was to escape it. There
was cultivation of Greek and Hebrew, fundamental for a
reform of science and religion. Francis I has savants and
poets at his court, as Marguerite at hers. LeFèvre, hellenist
and theologian, joins humanism with reform. Despériers
united reform with free thought and poetry. Marot, court
poet, is a Protestant. Marguerite combines poetry, mysticism, humanism, and zeal for reform. "One senses that in
this period there is an effort to realize the Italian ideal of
the complete man whose free physical and moral development shall not suffer restrictions or limitations."[4]

It is in this happy epoch that Calvin gets his training at
Paris, Orléans, and Bourges. The revival of art and science
was the great theme of conversation among the students,
like evolution before the World War. If Calvin knew
Rabelais in person it would help him undoubtedly to
appreciate the new culture, but it was not absolutely necessary for the spirit was everywhere in the air. Who could
help knowing of Marot the court poet, who had been present
at the victory of Marigan, and so doubly enthusiastic for
the new culture? No young student could help being affected
by the indignity Marot suffered when imprisoned for eating
pork in the Lent of 1527.[5] At all events, the Renaissance

---

[4] Ibid., p. 221 f.

[5] VIÉNOT, J., Histoire de la Réforme française, p. 137. Marot was
born c. 1495 in Cahors; his father was a poet. Young Clément served
as page in the family of Nicholas Neufville–Villeroy, then as valet de
chambre of Marguerite and (later) of the king. While with Marguerite
about 1521 he gets certain ideas of reform. In 1523 he hears the preaching of Farel, and comes under the influence of Erasmus and Aimé
Meigret. While in prison for eating pork he writes Epitre du lion et du
rat. In his Enfer he describes the horrors of the Châtelet. Through
Marguerite he begins to study the Bible about this time. Soon he acknowledges Erasmus as his master, and commences to translate the Colloquies. In 1532 he, together with Laurent and Louis Meigret and others,
is again charged with heresy (he had again eaten pork in Lent). In
1534 he flees to Reneé of Ferrara where he meets Calvin in 1536. Ibid.,
pp. 132–137.

winds blowing from Italy had so affected Calvin that in 1529 he trekked to Bourges when Alciati became professor of law there.[6]

In the following sections we shall study the French Renaissance in so far as it touched young Calvin.

### Section 2.  Lorenzo Valla

A narrative of the influence of the French Renaissance on Calvin must begin with a study of Lorenzo Valla. It should not appear strange to one acquainted with this period that a description of a French movement should commence with the story of an Italian. As has been said repeatedly, the French revival of learning takes its rise from the contacts of France with Italy. No scholar made a greater impact on the young Frenchmen since Charles VIII's time than Valla, "undoubtedly the hardest thinker and closest scholar that the Italian Renaissance had produced up to the middle of the 15th century."[7]  Born (1407) in Piacenza, he was soon to associate himself so closely with the city of Rome that he called himself a Roman.[8]  There he studied under Bruni, Poggio, and Aurispa (a Greek scholar from Constantinople). Leaving Rome in 1431 he taught in Pavia where he attacked the dialecticians and the jurists with his mordant tongue and pen.  After a brief sojourn in Genoa, Ferrara, and Mantua, he lived more permanently in Naples under the much-needed protection of Alphonso.

A constructive as well as destructive critic, his works are

---

[6] For interesting details on the early influence of the new spirit on Calvin, cf. Pannier, J., *Recherches sur la formation intellectuelle de Calvin*, a series of articles, of which the 5th is on "Influences étrangères," pp. 410–447, Revue d'Histoire et de Philosophie religieuses, Juillet-Octobre, 1930. Pp. 424–444 take up the question of the influence of Despériers, Marot, Rabelais, Dolet.

[7] Taylor, H. O., *Thought and Expression in the 16th Century*, p. 47; for Valla and the beginnings of modern criticism, see Creighton M., *History of the Papacy 1327–1527*, III, pp. 170–173; Gregorovius, F., *A History of Rome in the Middle Ages*, VII, pp. 103, 111, 122, 517; Hall, F. W., *A Companion to Classical Texts*, pp. 108–110.

[8] Voigt, G., *Die Wiederbelehung des classischen Alterthums*, I, p. 406 f.

almost all of a high order.[9] The most famous of these is the *De linguae latinae elegantia*. First printed in Venice, 1471, this amazing book ran through fifty-nine editions between that date and 1536.[10] In line with the Petrarchan tradition of contemning the post-classical and Medieval changes in Latin, and of conforming to classical models, the *Elegantiae* laid the foundations of modern classical philology.[11] Believing himself heir to the Roman classical culture, he loved to call himself "Patritius Romanus," and referring to himself and his fellow-humanists he would say "we Romans." He made the claim that the Roman Empire holds sway wherever the Roman language dominates.[12] "The unity of the Roman tongue is its unique glory. The Greeks had nothing like it, speaking dialects (Attice, Aeolice, Ionice, Dorice, κοινῶς)." "What lover of letters, he continues, what lover of the public weal can restrain his tears when he sees how horribly the Gallic invasion overturned this wonderful empire?"[13] "Donatus, Priscian, and Servius are the last respectable latinists, since whom everybody appears only to stutter. After them come Papias, and other ignorant fellows, Eberardus, Huguitio, Catholicon, Aymo, and still others unworthy of naming, getting paid for knowing nothing, or for rendering their students more stupid than they were before.[14] Valla praised the dignified Latin of the Justinian *Digest*.[15] He recommended them to lovers of the Roman language. It is evident that his appreciation of them is, broadly speaking, that of a humanist and not that of jurist particularly. The *Digests* were

---

[9] His independence was boundless, yet explainable, as in the case of his preference for Quintillian instead of Cicero. Cf. VOIGT, G., *op. cit.*, I, p. 457 ff., "Kein Zweifel, dass die seit Petrarca hergebrachte Vergötterung Cicero's den jungen Kritiker zum Widerspruch reizte." With Poggio and the cultured secretaries of the Curia he was involved in "mancher Wortstreit über die blasphemische Behandlung Cicero's." Cf. also *Opera Vallae*, pp. 253–366. " . . . *Antidoti in Poggium*," libri I–IV.

[10] TILLEY, A., *The Dawn of the French Renaissance*, p. 36. Voigt remarks that "in den Elegantien ständen 2000 Dinge, die vorher unbekannt gewesen," *op. cit.*, I, p. 468.

[11] TAYLOR, H. O., *op. cit.*, I, p. 48 ff.

[12] *Opera*, p. 3, "Nostra est Italia, nostra Gallia, nostra Hispania, Germania, Pannonia, Dalmatia, Illyricum, multaque aliae nationes. Ibi nanque imperium Romanum est, ubicunque Romana lingua dominatur."

[13] *Ibid.*, p. 4.

[14] *Ibid.*, p. 41.

[15] *Ibid.*, p. 79.

just part of the treasure he had unearthed. Little did he dream that some day his remarks on them would arouse in Budé the desire to re-edit them. Valla's consuming passion was to purify the Latin language. Prof. Taylor sums up his method as "reaching greater clarity by analyzing the meanings of words, or again by discovering the impossibilities hinging upon the inconsistencies of statement. So this incisive questing spirit, from the suggestions of a scientific philology, proceeded to attack grammarians, literati, jurists, dialecticians and philologians, and monks. By sifting the exact from the loose, realities from falsities, he passes to the broader criticism, historical or philosophical."[16]

Calvin had had two definite modes of contact with the *Elegantiae*. First as a student of Latin. Valla's book was one of the most popular and most important hand-books for this study. (Erasmus even published an abridged and handy edition of it for the convenience of students.) Calvin shows that he used it for the *Seneca Commentaries* by reference to it there.[17] The second contact was through his studies of the law. Apart from the fact that a young man of Calvin's curiosity would certainly look into Valla's fascinating Prefaces, his attention would be called to these by Budé's *Annotations on the Pandects*. The idol of every French humanist, Budé was even more worshiped by the young French law students, for he had made the outstanding contribution to the restoration of the Justinian *Digests* or *Pandects* in their original purity, by his *Annotations*. Now everybody would be interested to know how Budé, who was primarily a hellenist, got the impulse to edit the *Pandects*. The author himself explained this. Valla's eulogy on the *Pandects* had given him the idea of reading more closely this famous compilation.[18] He had been especially

---

16) *Op. cit.*, I, 48 ff.

17) *Comm.*, p. 31, "Observandum est verbum licentiae hic positum in malam partem, quemadmodum fere accipitur apud autores: ut Valla annotavit."

18) BUDE, G., *Annotationes in Pandectas*, pp. 12, 13. "De Pandectas vero quid sentiam, malo alienis verbis quam meis dicere. Prodeat igitur aliquis Latinorum operum aestimator idoneus. Is erit Laurentius Vallensis, vir certe cum latine doctissimus, tum vero alienorum scriptorum iudex ut optimus, sic minime ambitiosus, et veritatis amantissimus: id quod invidiosum nomen eius vulgo reddidit, ut iam publico consensu latine ignorantium tanquam iniquus iudex fere reiiciatur. Is igitur Laurentius censor ac criticus quamlibet etiam morosus, ut illis quidem vide-

struck by the sentence in which Valla had said that in three years he could make such sound glosses on the text that the Accursian glosses would no longer be useful. Budé thenceforth was the sworn enemy of the "blind ignorance" of the Bartholists and Accursians.[19] Thenceforth also, in this instance at least, he surpassed the great Valla in substantial scholarship; for the latter had used the *Pandects* primarily as a source for Latin elegance.[20] Now the *Annotations* of Budé, which had received their first inspiration from Valla, were closely studied by Calvin as a student of law. The *Antapologia* of Duchemin indicates the students' close acquaintance with Budé. The *Seneca Commentaries* refer to the *Annotations* by name.[21]

Valla gave proof of his ability in textual criticism of the classics in his *Emendationes sex librorum T. Livii de secundo bello punico,* written (1442) while he was secretary to King Alphonso of Naples, a king who, like the great Medicis, had made a name for himself as a patron of letters.[22] Calvin twice refers to this work.[23] The *Emendationes* grew out of his famous quarrel with Beccadelli (Panormita) over the meaning of "ire in sententiam pedibus" in Livy.[24] Ever since Petrarch the humanists had sought to improve the condition of the Livian text, and hitherto not even Bruni and Guarino had done it adequately. Beccadelli, at the court of Naples, now undertook the task.

---

tur, Elegentiarum suarum libro tertio sic inquit: Relegi proxime quinquaginta Digestorum libros ex plerisque voluminibus iurisconsultorum excerptos: et relegi cum libenter, tum vero quadam cum admiratione: Primum, quod nescias utrum diligentiane an gravitas, prudentia an aequitas, scientia rerum an orationis dignitas praestet, et maiori laude digna esse videatur: deinde . . . Verum illud Laurentii elogium me impulit ut diligentius Digestorum libros legerem, qua in lectione cum multis in locis volumina ipsa partim mutilata, partim mendosa inveni: tum vero (quod flagitosius esse multo arbitratus sum) verba multa non trivialis, sed antiquae ac probae monetae, in alienum usum ignorantia temporum translata esse animadverti." Cf. also BUDÉ's *Commentarii linguae graecae,* pp. 20, 46 f.; DELARUELLE, L., *Guillaume Budé,* p. 168 f.

19) *Ibid.,* p. 100.
20) *Ibid.,* p. 111 f.
21) *Comm.,* p. 77.
22) VOIGT, G., *op. cit.,* I, p. 461 ff.
23) *Comm.,* p. 68, " . . . Malim autem interrogative legere, quanquam sine interrogatione legitur in plerisque exemplaribus: et loquutio est ab autoribus recepta, licet Valla improbet." He disagrees with him in *Comm.,* p. 83, "Reperitur tamen active, contra observationem Vallae et Beroaldi, apud Livium libro XXII."
24) VOIGT, G., *op. cit.,* I, p. 457 ff.

Valla being present at this scholar's reading of Livy in the royal presence, was not slow to exhibit his superior skill. The story of how the two men, hitherto friends, became bitter enemies is interesting. Two hostile camps were formed. Alphonso appointed Bartolomeo Fazio (Valla's arch-enemy who was also the court historian) to edit and publish the text of Livy with his emendations. Valla at once wrote a polemical counter-edition of Livy (six books) against Fazio. It is this volume that Calvin used.[25]

Of unusual importance was Valla's book exposing the Donation of Constantine as a forgery *(De falsa credita et ementita Donatione Constantini Declamatio).*[26] It was written in the interest of Alphonso's throne against the papal claims. The author was not the first to attack this document, but the most forceful, and the book worked as a powerful leaven in preparing the Reformation. He also exposed the forgery of Christ's *Letter to Agbarus,* and questioned the authenticity of the Apostles' Creed.[27] In connection with the latter he had considerable trouble with the monks, one of whom preached special sermons against his reflections on the creed's authenticity.[28] It is remarkable that Calvin seems not to have had any desire to enter the monastery. Surely, writings by men like Valla were not calculated to cultivate such a desire. Full many a sermon young Calvin heard on Sundays must have contained appeals to take the vows, his confessor must have brought the matter to his attention, seeing some friend or acquaintance assume the "habit" could not but suggest it to him, discussions among the students on religious issues must often have skirted the subject. Yet on the other hand there was the growing spirit of secularism. There had been *The Praise of Folly,* there was the more "dangerous" thrust at the whole papal system by means of fresh criticism in the Vallan spirit of some of the main props of Rome's authority. The Roman Church calculated its strength in terms of the numbers that

---

25) *Ibid.,* I, p. 488,, II, p. 385; also Valla's Letter to Decembrio, *Opera,* pp. 633–643.

26) *Opera,* pp. 761–7,95. A good translation is that of COLEMAN, C. B., *The Treatise of Lorenzo Valla on the Donation of Constantine,* University of Yale Press, 1922.

27) VOIGT, G., *op. cit.,* I, p. 468 ff.

28) *Ibid.,* I, p. 468 ff.

take vows, as it does today. Meanwhile Calvin was moving farther away from them each year. His chaplaincy at Noyon was but a form of scholarship aid. He had abandoned theology. He would be a free spirit, though making his bow to the church. It was the spirit of Valla in essence.

We come to the *In Novum Testamentum Annotationes*.[29] The sleepless Valla gave considerable attention to the Scriptures. The critical apparatus he had developed for the restoration of the classical texts was now put to use in the same manner with respect to the New Testament. The first fundamental of his method is to compare the received text with other manuscripts. This was a revolutionary step. It is true that the Vulgate was not to be declared infallible till the Council of Trente, but de facto it was, which in effect precluded comparison with the codices. Secondly, he permits himself to suggest changes that are not required by the codices at hand. E. g., on Matthew V,[30] "Beati qui esuriunt et sitiunt iustitiam . . .," he remarks, "Ego dixissem, iustitia. De iis enim ipinor deum loqui, qui propter iustitiam esuriunt et sitiunt, cum addatur, quoniam satiabuntur." Again, he notes[31] that Mary's name is written in the genitive, though it is really indeclinable.

Erasmus was one of the first to appreciate what Valla had done, and accordingly had the work printed. In the Dedicatory Epistle to Fischer[32] he says that though a general stigma (generalis invidia) attaches to the name of Valla on account of his extreme candor, yet all who love good letters owe him grateful respect. Continuing, he says: "What if Valla was severe on others? . . . . As if Aristotle did not reprehend everybody in almost all respects; as if Brutus did not contemn the "totam Ciceronis dictionem"; or Caligula that of Maro (Virgil); Jerome that of Augustine and Rufinus . . . . . . !" The defense he makes of Valla shows how bold a thing it really was to recommend his work. The Reformers follow in the footsteps of Erasmus. What had begun as a purely humanistic venture in literary criticism remained a permanent element in the purified church of the Reforma-

---

[29] *Opera*, pp. 803–875.
[30] *Ibid.*, p. 808.
[31] *Ibid.*, p. 803, Mathh. I.
[32] *Ibid.*, pp. 801–803.

tion. Calvin is known to have used the *Annotations* of Valla. When the Council of Trente delivers its pronounce-ment about the infallibility of the Vulgate he writes: "What! are they not ashamed to make the Vulgate version of the New Testament authoritative, while the writings of Valla, Faber (Lefèvre), and Erasmus, which are in everybody's hands, demonstrate with the finger, even to children, that it is vitiated in innumerable places?"[33]

Besides making a beginning of re-editing the Scriptures Valla made a diligent study of them for the purpose of defending his humanism. This is a fact of the utmost importance for our thesis, for Calvin as a reformer developed a scriptural defense of humanism. What is more, Valla is very explicit in casting up a wall of Scrip-ture passages to validate his claim that a man has the right to enjoy life, and Calvin seconds this attempt (though much more soberly). One could indeed expect that the Christian humanist would seek to defend his pursuits by Scripture. In fact, the Reformation is largely a defense of the new age that the Renaissance had ushered in. Calvin did this in so many words when he propounded the theory of common grace.

In the Preface to Book IV of the *Elegantiae*[34] Valla says: "I know that there are some people who seem to themselves holier and more religious who will presume to criticize this work of mine as unworthy of a Christian man, whereas I exhort others to read secular books...... What! do you say that secular books must not be read, and do you advance the authority of Jerome for that?" He goes on to say that Jerome was a Ciceronian, and that as a Latin man he desired "the style of Cicero, the style I say, a style that he could use in questions of philosophy......, (for) he was a writer of sacred disputations...... If he was well-versed in Cicero, why not in Plato?..... Why not in philosophy or the other arts?..... I do not want to compare philosophy with elo-quence;..... (for) philosophy and Christianity can hardly live together, and heresies all derive from the founts of philosophy." Again,[35] "the Latin and Greek fathers culti-

---

[33] "On the Fourth Session," Beveridge's Transl., *Tracts*, III, p. 74.
[34] *Opera*, p. 117 f.
[35] *Ibid.*, p. 130.

vated good language, Hilary, Ambrose, Augustine, Lactantius, Basil, Gregory, Chrysostom, and many others who in every age embossed with the silver and gold of eloquence those precious gems of divine utterance......See how the apparel of Aaron distinguished him by its marvelous decoration,.....as also the temple of Solomon....... So also people decorate their own houses......Let us ornament the House of God."

Valla's study of the Bible is not limited to the *Elegantiae* It is spread throughout his works. Let us content ourselves with a few of the more prominent instances. In the *Invectives against Fazio and Becadelli* we find the observation that ecclesiastical words like synod, eucharist, etc., do not come from the Hebrews, but from the Greeks.[36] His essay of the *Freedom of the Will* contains copious references to the Scripture, quoting at length from Romans XI, in seeking to prove, against Boethius, that the will of God roots in his "praescientia."[37] On almost everyone of the last 18 folio pages of the *De Voluptate* is the Scripture quoted in a desperate attempt to prove that the Bible is not opposed to the proposition that voluptas is the true good.[38] The passages range from the "paradisus voluptatis" of Genesis to the joys and beauty of the heavenly city of Revelation.[39] Valla's *Apology,* defending his use of the word "voluptas," asks why indeed we should spurn the word of God. Was it not the Lord who said to Cain, "Nonne si beneficeris, accipies?.....Et ad Abraham: Noli timere Abraham, ego protector tuus, et merces tua magna nimis....." Again, "Ecce relinquimus omnia, et sequuti sumus te, quid erit nobis? deinde respondit dominus quae sit futura remuneratio....." And thus it is in the parable of Lazarus and the

---

36) L. Vallae in Barpt. Facium Ligurem (et Ant. Panhormitam), invectivarum seu recriminatiorum Libri I–IV, *Opera*, p. 513, "Ubi enim reperies apud eosdem ecclesia, episcopus, presbyter, diaconus, acoluthus, canonicus, papa? Ubi baptisma? Ubi eucharistia? Ubi schisma, ubi hebdomada? Ubi synodus? Ubi alia infinita? Quae tamen a sapientibus viris e Graecorum fontibus derivata sunt, non ut vestra fert opinio, ex Hebraeis: quod si ex istis non possim proferre exampla, possum ex Graecis Homero, Hesiodo, Euripide . . . aliisque quamplurimis, ut scias non imperitiorum haec, sed peritissimorum vetustissimorumque esse vocabula."
37) "Nam voluntas habet antecedentem causam quae sita est apud sapientiam dei." De libertate arbitrii, *Opera*, p. 1007.
38) *Opera*, pp. 977–994.
39) See below for a fuller discussion of the *De Voluptate*.

Rich Man. Valla was proving that the Scriptures had new possibilities.

The abundant reference to Valla's use of the Scriptures is made with the added purpose of indicating that the Bible was by no means lacking in the armory of the humanist. It is not altogether true that the Reformers revived the study of the Bible. They indeed popularized, but they did not initiate the study of it. The credit for that belongs to the humanists. There can be no doubt that at least among Valla's reasons for studying the Bible was his perception that it does not condemn the enjoyment of natural life. (His attempts to show this, as described above, cannot be said to be entirely unsuccessful.) After Valla would come Erasmus, Budé, Lefèvre, whose direct heirs are Luther and Calvin.

The student who had once got interested in Lorenzo Valla could not have helped reading his *De voluptate, ac de vero bono.*[40] The recognition of this book was so live that Badius had published an edition of it about 1515.[41] Four years later there was another edition.[42] This volume, Valla concedes, might with propriety have been called "Concerning the True Good," for though he frankly insists that "voluptas" (pleasure) is the true good, he does not advocate moral license. If there are passages that appear to indicate the latter, it must be remembered that the book is written in dialogue. It is a glorification of natural passion over against celibacy which he calls a most unnatural and unbearable disease.[43] It was not an accident that the reformers advocated marriage for the clergy. The step as such was a great one, for a long medieval tradition opposed it. But such literature as this was bound to break down the resistance of anyone who allowed himself to be swayed by the humanists. The latter were not interested solely in the classics as such, but also in their appreciation of the natural life, untrammelled by traditions and doctrines of men.

[40] *Opera*, pp. 896–999.
[41] TILLEY, A., *op. cit.*, p. 230.
[42] BEAULIEUX, CHAS., *Catalogue de la Réserve XVIe siècle (1510–1540) de la Bibliothèque de l'Université de Paris."* Paris (VIe) 1910.
[43] VOIGT, G., *op. cit.*, I, p. 465 ff.

For a better understanding of this work we present a sketch of the subject-matter:

Quod natura magis amemus turpia quam honesta, p. 907f.; de odio virtutum, p. 903; quod voluptas est bonum, p. 912; de pulchritudine virorum, p. 913ff.; de pulchritudine foeminarum, p. 915f.; de potu et laudibus vini, p. 917f.; de odoratu, p. 919ff.; quod voluptas est domina virtutum, p. 921; de fornicatione et adulterio non improbanda, p. 922; quae fuerit causa et origo constituendarum virginum, p. 924; book III makes Christianity triumph, and the Scripture is appealed to in defense of his principle that the true good and blessedness is voluptas; reference is made to the "paradisus voluptatis" of Genesis and the "poma et arbor voluptatis" in Ezechiel, p. 977f.; the pre-Christian (ante fidem) philosophers' precepts were depraved, he says, and he adds a radically orthodox appreciation of Christ, p. 978f.; God should be loved above all, p. 979; and the highest good is heaven, p. 980; after treating such matters as to what extent the love of God is declared in the Old and New Testaments, p. 983f., he speaks of the beauty and adornment of the angels, p. 987ff., of the sensuous delights (voluptates) of heaven, p. 990f., of the abundant, the better, and the greater (than earthly) joys of heaven, p. 991f., etc. Throughout there is copious reference to Scripture.

Valla's personal life tended to identify his book as a manifesto of libido or Epicureanism (invidioso nomine).[44]  In the *Seneca Commentaries* Calvin is explicit in his abhorrence of the Epicurean theology, preferring the Stoic.[45] Nevertheless the *Commentaries* contain a passage of unusual interest, since it reveals an appreciation of at least one of the fundamentals of Epicureanism.  In the first book, the first chapter, p. 29f., we have his comments on Seneca's words concerning untempered desires.  He says, "To be

---

[44] VOIGT, G., *op. cit.*, I, p. 466.

[45] *Comm.*, p. 18, "Epicurei tametsi deos non negant, at, quod proximum est, voluptarios nescio quos somniant, otiosos, mortalia non curantes, ne quid voluptatibus suis decedat, pronoean Stoicorum rident, quasi faticidam." The book of Valla contains two conversations in which the case for Epicureanism and against Stoicism is defended, *Opera Vallae*, p. 905 f., "Antonius pro Epicureis, et pro natura contra Stoicos" and, p. 908 f., "De bonitate naturae, et perversitate Stoicorum." ALLEN, P. S. *The Age of Erasmus*, p. 27 ff., quotes a letter of Hegius to Agricola: "I have been reading Valla's book on the True Good, and have become quite an Epicurean, estimating all things in terms of pleasure . . . ," which shows the reaction of a very sane humanist to the volume.

clearer, we may accept the division of Epicurus, to which
Cicero refers......"

> Desire (cupiditas) which is:
> Natural and necessary is very easily satisfied;
> Natural, not necessary, is content with a little;
> Neither natural nor necessary is insatiable.

In his acceptance, be it for the sake of clearness, of the
Epicurean division of concepts there is at least no condemnation, and certainly a tacit acceptance of the Epicurean
proposition *that natural and necessary desire is legitimate.*
Valla had shown that it was unnatural to inhibit the pro-
creative power by which, as by a natural law, we are born.[46]
Calvin's works contains passages like this: ".... While the
Lord calls the propagation of the race a blessing, Cenalis
orders it to be cut down by a knife as an unfortunate ex-
cressence, as if children were the off-spring of chance..."[47]
Calvin's opposition to celibacy was at bottom a defense of
natural law. Beyond the principle of inviolable natural
law Calvin will find little more in common with the
Epicureans, or with Valla for that matter. It may be said
that the latter was rather a Cyrenaic (one who simply concerned himself about getting the greatest amount of happiness out of life) than an Epicurean (one who combined this
hedonism with the Democritean atomism). Calvin's re-
jection of Epicureanism goes farther than that of Cyrenaism.
Yet both are criticized for their emphasis on hedonism.[48]
The criticism is not violent. There is a certain concession
in his language.[49] His view is not that Epicureanism and
Cyrenaism are *per se* hostile to the highest good, but that
they are *inadequate.* The Stoic motivation for being humane
is in his opinion broader and deeper than the Epicurean and
Cyrenaic with their appeal to the individual's happiness
only.

Like Valla, Calvin's authorities for what constitutes the

---

46) Cf. VOIGT, G., *op. cit.,* I, p. 466.

47) *Tracts,* III, Beveridge's translation, p. 340, "True Method of Giving Peace and of Reforming the Church."

48) *Comm.,* p. 40 f., "Verum statim Epicurei Cyrenaicique reclama-
bunt, qui ut nihil suis voluptatibus decedere volunt . . ." " . . . Hoc
pro Cyrenaicis, qui in omnibus prospectum volunt suae utilitati."

49) *Comm.,* p. 41, "Serviunt autem maxime voluptati et utilitati, pax
quies, otium."

Christian view of life almost never are more recent than Gregory the Great, who died in 604. Augustine is Calvin's favorite father, while Jerome is Valla's. In this attachment to the early fathers both are true to the humanistic tradition since Petrarch. All of them passed by the medieval centuries with their neglect of the natural for the supernatural. If Calvin discovers the limitations of the Stoics, he nevertheless credits them with all that the early fathers did. Valla makes the Christian theory of life triumph, just as Calvin does when he makes "nostra religio" the ultimate standard of judgment, but neither identifies the views of the contemporary church with those of the Christian religion.[50]

### Section 3. Guillaume Budé

Among Calvin's elder contemporaries none exceeds Budé in influence upon the young French humanists. Not brilliant as a writer, he used the entire force of his vast intellect to set up a standard of accuracy and substantialness of scholarship unknown among his countrymen. Less versatile than Erasmus, with whom he has often been compared, he excelled him in depth and exactness of erudition. Not as imaginative a literary man as the great Rotterdammer, he never wrote anything unworthy of a scholar.[51] Budé did not find readers among the common people, as Erasmus did, but his authority among savants was quite as great. His popularity in France was greater than that of Erasmus, first because he had removed from the French scholarship the reproach that it was inferior to the Italian,[52] and secondly because in him French scholarship had equalled the best of Germany, Holland, and England.[53]

---

[50] For a general summary of Valla's life, character, and work, cf. MONNIER, PH., Le Quattrocento, essai sur l'histoire littéraire du XVe siècle italien, 1912, pp. 274–290.

[51] Budé would criticize Erasmus for his carelessness in this respect, e. g., in a letter (July 7, 1516) to him Budé remarks that his De Copia contains things that are unworthy of him. DELARUELLE, L., Répertoire analytique et chronologique de la correspondance de Guillaume Budé, p. 8 f.

[52] DELARUELLE, L., op. cit., p. 5; TRIWUNATZ, M., Guillaume Budé's De l'institution du prince, p. 26 f.; TILLEY, A., The Dawn of the French Renaissance, p. 277; cf. our discussion on Budé's De Asse below.

[53] He corresponded as an equal with Erasmus, More, Tunstall, Zazius, to name a few prominent ones. Cf. DELARUELLE, L., op. cit., passim. When Erasmus coupled the name of Budè with that of Badius, all France

The proposition that in Budé we have the epitome of French solidity of learning as contrasted with Italian superficiality is frequently advanced, but it needs qualification.[54] It was enough for French humanism to have equalled the Italian. The succeeding years would show that the Italian Renaissance had spent itself, while the French continued (with the entire Italian humanistic achievement behind it).[55]

---

was aroused to fury against the Hollander, showing that the attachment of France to Budé was deeply dyed with nationalism (for the cause of the trouble was insignificant and could easily have been explained). Cf. SCOTT, I., *Controversies over the Imitation of Cicero*, p. 31 ff. Calvin undoubtedly shared this French lionizing of Budé. Cf. *Comm.*, p. 54, "Guilielmus Budaeus, primum rei literariae decus et columen, cuius beneficio palmam eruditionis hodie sibi vendicat ("vindicat" is meant) nostra Gallia." The clause, "on account of whose service our Gaul lays claim to the palm of erudition," means nothing else but that France has bested not only the Italians but Erasmus, etc.

[54] After all Valla had been the father of modern literary criticism. His *Elegantiae* is as substantial a piece of work as one might wish for. His criticism of the Donation of Constantine is still studied in the science of historiography. Add that HENRI ESTIENNE'S *Thesaurus* rests largely upon the early work of Perotti and Calepino. Again, Alciati, though attempting to present his studies in the more palatable form of literary art, made a very solid contribution to the science of jurisprudence. Budé at least regards Alciati capable of continuing the work begun in the *Annotations on the Pandects*, DELARUELLE, L., *op. cit.*, p. 136 f. He recommends Alciati as an excellent teacher for young men, *Ibid.*, p. 255 ff. The latter we learn from a letter to Alciati, written September 24, 1529, which relates that he (Budé) had recommended Alciati to two students in the course of the summer. Now this was the very summer that Calvin and his three friends began to study under Alciati. Budé' "recommendation" may have helped them to make up their minds.

[55] TRIWUNATZ, M., *op. cit.*, p. 26 f., says, "Es ist bekannt dass sich die französische Renaissance, im Gegensatze zur italianischen, nicht sowohl durch die Kunst, als besonders durch die Gelehrsamkeit, nicht durch die form, sondern durch den Inhalt kennzeichnet." Such statements are sometimes misleading, for they hint that the Italian's sense of form made him indifferent to content. The truth is that he had both form and content. The two magnitudes of the Italian and French Renaissance, respectively, can be appreciated when one perceives that both had a common plane in philology, and that they differed in that Italy had an art while France had none. It was comparatively easy to increase the bulk of philological erudition, as Budé did, while it would take a century and a half to create anything equal to Italian art. From the point of view of the Renaissance of the 15th and 16th century, Italy had the disadvantage of being caught in a wave of a-moralism which made it simple for the church of the Caraffas to carry out a violent program of religious reaction, while in France and the rest of northern Europe there was a moral sturdiness that prevented a violent reaction. The result was the Protestant Reformation, through which the humanistic spirit kept alive, e. g., in its appreciation of natural life over against celibacy, and its claims to possess the right to investigate all things, even to challenge all human authority if need be.

The life of Budé illustrates how far French humanism was lagging behind the Italian up to his time. The most famous French scholar of his youth was Lefèvre who, though having an international reputation for profound erudition, was only partially interested in the new classical learning. He divided his efforts between Aristotle, mathematics, music, mysticism, and theology. His exegetical work on the Epistles of Paul (1512), e. g., gives him a place of importance in the history of the French Reformation, but as a precursor of Budé his labors are next to worthless.[56] For the achievements of Budé were to require the most exact knowledge of Greek as well as Latin, while Lefèvre knew so little Greek that the only text he had of Aristotle (on whom he was *the* authority) was the translations of Bruni and others.[57] As to Latin, when Erasmus sought for a teacher at the University of Paris, who could induct him into the mysteries of Jerome, he could scarcely find three who were interested in the old father, and none who could help him much. Everybody was crying for Scotus and Albertus Magnus.[58] Of course, there were the exiled Greeks. Budé had studied under Georges Hermomynos who had come to Paris on his return from a diplomatic mission in England. He was a copyist who possessed a few classical texts and many Byzantine. David Chambellan, Reuchlin, Lefèvre, Erasmus, Beatus Rhenanus had availed themselves of his instruction. But he was a mediocre teacher, and more concerned about his wages than excellence of instruction. Erasmus called him "that ever hungry Greek." Budé writes to Tunstall, "I met a certain Greek, already an old man, or rather he took possession of me, to make of his pupil a milch-cow; and he certainly knew how to get a good deal of money out of me. Though not a lettered man, he taught me how to read his language, and how to pronounce it well; but for the rest the task was beyond his ability...... Meanwhile I understood

56) DELARUELLE, L., *Guillaume Budé, ses origines, les débuts, les idées maitresses*, pp. 45–54; TILLEY, A., *The Dawn of the French Renaissance*, pp. 233–256; IMBART DE LA TOUR, *Les origines de la réforme*, II, pp.382–395; for his work as a theologian and reformer, cf. GRAF, K. H., "Jacobus Faber Stapulensis," in *Zeitschrift für die historische Theologie*, Hamburg and Gotha, 1852, pp. 3–86 and 165–237.

57) DELARUELLE, L., *op. cit.*, p. 51 f.

58) *Ibid.*, p. 55 f.

that there was no Greek in France.......But little by little
the luster of the new studies in Italy spread some gleams in
our land. Being provided with some books, I began again,
this time to study alone, making each day double speed.....
In brief, this master of Greek taught me only the alphabet,
and on this point his lessons might even have been better."[59]
Then there was Janus Lascaris of Phrygia, an excellent
scholar, whom Budé had wished to engage as teacher. But
Lascaris was too involved in diplomatic activities to do more
than encourage him.[60] Even the Italians had done incom-
plete work in philology. The grammars were mediocre, the
lexicons imperfect, the manuscripts incorrect. Budé had in
many respects a virgin field to cultivate.[61]

Overcoming all the disadvantages described above, Budé
schooled himself so well in the Greek that in 1503 he
published a translation of a tract of Plutarch, *De placitis
philosophorum*. In 1505 he added two more translations of
Plutarch, together with a translation of St. Basil's famous
letter, *De vita per solitudinem transigenda*. Ever since the
first tract was published Budé's reputation as a hellenist
was secure.[62] In the meantime, between 1501 and 1505, he
had made two visits to Italy, where he had met men like
Pietro Ricci and had seen the famous Pisan Pandects (of
which he was soon to make use for his *Annotationes in Pandectas*). By 1508 he is *the* humanist of France, his reputation having been secured against every possible derogation
of it, by the publication of the work just mentioned. The
rest of our narrative of this man will be given in terms of
his works, for it is these that Calvin undoubtedly knew well.

---

[59] DE BUDÉ, E., *Vie de Guillaume de Budé, Fondateur du Collège de
France (1467–1540)*, p. 12; cf. also DELARUELLE, L., *op. cit.*, pp. 69–72;
REBITTÉ, D., *Guilaume Budé, restaurateur des études grecques en
France*, p. 144 ff.; OMONT, H., "Georges Hermomyne de Sparte, maitre
de grec à Paris," in *Memoires de la Société de l'histoire de Paris*, t. XII
(1885), pp. 65–97.

[60] DELARUELLE, L., *op. cit.*, p. 74 f.; DE BUDÉ, E., *op. cit.*, p. 14, note 2.

[61] VOIGT, G., *Die Wiederbelebung des classischen Alterthums*, II,
pp. 372–393.

[62] DELARUELLE, L., *op. cit.*, p. 75 f. Calvin's first reference in the
*Seneca Commentaries* is to an apophthegm of Plutarch. Cf. *Comm.*,
p. 15.

Meantime it may be borne in mind that Calvin must have known Budé personally through the family of Dr. Cop.[63]

The *Annotationes in quattuor et viginti Pandectarum libros* appeared in the spring of 1508. Although to a large extent it was a philological work, and as such won the admiration and praise of all men, it was also an unusually courageaous achievement, for most of the author's daily associates at the court were jurists and lawyers, and these in turn were to a man Bartholists. They had all been brought up on the *Magna Glossa* of Accursius and the post-glossal works of Bartholus and his successors.[64]

The *Annotations* are a mile-stone in philology. Budé brought his immense knowledge of the classics to bear on the language of the *Pandects*. His first care was to get the best manuscripts, which he knew to be the Pisan. He proceeded to correct these in the manner of Valla. But he did more than Valla. For the latter's work was after all chiefly to return to Latin purity as such; it was a book of Latin elegances, as he himself termed it. But Budé established the meanings of words from their usage, and his work becomes correspondingly more meaty. So in explaining a juridical term he not only gives the abstract meaning, but shows to what institutions it "responds," and often gives a

[63] Budé was largely instrumental in the founding of two great French institutions. First in the creation of the Library of Fontaine-bleau of which he was the first director. Today this is the Bibliothèque National. By order of Henry IV it had been transferred to Paris in 1595. Lascaris compared Budé's work to that of Varro for Augustus. Lascaris has the honor of having given the first books to the new Library,—sixty Greek manuscripts. To this library was also joined the Library of Blois, which was the first library in France, founded by Charles VIII, and much enriched by Louis XII. The second institution was that of the Lecteurs Royaux, which has been described before. On the library cf. DE BUDÉ, E., *op. cit.*, p. 28 f.

[64] DELARUELLE, L., *op. cit.*, pp. 95–99. The Italian humanists had attacked the glossators, for the history of which cf. VOIGT, G., *op. cit.*, II, pp. 479–485. Budé did not withhold appreciation for the merits of either Accursius or Bartholus. Cf. *Annotations in Pandectas*, Basel apud Nic. Episcopum Juniorem, MDLVII, p. 7, where Bartholus is given a place among men "primi nominis iurisperitia." Again his commentaries are among "paucorum amplissimi nominis et primariae autoritatis." Budé speaks of Accursius' ignorance, but blames it rather on his century, *Ibid.*, p. 9, " . . . similis est ignorantia Accursii, vel seculi potius Accursiani." Cf also pp. 31, 70. p. 105—Budé says that when the *Annotations* were published the Accursians will regard them heretical, but adds parenthetically that Accursius and Bartholus were able and studious men who had the ill-luck to live in bad times. The Accursians of his own day are stupid, ignorant of Latin.

French equivalent.[65]   The lexicographical value of the work was so great that Robert Estienne's *Thesaurus* of the Latin Language (1531) was based for the largest part on it. Budé went farther still. He investigated the nature of the Roman institutions, thereby, for example, ending the loose references to the French Parlement as the equivalent of the Roman Senate.[66]

In the 1526 edition of the *Annotations* the author inserted his *Annotations on the New Testament*. In the Abbey of St. Victor he had found a very old manuscript, and proceeded to study it. Comparing the Vulgate with it he told the world that the latter contained sundry errors, yes, that in his opinion there was reason to think that Jerome had little to do with its final editing. His language is very sharp when he rebukes the clerics who opposed these new discoveries. He had written these notes already in 1516, but had withheld them because Erasmus had not long before published his edition of the New Testament.[67]

The *Annotations on the Pandects* is not as orderly a work as his critics might desire. There are numerous digressions. But these digressions are very interesting and significant. They reveal much about the author as a thinker and a man. For example, he holds that the classical literature is not only a body eloquence and poetry, but an "encyclopedia" of true political science and of philosophy. He calls attention to the fact that Plato and Aristotle are still the greatest in both of these disciplines.[68]   Moreover, we find in these digressions many a devastating line of criticism of the morals of the jurists, judges, lawyers, clergy, soldiers—not a single class escapes. He voices the miseries of the common people at whose expense the upper classes live in luxury. His patriotism is his consuming passion. He made excursions into French history, and did it scientifically. He went through the Archives for the sake of history purely, not like

---

[65] For example, à propos of "lege agere," "mulctam dicere;" cf. DE-LARUELLE, L., *op. cit.*, p. 110, note 4.

[66] *Ibid.*, pp. 103–116; DE BUDÉ, E., *op. cit.*, pp. 64–68; VOIGT, G., *op. cit.*, II, p. 378.

[67] DELARUELLE, L., *op. cit.*, p. 117 f.; Idem, *Repertoire analytique et chronologique de la correspondance de Guillaume Budé*, p. 11.

[68] Cf. BUDÉ, G., *Annott. in Pandectas*, pp. 5, 177, 211, for elaborations of the idea of "Encyclopedia." Cf. Valla's praises of culture, and Calvin's defense of humanism in the Institutes. (See our last chapter.)

a lawyer who looks for precedents for policies the king wants to follow, as Robert Gaguin and Paul Emile had largely done in their works. As an historian Budé approaches the best of the Italians.[69]

In March, 1515, Budé published another opus magnum, a work that appeared colossal to his contemporaries, the *"De asse et partibus eius."* The humanists were very curious to know in detail how the Greeks and Romans lived, and Budé satisfied their curiosity with such learning in this book that it was used as a work of reference for at least a hundred years. Calvin's frequent use of it will be noted later.

As in the case of the *Annotations on the Pandects,* the digressions in this book are significant. First there is a protest against the Italian superiority complex. Julius II had called the French "i barbari," and there were not a few Frenchmen who went so far in their worship of Italian humanism that they offended the patriotic Budé. Cardinal Georges d'Amboise and Chancellor Guy de Rochefort were among these. Budé vigorously criticised this pro-Italianism. He contended strongly for Frenchizing the Court which under Louis XII had been full of Italians.[70] Calvin's "nostra Gallia" breathes the same spirit. As a Christian Budé is a preacher of righteousness. He does not fear to condemn the selfish policies of the pope, nor does he deem it disloyal to appeal to the testimony of the Scriptures for his standards of judgment. His diatribes against the clergy are particularly pointed. He asks them, for instance, "What if the laymen should follow your example?"[71] The disease of Ciceronianism to an extent infected the *De asse.* Speaking as a Christian, the author uses Ciceronian terms, calling the devil "primigeniae noxae suasor," Isaiah is called "sacrorum vatum Homerus," the conclave of cardinals is the "senatus purpuratus."[72] His estimate of pagan doctrine is that it is sterile compared to the Christian. "Quae (monuments of Christian doctrine) si satis animo comprehensas haberemus, omnem antiquam philosophiam (quod mores attinet, et institutionem animi) nugas meras esse iudica-

---

[69] DELARUELLE, L., *Guillaume Budé,* pp. 119–126.

[70] *Ibid.,* pp. 160–180.

[71] *Ibid.,* pp. 181–187.

[72] *Ibid.,* p. 190 f.

remus."[73]   This is exactly the estimate Calvin gives in the
second edition of the *Institutes*.[74]  Budé speaks of Tacitus
as a criminal author in so far as he speaks evil of the
Christians.[75]   But philology leads to Christian theology
which is the crown, the "encylopædia" to which the human
mind attains.   One may pass without effort from pagan
wisdom to Christian wisdom, a principle expounded at
length in the *De transitu Hellenismi ad Chritianismum*.[76]
Budé passes in review the principal books of the Old and
New Testaments, indicating briefly their contents.   He
remarks that the sacred text furnishes models of eloquence,
though it should not be appreciated from that point of view
primarily.[77]   Christianity is not a complicated theology.
After all man's knowledge has been canvassed there remain
the Scriptures with their simple message for everybody.
Christianity is obedience to the commandments of Christ,
an imitation of the Master's life upon earth.[78]   This was the
essential note of the Reformation.

Between 1515 and 1519 appeared Budé's *L'institution du
Prince*.[79]  This work, written so early in the reign of Francis
I, is a collection of "apophthegms" from Plutarch's work of
that name, which Budé offered to his young king.  They
were calculated to be of the nature of advice to the new
monarch.  Apophthegms like these were extremely popular
during the Renaissance, doubtless because the subject of
educating princes was the concern of so many humanists.
Erasmus had published his *Institutio Principis Christiani*
in 1515, Machiavelli his *Il Principe* in 1513, besides which
there was the treatise of Francesco Patrizii on the same
theme.  It is very interesting to observe that Calvin's *Seneca
Commentaries* are to an extent charged with the same purpose.  The very first sentence of the *Commentaries* is a
quotation from the apophthegms of Plutarch, and throughout the subject of the nature of authority is touched on.

73) *Ibid.*, p. 192, note 2.
74) Opera Calvini, I, p. 297.
75) DELARUELLE, L., *op. cit.*, p. 192 .
76) *Ibid.*, p. 194.
77) *Ibid.*, p. 195, note 3.
78) *Ibid.*, p. 195 f.
79) TRIWANUTZ, M., *Budé's l' institution du Prince*, pp. 37–43, and DE-
LARUELLE, L., *op. cit.*, p. 200 f., for discussion of the date.

Budé's book therefore has unusual importance for our thesis.

The *L'institution* contains a spirited appeal to the king to remember the interest of humanism, to be a Macenas to it. Plato's proposition as a basis for royalty is urged, namely, that philosophers be kings, and kings philosophers. Since royalty is hereditary, the former is beyond control, but the latter remains a possibility. So Francis may be a philosopher if he but desires. It is especially necessary for kings to have a broad outlook and to know history. They should read Plutarch above all. He should honor those who promote learning, as Alexander did when he praised Aristotle. Let him shun worldly pleasures. Let him study rhetoric and eloquence, like Pericles. He should be humane. Though he is not subject to law like common men, he should be so possessed of the inner principle of righteousness that he takes no advantage of his position of exemptness from obligation to the laws of the realm.[80] If a king respects not divine law he is unworthy of his office; he should at least set an example for his people, if he cares not for righteousness as such. Ideally he is a father, and his people his family. The king's duty in war is to encourage his soldiers. He must be careful about his friends, having among them men of learning. Let him remember that he is mortal. Budé again shows himself the patriot when he compares France with Germany to the advantage of the former. He quotes Machiavelli who had said that France was well organized and excellently ruled. This is a quotation from *The Prince,* and shows that it was read in France.[81]

Triwunatz draws an interesting comparison between the *L'institution du prince* and Machiavelli's *The Prince* and Erasmus's *Institutio principis Christiani*. All three of these books had been written in the space of about six years at most. Machiavelli's ideal is Alexander Borgia, Budé's is Pompey, while Erasmus's is a utopian figure. The difference between Budé and Machiavelli consists first in their contrasting views of morality, and secondly in that Machia-

---

[80] Calvin will reflect this position, but with more force, in the *Seneca Commentaries;* essentially he ageed with Budé's interpretation of "princeps legibus solutus est."

[81] TRIWANUTZ, M., *op. cit.,* pp. 44–67.

velli has before his mind a prince in a newly established realm or a prince who still has to create his throne, while Budé has in mind a king in a well-established kingdom. Erasmus's prince is unreal, an over-done Christian. He can find in the classics no exemplary king. Budé takes no examples from Christian history, though Christianity is his standard for judging the pagans. He exhibits his reverence for Alexander whom he calls "the Great," while Erasmus warns against him as an "exemplum magnorum sed stultorum principum." Aristotle had said that basically the king receives his authority from the voluntary submission of the people to him. Both Budé and Erasmus concede this principle. But Erasmus concludes that the people may take away the authority they once had given, while Budé leaves the punishment of unworthy kings to divine providence. Of course, he was a patriot and loved his king, while Erasmus was a homeless scholar, a cosmopolitan. Calvinism would have to pass through a generation of persecution before the position of Erasmus was adopted.

This volume is full of passion for humanism. Budé pleads for a knowledge of the classics, without which a man is not fully developed as a human being. Latin, and especially Greek, are important. He gives the king broad hints about establishing the Lecteurs Royaux. He adduces the examples of Augustus endowing Virgil, of Alexander making Aristotle's work on Animals possible, of Quintillian's annuity. The ignorance of the church and of the University of Paris is appalling. Little Greek has been known since Jerome. In many places men rather are "doctor" than "doctus." Let them study Moses and Daniel who knew the wisdom of Egypt and Chaldea. Let them study the fathers who were well-versed in the Greek. The University of Paris had not made provision for the study of eloquence, a shame for an institution that had always been honored as "l'eschole metropolitaine de l'Occident." Let there be an independent faculty of eloquence, therefore. After reflecting on the superficial philosophers who lack the foundation for building higher, and on those who hurriedly become doctors with the help of compendiums, so that they may get chairs from which they may criticize all sciences, he turns to the king, assuring him that he can prove "que toutes leurs facultés sans les bonnes lettres, ne sont que gueines et fourreaulx sans espées et sans ascier esmoulu, faictz pour monatre aux ignorans, ey aux enfans."[82]

*L'institution* was written in French. It was meant to be read by the king, and Francis knew Latin very imperfectly, if he knew any at all.[83] Budé wrote Latin when he wanted his work to endure, Greek if need be, but French he did not regard as capable of expressing deep thought or of being a literary language. The next generation would fight this prejudice. Calvin would be the first to compose a weighty French work. "Le triomphe de l'humanisme eût été la mort de l'esprit française."[84]

In 1529 Budé published his *Commentarii linguae graecae,* a vast work of about a thousand pages folio, the first learned volume on Greek in France, and destined some day to be the foundation for Henri Estienne's *Thesaurus of the Greek language,* as the *Annotations on the Pandects* had been for Robert Estienne's *Thesaurus of the Latin.*[85] About five thousand Greek words and phrases are explained, some discussed at length, and about five hundred Latin expressions are commented on. The originality of the work is obvious, though the author has made use of other Latin scholars. Of the latter he has named only Lorenzo Valla, so far as I have been able to determine, and he takes advantage of the opportunity to animadvert on his *De*

---

[82] *Ibid.,* pp. 67–86.

[83] MARMELSTEIN, J. W., calls attention to the fact that the *Epistre au Roy de France,* prefacing the French translation of the *Institutes* (1541), is dated August 23, 1535, and adds corollary evidence that when Calvin published his first edition of the *Institutes* (prefaced by his Latin letter to the king), he made a translation of this letter and sent it under separate cover to Francis, for he was anxious to have it read by the king who could not have deciphered the Latin. "Calviniana," in *Neophilogus,* onder redaktie van Proff. J. J. Salverda de Grave, K. R. Gallas, enz. J. B. Wolters, Groningen en Den Haag, 1930, 16e jaargang, 1ste aflevering, pp. 1–6.

[84] DELARUELLE, L., *op. cit.,* p. 220; DU BELLAY produced the first defense of the French language, *La Deffense et illustration de la langue françoyse* (1549), Édition critique par Henri Chamard, Paris, 1904. On this book see SAINTSBURY, GEORGE, *A History of Criticism and Literary Taste in Europe, from the Earliest Texts to the Present Day,* 1900, II, p. 112 f.

[85] CLEMENT, L., "Henri Estienne et son oeuvre française," p. 185.

*linguae latinae elegantia.*[86]   Just one year before, 1528, the
*Ciceronianus* of Erasmus had been published.   The Ciceronian controversy was at white heat therefore.   The wide
digressions on Cicero are consequently not surprising in this
volume on Greek language, for Budé has been known to
have indulged in many digressions in other works.   (It must
be remembered however that Cicero used a good deal of
Greek.)   Although Budé praises Cicero as "parens linguae,"
he is too good a latinist to be his slave.[87]

The letter dedicating the *Commentaries* to Francis I,
written in Greek, is famous in the annals of the Collège de
France.   It is the last and most eloquent appeal of the great
humanist to his sovereign to establish the Lecteurs
Royaux.[88]   Now this book was so outstanding an achievement, bringing so much honor to the French name, and the
letter to the king was written in a language that was subtly
calculated to touch his pride, that Francis could no longer
postpone the project.   It is this letter that caused the Lecteurs Royaux to become an established fact the next year.[89]

### Section 4.   The Revival of Latin and Greek

John Calvin became one of the best latinists of the sixteenth century.   The state of latinity in his youth is illustrated by the fact that when he was at the Collège de Montaigu it was unusual for teachers, clerics, or jurists to use

86) *Commentarii linguae graecae,* venundatur Iodoco Badio Ascensio,
1529, pp. 46, 47.   A note of admiration for Valla is heard in the following.   "Ego vero Laurentium Vallensem egregrii spiritus virum existimo
seculi sui imperitia offensum: primum latine loquendi consuetudinem
constituere summa religione institisse . . . "   At the same time he feels
free to differ from him, and to criticize him for his "iudicii acrimonia
singulari."   Cf. p 20 where he speaks of "Laurentius . . . homo summa
laude dignus."   Cf. also BUDÉ's *Annott. in Pandectas,* p. 12.

87) *Comm. ling. graecae.*   Compare p. 873 with p. 19 f. and p. 886.

88) *Ibid.,* a ii–a v; cf. also p. 217 f.

89) Much more can be said about Budé.   For example, it is worth
noting his scientific probity, compared with some of the Italian savants.
Alciati "n' hesitait pas à fabriquer des inscriptions." (VOIR, *Melanges de
Rossi,* p. 41, l'article de l'abbé Duchesne sur St. Barnabé), DELARUELLE,
L., *op. cit.,* p. 155, note 1.

Budé's scholarship was close and unusually painstaking.   ALFRED P.
DORJAHN has given testimony of this in his *On Readings in the Hand of
Budaeus (i) inserted in his deck copy of Pliny's Letters,* Seminar report,
October, 1922–June, 1923, Chicago, 1923.

Further biographical material on Budé can be found in WINKLER
PRINS, *Geïllustreerde Encyclopaedie,* 3de Druk, Amsterdam, 1906; and
especially in BAYLE's *Dictionaire Historique et Critique,* Rotterdam, 1720.

pure Latin. A sketch of the study of this language in France up to this time will help us appreciate his achievement.

Ever since the Carolingian Renaissance classical models like Cicero had been used in the schools in the courses on grammar and rhetoric, so that the writing of Latin had gradually improved, and the Twelfth Century found many writers living or educated in France who could express themselves in forcible and correct Latin. That their style was not classical was due to both the theological and philosophical subject matter and to the fact that the greatest writers were men of exceptionally strong individuality (Abelard, St. Bernard, John of Salisbury, and others). As Scholasticism became more refined and scholars' interests were occupied by abstract ideas, to which the Latin was ill-suited, it declined as a vehicle of style. After Occam (died, 1350) "Latin writing became as barbarous in style as it was feeble in thought."[90]

It was humanism that swung the pendulum back to good latinity. The wise Louis XI had encouraged Italians to settle first at Lyons, then at Tours, to promote a revival of trade.[91] This courtesy was soon accorded to the Swiss, Spanish, Flemings, and many others. One of these foreigners, Guillaume Fichet, a Savoyard, introduced into France the printing-press. Having been made a doctor by the Sorbonne in 1468, he and John Heynlin, a colleague, were instrumental in setting up the press within the very precincts of the Sorbonne (1470). It was managed by Michel Friburger, Ulrich Gering, and Martin Kranz. From the beginning most of the books they printed were humanistic. It is interesting to know that the first was a collection of model letters by Gasparino da Barzizza who has been called "the founder of the Ciceronian school."[92] Late in 1472 Fichet left France and the press was removed to another location. Twenty-five books had issued from this first effort to promote humanism by printing. Though two other presses were set up alongside that of Fichet's colleagues, the pure humanistic character of their issue was on the decline. From 1477 to 1492 an

[90] TILLEY, A., *The Dawn of the French Renaissance*, p. 186 ff.
[91] IMBART DE LA TOUR, *Les Origines de la Réforme*, I, 287 ff.
[92] VOIGT, G., *op. cit.*, I, p. 506 f.

inferior grade of literature was printed. Humanism did not pay.[93]

The torch was passed on from Fichet to Robert Gaguin (1433-1500). The little Greek he knew he had learned from Città di Castello. His Latin he had improved under Fichet, his teacher and friend. He was also connected with the establishment of the first press, and when Fichet left he took up his friend's task (1473). He lectured on Latin composition, and soon published his first textbook *Ars versificandi*.[94] Much in demand as a diplomatist, he was too often distracted from his humanistic pursuits. His tastes turned to history, and some translations of Roman historians are the result. In 1495 his magnum opus appears, which is a history of the French people, *De origine et gestis Francorum Compendium*, for which Erasmus, then in Paris, wrote a laudatory epistle (which was printed at the end of the volume). The style of this history is not that of a finished latinist, but it shows the author's effort to cultivate conciseness and force.[95]

Lacking in profound learning and accurate scholarship and in grace of style, Gaguin nevertheless was a significant figure in French humanism. For twenty-five years he was the center of a group of humanists in the University of Paris. By character and bearing respected, his position of diplomatist gave him international standing, which in turn gave standing to humanism. He was the friend of Marsilio Ficino and Pico della Mirandola, and these were valuable friends indeed. One of his most important contributions to the cause of revived learning was the founding of a library in the Mathurin monastery, which grew to considerable proportions.[96]

The last years of the Fifteenth Century were not entirely barren of humanists in France. A list of Gaguin's friends

---

[93] TILLEY, A., *op. cit.*, p. 88. On Fichet see PHILIPPE, J., *Guillaume Fichet, sa vie, ses oeuvres;* FRANKLIN A., *Dictionnaire historique des arts, métiers, et professions* . . . , p. 394; CHRISTIAN, M., A., *Origines de l'imprimerie en France,* p. 11; BAYLE, *Dictionaire historique et critique,* in loc.

[94] TILLEY, A., *op. cit.*, p. 188.

[95] *Ibid.*, p. 192 f.

[96] For example, in March, 1500, Erasmus writes for a loan of a Macrobius and a Quintillian, ALLEN, P. S., *Opus Epistolarum Des. Eras.,* I, p. 283 f. Cf. also *Ibid.*, p. 195.

and followers or supporters is impressive: Laurent Bureau, Angelo Cato, Guillaume Rochefort, Jean Ganay (to whom Budé dedicated the *Annotations on the Pandects,* and Dr. Cop his *Prognostics of Hippocrates*), Stephen Poncher, Trithemius, Charles Fernand (who had edited Seneca's *Tragedies* in 1488), Jean Fernand, Guido Juvenalis (who had published an abridgment with comments of Valla's *Elegantiae,* which became a favorite text-book in several universities), Pierre de Bur or Burry (often called the French Horace), Gilles de Delft (who though a doctor of the Sorbonne published a commentary on *De remedio amoris*), the poet Guillaume de la Mare, Guy de Fontenay, the blind professor Pierre van der Brugge, Michel l'Anglois, Tardif (whose lectures at Navarre had been attended by Reuchlin in 1473, who also had translated Poggio's *Facitae* and Valla's *Facitiae morales*), Arnold Bost of Ghent. Among these there is a liberal sprinkling of Flemings and men from other parts of the Low Countries. Gaguin himself, though of French descent, was born in the Flemish province of Artois. Hailing from the Low Countries were the Fernand brothers, Pierre de Bur, Pierre van der Brugge, Michel l'Anglois, Gilles and Martin (Delft), and Arnold Bost. Again, a good number of Gaguin's immediate circle were in the first place theologians and humanists only in the second. Laurent Bureau and Arnold Bost were Carmelites, Gaguin himself was a Trinitarian, Juvenalis and the two Fernands left the University for the Benedictine monastery, Gilles and Martin de Delft were doctors of theology. According to this the Sorbonne was not opposed to humanism in the Fifteenth and early Sixteenth Centuries. The first press had been set up on its property, and leading humanists were on its faculty. It was not till the Reuchlin controversy that the Sorbonne altered its policy. For the issue there was "whether all branches of learning and science were to be subordinate to theology!"[97]

The story of Latin scholarship in particular, and of French humanism generally, cannot omit the person and work of Josse Badius Ascensius. Born c. 1462 in Ghent, his family name was perhaps Van Asche (whence Ascensius). It is

---

[97] TILLEY, A., *op. cit.,* p. 211 f.

erroneous to say that Badius was "a printer of no great reputation."[98] The very fact that in the *Ciceronianus* Erasmus had coupled the name of Badius with that of Budé indicated the respect he had for the Parisian printer. It needed not at all have been interpreted as an insult for Budé. After all the *Ciceronianus* is about latinity. Had the subject been hellenism the collation of these two names had been inexcusable. As for the story of the promotion of good Latin, Badius runs at least a close second to Budé.

After the death of Gaguin in 1500, and before the emergence of Budé, Badius is the leading humanist in Paris. He lacked the old master's (Gaguin's) prestige and advantage of position, but he was a better scholar. He not only had a better mastery of Latin, but unlike Gaguin knew considerable Greek. "His services to humanistic education as an editor of Latin classics and as a reformer of text books were very great, but perhaps his greatest service consisted in the impulse which he gave to the printing of humanistic literature, whether of Latin classics, or of Latin translations of the Greek classics, or of works in prose and verse by Italian humanists."[99]

Badius was one of the famous humanist printers, like Aldus and Froben, a class of men without whom the revival of learning had been impossible. Manager of the Trechsel Press in Lyons from 1493 to 1498, he migrated to Paris and became general advisor to Jean Petit who in 1495 had founded the great house that was to be Paris's leading book-store and publishing center for almost a century. When Badius became its master he christened it the *Aedes ascensianus,* a name that is celebrated in the history of printing.[100] Latin classics flowed from his presses in a steady stream. John Calvin would find them ready for his perusal. Other Parisian printers doing the same were Louis Hanken and Guillame le Rouge. Badius however outranks them all in both volume and variety. He took a deep interest in producing the new and better grammars to replace such medieval favorites as the *Doctrinale of Alexander de Villa*

---

98) SCOTT, I., *Controversies over the Imitation of Cicero*, p. 31.

99) TILLEY, A., *op. cit.*, p. 214.

100) FRANKLIN, A., *op. cit.*, p. 214; RENOUARD, PH., *Bibliogaphie des impressions et des oeuvres de Josse Badius Ascensius, imprimeur et humaniste*, I, p. 40; BROCKHAUS, F. A., *Konversations-Lexicon*, "Badius."

*Dei.*[101]  Ever since Valla's *Elegantiae* had attacked these
old text-books, there had been a barrage of efforts to upset
the firmly entrenched position of the *Doctrinale.* The name
of Niccolo Perotti is the greatest among the attackers.[102]
Perotti's *Grammar* (1468) was frequently printed, and
praised by Erasmus; his *Cornucopia* and other volumes are
called "a mine of latinity and Latin knowledge in every
direction."[103]  But the *Doctrinale* was not easy to remove.
It was written in verse that was calculated to aid memoriza-
tion. Wise man that he was, Badius prepared a new edition
of this book, making necessary omissions, additions, and
corrections. It was popular over night, and scandalously
pirated. In 1504 he ventured to print the *Grammar* of
Perotti, and lest this prose work fail of a market he worked
in a versified grammar of his own which he called the
*Textus Ascensianus.* He also edited the *Dictionary* of Am-
brogio Calepino, and reprinted it four times.

To Badius the early Sixteenth Century students owed
several treatises on composition which usually contained
model letters. While in Lyons, he had edited *Illustrium
virorum epistolae,* collected by Politian, and in 1512 he
printed the complete works of this humanist. Beroaldo was
his favorite author, whose *Varia opuscula* were printed five
times before 1515. Beroaldo was not only quoted by Calvin
in the *Commentaries* on Seneca, but appears to have been a
general favorite in Paris.[104]  This may have been due to the
fact that he had lectured there, but it was also because of
his preoccupation with moral questions, and his wealth of
illustration and quotation drawn from a wide range of
classical literature. It is a sign that the French humanists
were not superstitious admirers of Cicero; for Beroaldo
"cultivated the simple non-periodic structure and other
archaic effects by which Fronto and Apuleius had dealt the
final death-blow to Ciceronian prose as a living style."[105]

Thus far I have mentioned only a few of the Badian

---

101) Cf. REICHLING, D., *Das Doctrinale des Alexander de Villa Dei*
(Monumenta Germanische Paedagogica, XII), Berlin, 1893.
102) VOIGT, G., *op. cit:,* II, pp. 133 f., 136 f.
103) *Ibid.,* II, p. 137.
104) CLÉMENT MAROT had translated some of his verse in 1514, "Les
tristes vers de Béroalde sur le jour du vendredi saint, *Oeuvres complètes,* III, p. 138 ff.
105) TILLEY, A., *op. cit.,* p. 225 f.

editions of such authors as were quoted by Calvin in the *Seneca Commentaries*. He published many more, of course. No mention has been made of the Ciceros, the Senecas, and numerous others of whom he published numerous editions. In his zeal to bring to the studious public all that the Renaissance had to offer he even printed Valla's *De Voluptate*. "As a printer, and editor and commentator of Latin and Neo-Latin authors, and a writer of manuals of grammar and rhetoric he fully merits the claim to be regarded as the chief promoter of Latin studies in France during the reign of Louis XII."[106]

Badius died in 1535. Over four hundred workman-like volumes had come from his presses. Humanism was at high-tide during the last half of his life. Never again would his record be duplicated. Humanism was about to ebb. Latinity was to give way to French. Marot, Marguerite, Rabelais, had already produced some of their best work before Badius died; the very year of his death Olivètan published his French Bible, and Calvin sends a French Dedicatory Letter of the *Institutes* to Francis I. That is after Calvin's conversion, however. His discovery of the French language is synchronous with his discovery of the common people who have needs and rights despite their lack of a humanistic education. There was also an economic factor. Calvin had to realize that the invention of printing was one of the fundamental causes of the decline of the Latin language. A printing-press subsists on volume production; the greater the sale of a book, the richer the printer becomes. The great masses of people would never learn the Latin well enough to read it with any degree of pleasure. Therefore authors had better develop their vernacular.[107]

---

[106] *Ibid.*, p. 230.

[107] Cf. BRUNOT, F., *Histoire de la langue française dès origines à 1900*, Tome II, "Seizième siècle," p. 20 f. On Badius see furthermore RENOUARD, PH., *Imprimeurs parisiens, libraires*, etc., p. 11 ff.; BAYLE, P., *op. cit.*, "Badius." General works: TIMPERLEY, C. H., *A Dictionary of Printers and Printing*, etc.; OSWALD, J. C., *A History of Printing; Its Development Through Five Hundred Years*.

Calvin dealt with at least two printers in Paris. The *Antapologia* of Duchemin was printed by Gerard Morrhy, a distinguished hellenist, a warm friend of Erasmus ,and author of *Lexicon Graeco-Latinum*. After 1532 nothing is heard of him. Cf. TIMPERLEY, C. H., *op. cit.*, p. 255 f.; REBITTÉ, D.,*Guillaume Budé*, pp. 25, 44 (works published); RENOUARD, PH., *Imprimeurs parisiens*, p. 277, who tells us that Morrhy was associated with Jean Pierre of whom Aleander relates that "he sells Aldus'

While Latin was very popular in early Sixteenth Century France, Greek was almost unknown, and was regarded as a curiosity.[108] Rebitté outlines three Greek periods in France: (1) 1500-1530 when Budé stood almost alone as a really outstanding Greek scholar. (2) From the founding of the Lecteurs Royaux in 1530 to 1560 when Henri Estienne published his *Thesaurus.* It may be remarked that it is during this period that Calvin did his reformatory work. Himself a product of the Royal College, he can be said to be of the second generation of Greek scholars, just as he belongs to the second generation of Reformers. It will help one appreciate his eminence as a Greek scholar to remember that this second period was one in which an enormous amount of research had still to be done. Estienne, the peer of French hellenism, could have done little without the pioneering of Budé; so too Calvin had been unable to make his high mark in exegesis without Budé and the Royal College; but their diligence in exploiting their respective Greek fields was in itself a herculean task. (3) The third period, when Greek had come to its own, runs from 1560 to the end of the century.[109]

The work of Budé has been discussed in another section, so that nothing need be said about him here. Certain of his contemporaries in Greek studies are worth telling about. Besides Lefèvre, of whom we have told before, there was Tissard, concerning whom we know too little. In 1505 he published Valla's *Annotations on the New Testament* on which he made many comments in Greek. In the preface he asks the readers' indulgence for the words he accents wrongly. In 1507 his *Liber gnomaricus* appears which, if the first Greek grammar in France, was as imperfect as first

---

books at three times their original price," making Greek studies very expensive; cf. OMONT, H., *Essai sur les débuts de la typographie grecque à Paris,* Memoires de la Societe de l'histoire de Paris, XVIII, 1892, p. 68 ff.

Calvin had the *Seneca Commentaries* printed by Louis Cyaneus, whose name is a Latin translation for the Flemish Blaublom, or Blaamobloeme (-bluet). He hails from Ghent, and is in the printing business from 1528 to 1546. Little is known about him. Cf. RENOUARD, PH., *Imprimeurs parisiens,* p. 89; Idem, *Les marques typographiques parisiennes des XVe et XVIe siècles,* p. 62.

108) Lacroix counted more than six thousand French latinists; Robert Estienne allowed nothing but Latin to be spoken in his house; cf. REBITTÉ, D., *op. cit.,* p. 2 ff.

109) *Ibid.,* p. 4 f.

things often are.[110)]   Still in 1508 he brought out four little works which formed a rather considerable collection of Greek texts, which opened, despite all sorts of obstacles, the series of Greek publications that has been of good service to the renaissance of philology.[111)]

After Tissard comes Vatable who undoubtedly knew Greek, though his reputation rests mainly on his knowledge of Hebrew. More famous as a hellenist was Joannes Cheradamus of whom Beza says: "About the year 1517 the Greek language was publicly taught at Paris by a Frenchman called Cheradamus, a man well-versed in Hebrew as in Greek letters."[112)]   That Francis I did not appoint him to a lectureship in the Royal College perhaps indicates that he had not won great fame. Still he advanced Greek studies actively. He published a Grammar in the preface of which he complains about the scarcity of Greek books. In the same place he says that he is preparing a Greek dictionary. He was close enough to Budé to be among his correspondents. He took part in editing the Greek dictionary of Guillaume Main, friend and protégé of Budé. In 1526 he reëdited Barlandus's abridged edition of Erasmus's *Adagia*. In 1528 he published nine comedies of Aristophanes, whereafter he is no more heard of until 1543 when his promised dictionary appears.[113)]

More significant than any of the foregoing scholars was Jacques Toussain (Tusanus). In a letter to Erasmus Budé calls him a man learned in two languages, meaning Greek and Hebrew.[114)]   Originally from Troyes (whence he is known as Tusanus Trecensis), he came to Paris in 1517 where he took his degree in the arts. He made his home with Ruzé, the intimate friend of Budé.[115)]   He was privately coached in the Greek by Budé himself, and in 1527 began teaching it at the University of Paris. Budé had long had him in mind as one of the first professors for the Royal College, and had recommended him to the king. Calvin must fre-

---

[110)] *Ibid.*, p. 9.
[111)] *Ibid.*, p. 54; Bayle, P., *op. cit.*, "Tissard."
[112)] *Histoire ecclésiastique*, I, p. 17.
[113)] For further details on Cheradamus, cf. Rebitté, D., *op. cit.*, pp. 56–62; Bayle, P., *op. cit.*, "Cheradamus."
[114)] April 12, 1518, Delaruelle, L., *Repertoire*, p. 33 f.
[115)] Tilley, A., *Down of the French Renaissance*, p. 274; Delaruelle, *op. cit.*, p. 33, note 4.

quently have met him there, though he did not study under his direction. One of Toussain's first publications was a collection of Budé's letters in 1520.[116] About the same time he helped Cheradamus publish his grammar. He contributed to completing the Latin translation of Theodore of Gaza's *Grammar* of which Erasmus had translated the first two books. His own *Lexicon graecolatinum* appeared posthumously in 1552, six years after his death. He was a teacher of Greek grammar rather than literature, which likely is the reason why Calvin (who had taken the elements of grammar under Wolmar) did not study under him.[117]

Pierre Danès (Danesius), Calvin's teacher at the Royal College, was younger than Toussain, but was accorded the first title of professor regius of Greek. He began the study of Greek at the age of about twenty, and during the next thirteen or fourteen years he perfected himself as a hellenist, at the same time amassing a financial fortune. His most considerable work is an edition of Pliny the Elder (1533). An ardent admirer of Aristotle he expounded mainly the Organon at the Collège Royal. He was involved in the trouble over the contest of Ramus against Aristotle (1543), which resulted in the order to suppress the latter's *Institutiones dialecticae* and *Animadversiones aristotelicae.* Ramus was furthermore forbidden to publish any book on philosophy without the express permission of his Royal Majesty. Over against the partizanship of Danès for Aristotle stands his unselfishness and high-minded independence. He was free from the contagion of avarice and lust for fame.[118] At the Royal College he refused to give instruction to the sons of the most important magistrates of Paris, in spite of entreaties and promises. At the same time he spared himself no pains to give his best to the students of his choice. Two motives determined his selection: his affection for the father of the student, and the promise the student gave of a brilliant future. Henri Estienne, one of his students, leaves a record full of praise for the master. Calvin must have impressed him as a promising young man, for he too sat under him.

---

[116] *Epistolae Gulielmi Budaei Regii Secretarii,* 1520.
[117] On Toussain cf. DELARUELLE, L., *op cit.,* pp. 33 f., 107, 124 f., 133 ff., 212, 217; REBITTÉ, D., *op. cit.,* pp. 30 *(Lexicon graecolatinum),* 49, 62–65; LEFRANC, *Histoire du Collège de France,* p. 173 ff.
[118] For examples of which cf. REBITTÉ, D., *op. cit.,* p. 70 f.

## Section 5.  The Revival of the Roman Law

The Emperor Justinian (527-565 A. D.) in the first year of his reign directed that Tribonian and nine learned associates "revise the ordinances of his predecessors, as they were contained, since the time of Adrian, in the Gregorian, Hermogenian, and Theodosian codes, to purge the errors and contradictions, to retrench whatever was obsolete or superfluous, and to select the wise and salutary laws best adapted to the practice of the tribunals and the use of his subjects."[119]  The result was the famous *Code of Justinian,* which was ordered thenceforth to be the only legal authority of the Empire.  But a heavier task was still to follow: "to extract the spirit of jurisprudence from the decisions and conjectures, the questions and disputes of the Roman civilians. . . . . Two thousand treatises were comprised in an abridgment of fifty books; and it had been carefully reduced, in this abstract, to the moderate number of one hundred fifty thousand."[120]  Thus came into being the *Pandects* or *Digest,* which together with the *Institutes* and the *Code* were "declared to be the legitimate system of jurisprudence."[121]  When we speak of the revival of Roman Law, special reference is had to the Justinian *Digest* or *Pandects.*

Now Western European "medieval political theory was based upon aᶀ tripod: the Roman law, the teachings of the Fathers, and Germanic legal traditions and social institutions.  Antiquity believed the State to be real, supreme, immutable, permanent, above all, and not responsible to its subjects.  Christianity, through St. Augustine, taught that civil society, i. e., the State, being derived from sinful man (Nimrod was its founder), was ex origine evil; that the church was the perfect form of society, and the State at best was only to be tolerated within and subordinate to the Church.  With the primitive Germans, on the other hand, even when the inchoate State began among them, the emphasis was laid upon the rights of the individual.  All three of these antithetical conceptions entered into the

---

119) GIBBON, E., *The Decline and Fall of the Roman Empire,* III, p. 673.
120) *Ibid.,* III, p. 673 f.
121) *Ibid.,* III, p. 674.

fabric of the Medieval State." The dissolution of feudalism left the field to the remaining contenders: the Roman Law, championed by the emperors, and the doctrines of Augustine defended by the papacy.[122]

That the emperors sustained their claims by the Roman law is illustrated by the life of Frederick I.[123] But it was more than an instrument for the convenience of monarchs. Had it not offered advantages to a larger class of men, the Roman law had never enjoyed the popularity it was destined to have. Feudal law was feasible for the regulation of simple communal relations, but it was quite incapable of dealing with situations so complex as the new commercial and political society that, at least in Italy, was resulting largely from the Crusades and the rapidly growing trade relations between the Orient and Western Europe. "In the commercial and political society of the Italian cities there arose a demand for fruitful knowledge, for science applied to the regulation of social life—for *civilization* in the strictest sense of the word. And this demand was met by a revived study of the long-neglected but never wholly forgotten monuments of Roman Jurisprudence."[124] Professor

---

122) THOMPSON, J. W., *Economic and Social History of the Middle Ages*, p. 699. Augustine did not identify the Civitas Dei at all points with the Roman Church, but rather with the communio sanctorum, cf. *Civitas Dei*, II, 21. For the relation between the Civitas Dei and Civitas terrena, cf. FIGGIS, J. N., *Political Aspects of St. Augustine's Civitas Dei*, Chapt. IV. The Medieval Church overlooked the fine points of Augustine's thought in its consuming desire to find in so great an authority the props it needed for its claims. Such props could be found easily, of course, for Augustine was unequivocally opposed to the nationalistic aspirations of the Donatists, and equally so to the idea of an unchristian State. His grand ideal was a res *publica christiana* in which the State should be sanctified by the Church, and the Church given security by the State.

123) THOMPSON, J. W., *Feudal Germany*, p. 227, "Frederick I's caesaristic madness and his mania for the application of the Roman law was destructive of the best political traditions of Medieval Germany. It is ineffectual argument for his admirers to claim that he never had any intention of introducing the Roman law into Germany, and to cite the decision of 1181 as evidence thereof. For the same man had earlier, in 1165, repudiated German law in the face of the bitter opposition of Worms on the ground of the decrees of his 'predecessors.' And whom did he mean by the word? Constantine and Valentinian, whose 'sacred laws' he venerated as 'oracles'."

124) Rashdall, quoted in THOMPSON, J. W., *Econ. and Soc. Hist.*, p. 445, note 3.

Thompson gives an excellent illustration of the greater adequacy of the Roman law:

> Roman law had viewed the relation of rivers to the public interest in a sane and practical way. Navigable rivers were public. Private right pertained only to the banks and islands in the stream; in event of a change of course the abandoned channel was held to belong to the abutting property owners. But feudal law had reversed all this, and the medieval nobles extended their private proprietorship over the waters of navigable streams, hung chains across or placed weirs to intercept traffic and imposed tolls upon all traffic up and down stream....... But at the Peace of Constance in 1183 (art. 3) Roman law, never dead in Italy, was reasserted, and the Lombard cities recovered all the rights previously usurped by the feudality.....It was not an accident that the study of Roman law was intently pursued in the Lombard cities.[125]

The revival of the Roman law occasioned the creation of a new profession, that of the glossators who flourished from the Twelfth to well into the Sixteenth Century. The greatest of the early glossators (after Irnerius who founded the school of Roman law in Bologna) was Accursius whose work had been "primarily to restore the text of the law books, then to interpret the text literally."[126] Since the life of the Sixth Century (the century of Justinian) was different from that of the Twelfth, the glossater had "to bend facts to meet a literal interpretation of the law, or else make concessions to fact."[127] The great work of Accursius was generally called the *Glossa Magna*.

His famous successor as interpretor of the law was Bartholus of Sassoferrato. "For two centuries after his death he was recognized as the 'prince of jurists'; from the invention of printing to the close of the Sixteenth Century, one edition of his works followed another.[128] He was born in 1314. At thirteen or fourteen he studied law under Cino da Pistoia (friend of Dante and Petrarch) at Perugia. A doctor in 1334, he became professor at the University of Pisa in

---

[125] *Ibid.*, p. 445 and note 3.

[126] WOOLF, C. N. S., *Bartolus of Sassoferrato, His Position in the History of Medieval Thought*, p. 4.

[127] *Ibid.*, p. 4 f.

[128] *Ibid.*, p. vii f.

1339, and in 1343 at the University of Perugia (where he did his greatest work). He died in 1357.[129] Bartholus was rather a postglossater. Though his work made no break with that of the Accursians, his task was a different one. For while he interpreted the text of the *Pandects* he had also to deal with the *Glossa Magna*, and he had rather "to evolve a law practically effective for the world in which he lived than to expound a law scientifically correct according to the texts."[130]

The Roman law naturally conflicted with the Canon law. Bartholus placed Civil law on a level with the highest branches of learning, calling it perfect in itself, and second to none save theology. Cino, his master, had been a bitter opponent of the Canonists, but Bartholus was more temperate in his opinions. After him the great jurists are usually doctors of both Civil and Canon law.[131]

Great as the interpretations of the glossaters and postglossators had been, the age of Accursius and Bartholus was past, and the age of the latter's more radical teacher, Cino, was dawning. The great contenders for the principle of absolutism for national monarchy were about to be born. The times were full for the appearance of Henry VIII and Francis I. The Roman law was destined to play a rôle in this new phase of history, and would go far in the validation of the claims of these rulers. Even in discordant Germany it would find echo in the phrase "cuius regio, huius religio." Feudal law was daily proving its inability to cope with the new organization of society, which is illustrated by the German knights, against whose "arbitrariness Peter von Andlo, the German patriot, hopes the Roman law will cast up an effective wall of defense."[132]

---

[129] *Ibid.*, p. 2 ff.
[130] *Ibid.*, pp. 5–9.
[131] *Ibid.*, pp. 13–19; cf. also STINZING, R., *Ulrich Zazius, Ein Beitrag zur Geschichte der Rechtswissenschaft im Zeitalter der Reformation*, Beilage II, Ueber die Vertretung des Römischen Rechts auf den deutschen Universitäten im vierzehnten und fünfzehnten Jahrhundert, pp. 323–344. Stinzing shows the growing frequency of the title "Juris utriusque doctor" since the end of the Fourteenth Century. Even the "Stiftungsbullen" of the popes permit both at the opening of the Fifteenth Century, as is exemplified in that of Alexander V for Leipzig (1409), which mentions the "studium . . . ac utroque Jure, videlicet Canonica et Civili."
[132] STINZING, R., *Ulrich Zazius*, p. 91.

It will help one appreciate the close connection of Calvin with the movement to revive the Roman law, if it is realized that he was in contact with either the persons or the writings of the greatest promoters of this revival. Besides Valla, Budé, and Alciati, there was also Zasius of Freiburg. The last three generally were referred to as the great triumvirate of the new jurisprudence.

Lorenzo Valla's criticism of the glossators and postglossators was in direct line with the spirit of humanism. That is, he aimed his thrusts first of all at their uncouth Latin. Take, for example, the splenatic invective which peppers his letter to Decembri, in which he asks why the many terribly unlearned books, most ineptly written by the jurists, are not thrown into the fire.[133] Of the jurists there is scarcely one who is not contemptible and ridiculous.[134] Coupled with their bad Latin is their ignorance of law.[135] Why, given three years for the task, Valla says that he could write glosses for the *Digest* that would be far more useful than those of the Accursians.[136] As for the style of the *Digest* he has high admiration. He tells us that he had read about fifty books of it with pleasure.[137]

133) *Opera*, p. 633, "Nonne indignum est Candidem et aegre nobis ferendum, quod tot ineruditissimi libri, et ineptissimi scripti, non modo non iniiciuntur flammis in publica positis, more maiorum, sed et multos ita amatores, laudatoresque habent . . . ?"

134) *Ibid.*, " . . . Horum quos dico Jurisperitorum, nemo fere est, qui non contemnendus plane ac ridiculus videatur. . . . Itaque vide quid feceris, et ubicunque es, fateare te male inconsiderateque fecisse; nisi forte gaudes nostro male, in locum Sulpitii, Scaevolae, Pauli, Ulpiani, aliorumque, ut leviter loquar, cygnorum, quos tua aquila saevissime intermit, successerunt auseres Bartolus Baldus, Accursius, Dinus, caeterique id genus hominum, qui non Romana lingua loquantur sed babare: non urbanam quandam morum civilitatem, sed aegrestem rusticanamque immanitatem prae se ferant . . . " He charges "iste Bartolinus sol" with having left the house pretty dark (p. 634).

135) *De lingua latinae elegantia, Opera*, p. 80. "Nota sunt eorum, et nimis nota nomina . . . qui vix quintam partem iuris civilis intelligunt, ob imperitiae suae velamen tum aiunt non posse doctos evadere in iure civili facundiae studiosos, quasi iurisconsulti illi aut rustice locuti sunt, id est, istorum more, aut huic scientiae non plane satisfecerint . . . "

136) *Ibid.* "Quod si Cicero ait, sibi homini vehementer occupato, si stomachum moveant, triduo se iurisconsultum fore, nonne et ipse audebo dicere, si iurisperiti (nolo dicere iurisimperiti) stomachum mihi moveant, aut etiam sine stomacho me glossas in Digesta triennio conscriptorum, longe utiliores Accursianis?" Valla is perhaps jesting.

137) *Ibid.*, p. 79, "Perlegi proxime quinquaginta Digestorum libros ex plerique iurisconsultorum voluminibus excerptos, et relegi quum libenter, tum vero quaedam cum admiratione. Primum, quod nescias utrum diligentia ne an gravitas, prudentia an aequitas, scientia rerum an orationis dignitas praestet, et maiori laude digna esse videatur."

Valla never went beyond jesting about his being able to write a commentary on the *Digest* in three years, but his jest and his praises of the *Digest's* dignified Latin awakened in Budé the desire to annotate this great compilation of laws, as we have seen before.[138]   The difference between Valla and Budé with respect to the glossators is that the latter was ready to appreciate at least Accursius and Bartholus as men of worth, deprecating the times in which they lived, while Valla would have nothing of them.   Again, Budé had a profounder appreciation of the *Digest* as such, for he had actually accomplished the task of commenting on twenty-four books.   Calvin was very fortunate to live in Budé's time instead of Valla's, for if Budé had not discovered any new principles for literary criticism, he had at all events produced a vast body of work in which the best of these principles were exhibited; besides, for a student of law the *Digest* or *Pandects* were the most significant text to study. Calvin had studied the glossaters under de l'Estoile, but the latter had not been hostile to the new method of consulting the Justinian text in the setting given to it by Budé (whose method, as we know, was to put the text in the context of the institutions and usages originally belonging therewith). Duchemin's *Antapologia* shows that de l'Estoile's students were well acquainted with Budé. The *Annotationes in Pandectas* was to Calvin another avenue of escape from the influence of the Middle Ages.   We are not aware that he ever took up a study of Canon law; the auspices under which he pursued his legal studies were humanistic, and therefore not of the sort to encourage it.   The glossators had interpreted the law with a view to making it fit somehow or other the actual conditions in Europe, with the result that often there was the form of Roman law without its spirit.   The humanists went to the original text, penetrated its signification, extracted its spirit, and from the new point of vantage looked at life, with the result that the existing conditions were, so to say, on trial.   Few thought of questioning the principles of the Roman law; its authority was very great, what of its obvious sanity for the regulation of society, and its venerable age.   The thinking man of that age found a

---

[138]  Cf. our section on Guillaume Budé.

vast element of society that had intellectually and spiritually broken with the authority of the Canon law; he also found a society that could not use the old feudal law; and the natural thing to do was to contemplate a reconstruction of human relations in accordance with certain fundamental conceptions of the Roman law.

In our opinion Calvin deferred to Budé's *Annotations* primarily in his studies of law, but he could not help learning something from Alciati who was after all a great teacher. Alciati had published his *In tres posteriores Codici Iustiniani libros annotatiunculae* in 1513, which was his first work and of a purely philological character. Fundamentally his and Budé's methods were the same, namely, as has been said, to expound the text by the context of the institutions and usages of antiquity.[139] From our knowledge of Alciati as Calvin's teacher it appears that he impressed the young man with his esthetic appreciation of the classics rather than as an authority on law. Calvin seems not to have taken much confidence in his erudition; the attack on Alciati in the *Seneca Commentaries* indicates that Calvin expected much more of a teacher in this respect than he found in Alciati. The strength of the Italian professor lay in his power of inspiring the student with the beauty of the classical literature first of all, and incidentally presenting the subject of law in accordance with the basically sound method of illuminating the text.

There was also Ulrich Zazius, whom Calvin had read.[140] This man was introducing the Roman law into Germany, where its regulations appeared certainly to have been needed.[141] He was born in Constance, 1461, and attended the Cathedral school there. Though Hegius, Dringenberg, Wimpheling were in those years coming to the fore, Zasius had not the good fortune to have a man of their type as teacher. In 1481 he goes to the then recently founded (1477) school at Tübingen where the jurists were mostly Doctors of Canon Law, and where at any rate he had indulged in too much pleasure to learn much. Soon after leaving this school

---

[139] Cf. Delaruelle, L., *Répertoire analytique et chronologique de la correspondance de Guillaume Budé*, p. 69 and note 7.

[140] *Comm.*, p. 112, where he remarks that "scitissime docuit Zazius iurisconsultus" on some detail in the Roman law.

[141] Cf. Stinzing, R., *op. cit.*, pp. 80–99.

he accepts the position of court secretary to the bishop of Constance, and becomes an expert in Canon law. Then he is called to take the position of city clerk of Freiburg (1491). Here he gets an excellent reputation for his legal talent. Meanwhile he enrolls as a law student at the University of Freiburg. Gabriel Ghabot is professor of Roman law. Paulus Cittidanus of Milan (Alciati's city) is there also, and wins Zasius entirely for the cause of Civil law. Cittidanus had been a student of Jason who had been Alciati's professor. In this manner Zasius fell heir to the same training that had produced Alciati.[142] In fact, "on the whole it can be said that the same ideal was being pursued (at the Universities of Freiburg, Heidelberg, Basel, etc.) that had been in the mind of Lorenzo Valla half a century before."[143]

We come to a discussion of what the *Seneca Commentaries* have to say about their author's debt to the Roman law. It will be obvious to the reader of Beyerhaus's book on *Staatsanschauung Calvins* that we are following his plan of treating the subject.

As to the question of the origin of authority, we have two references in the *Commentaries*. The first in connection with his comments on Nero's speech in the beginning of the book,[144] where, in accordance with Romans XIII, he derives all authority from God, as also the noble pagans assert. The notable feature about this passage is that there is not a single note about the part sin plays in the origin of government. Calvin is still a thorough humanist. In another passage Calvin calls attention to Seneca's position that the communal nature of man is a ground for "potentia," and though he quotes copiously from Plato, Aristotle, Cicero, and Seneca's letters to show that this was universally held, he limits himself to its ethical meaning. Calvin does not reject the Stoic metaphysics, but modifies it.[145]

The ancients had differentiated between positive right (ius civile) and natural right (ius naturale), a distinction that was maintained throughout the Middle Ages and remained the firm basis of thought in the Sixteenth Century.

---

[142] *Ibid.*, pp. 1–26.
[143] *Ibid.*, p. 27. The most adequate discussion of Zasius is still Stinzing's book, which see for further particulars.
[144] *Comm.*, p. 18.
[145] *Ibid.*, p. 40.

All men regarded the State as an entity independent of society and above it. The State had no inherent responsibility to society as such. But there was of course a nexus, a provision by which the State was indirectly bound to promote the welfare of man. This was called natural right. After all even kings were human; they were born, they lived, and died as other men did. So though as kings they were exempt from obligation to the subject, as men they were expected to be just and good. Seneca had said that the royal power "need not be bad if it respects natural law (naturae lex)." Calvin takes over this whole conception uncritically, calling this universal law "lex naturalis." Let kings treat their subjects with the same goodness wherewith God has favored them, is as far as he goes. He speaks of a fundamental "aequum" which must go hand in hand with "ius" to make the State happy.[146] The idea of "aequum" comes up more than once in the *Commentaries*. A ruler should not always treat his subjects according to the strictest justice; circumstances, humors, and so forth, must be reckoned with.[147] Aequum (fairness) is coupled with "bonum," and is even defined as that which opposes requiring the uttermost farthing.[148]

From our previous references to the expression "princeps legibus solutus est" it may be gathered that it is an important one. Literally it means that the prince is bound to keep the laws of the realm, just as his subjects are. That was its original meaning. In the Justinian Codes it means exactly the opposite, namely, that the prince is free from the obligation to observe the laws. That was also the view of the Twelfth Century.[149] In the Sixteenth Century the same view still obtains. Budé is unequivocal in his endorsement of it. Beginning with the principle that the prince "must be thought as the equal as it were of some god among men (he takes his cue from Aristotle), and that equals are

---

146) *Ibid.*, p. 61.

147) *Ibid.*, p. 34 f.

148) *Ibid.*, p. 119, "Aequm et bonum, quod iuri summo seu rigori iuris oppositur."

149) Beyerhaus, G., *op. cit.*, p. 10 f. Cf. also *Corpus Juris Civilis*, Lib. I, tit. 3, loc. 31: "Ulpianus, ad Edictum: Qui legibus soluti sunt . . . Princeps legibus solutus est. Augusta autem, licet legibus soluta non est: principes tamen eadem illi privilegia tribuunt, quae ipsi habent." Concerning Ulpian cf. Karlowa, O., *Römische Rechtsgeschichte*, pp. 739–744.

under legal obligation only to equals," he concludes that the
laws are absolutely not intended for them.[150]    Alciati's
view coincided with that of Dio Cassius: "Significat hoc
(princ. leg. sol.) ab omni legum necessitate liberum."[151]

Calvin agrees with this principle.[152]   Commenting on the
words "sic me custodio, tamquam legibus.....," he says:

> "He (Seneca) does well to add this, however; for the
> prince is certainly not bound by the laws: but as the
> voice of one worthy of reigning in majesty he is held as
> prince to bind himself by the laws.  And it is actually
> better for the empire that the throne submits to the
> laws: as in the Rescript of Valerian and Theodosius and
> in the Rescript of Severus and Antoninus, 'It behooves
> that we are not under the laws, but we live according
> to the laws nevertheless.'  Pliny, in the panegyricus,
> 'The emperor should become accustomed to placing the
> ballot with the empire; thus he may come in, thus he
> may retire, though one who is of a mind to renounce
> this plan should make known what he has withdrawn
> .....'  Likewise, 'You ought to have no greater strength
> than we.  The prince is not above the laws, but the laws
> above the prince.'  Thus even Augustus proposed in the
> senate a method of ruling the empire with reason."[153]

---

150) *Annotationes in Pandectas*, p. 67 f.  Budé then proceeds to discuss
the necessity of the State's promoting liberty, wealth, virtue, and equality among the citizens; adding that the very character of a ruler implies
that he be generous, "quod vocant generis nobiltatem."  There is therefore a certain mutuality between king and people, which is basic to the
idea of the "res publica."  He points out that "we have kings today, who
have everything in their power, and who, like the very Homeric Jupiter,
stalk about wherever they please to turn, making everything tremble by
their nod alone.  But, as Plautus says, they die off after the manner of
men."  This, of course, is intended as an illustration of kings who do
not realize the true character of their high position.  Then comes the
passage in which Budé gives compactly his principles which lead to the
proposition that the prince is not bound by the laws of the realm:  "Hoc
autem regni genus est, inquit Aristoteles, cum unus omnium potestatem
habet tum communium tum publicarum rerum, non aliter atque civitas
una, aut populus habent.  Haec autem species quinta (liberty, wealth,
virtue, equality, generosity), oeconomica est ratione instituta.  Ut enim
oeconomia regnum est domesticum, sic regnum oeconomia est civitatis
aut populi unius aut plurium, id est domestica dispensatio.  Propterea
reges Persarum non reges, sed tyranni esse censebantur, qui populus
sibi subditos feruos esse existimabant, non liberum loco familiaeque ha-
bendos. . . . Ex supradictis igitur demonstrari potest, ut arbitror, Prin-
cipem non modo legibus esse solutum, id quod Ulpianus dixit, sed etiam
legibus non teneri."
151) BEYERHAUS, G., *op. cit.*, p. 33.  Zazius and Cujas stand almost
alone in their war on this opinion, *ibid.*, p. 12.
152) *Comm.*, p. 53, "Imperant leges privatis hominibus.  Statuunt leges
quid marito liceat in uxorem . . . "
153) *Ibid.*, p. 23.

It is clear from this quotation that Calvin accepts the medieval concept, but that he will brook no tyranny, no arbitrariness on the part of the ruler. He must bind himself to the laws of his own volition, if he would reign successfully, even though he is not as such bound to do so.

Calvin makes no mention of the Israelitish State; the only fundamental form of State for his mind is the Roman. His judgment of this State is not mild, as is shown by his application to it of Augustine's expression "magnum latrocinium" to it.[154] However, the Roman monarchy was inevitable; despite its bad features it was a positive necessity, for without it "that well-knit body (of the State) had dissipated." It is true that the Roman people loved nothing more than liberty, but it had had no liberty except for the "liberality of the prince."[155] The ground of the imperial authority is, according to the *Commentaries,* a sort of "Lex regia de imperio" by which the people transferred all right to the Caesars (omne ius in Caesares transtulit).[156] Hence this authority is the result of the people's consent. Whether this is revocable has been debated throughout history, the watchword of the opposing views being "translatio" and "concessio" respectively. Calvin uses the term "translatio," but in another connection he says that the people have given the emperor not so much a "regnum" as a "procurationem civilem."[157] Antiquity presumed that the imperial government was ideally universal. To the medieval man this rested on the universality and unity of divine government.[158] There is no trace of this view in the *Seneca Commentaries.* The only place where opportunity could have been found to enlarge upon it is Seneca's sentence about the bees which "never suffer more than one (queen)." Calvin refers here to Jerome's *Ad rusticam* where it is said that "in apibus princeps unus est." This statement was used in the Middle Ages to support the theory of monarchy or universal empire on the pattern of the unity of nature. Calvin does no more

---

[154] *De Civitatis Dei,* Bk. IV, Ch. 4; *Comm.,* p. 19.
[155] *Comm.,* p. 31.
[156] *Ibid.,* p. 20 f.
[157] *Comm.,* p. 31.
[158] Cf. Dante's *De Monarchia,* Translation by Aurelia Henry, 1904, Bk. I, Ch. 3, 4.

than point out that to have more than one king will lead to internecine strife.[159]

Seneca's treatise on Clemency is what is known as a "Fürstenspiegel," a Mirror for Princes. Calvin agrees wholly with the author's attempt to combat all forms of despotic arbitrariness. The *De Clementia* was not intended as an ethical-philosophical treatise of academic character, but a political "Tendenzschrift" rooting in a definite historical context.[160] To appreciate Calvin's work one must look, of course, for the origins of his *Commentaries* in the political absolutism of monarchs like Francis I. His concession of the principle of absolutism to the prince is therefore a concession of it to his own king. On the ground of the Roman law he permits him to stand above "ius civile." He calls the king "lex animata," and believes in the principle of hereditary royalty.[161] Withal it must be remembered that Calvin writes on Clemency, which puts as effective a check on monarchial arbitrariness as is possible under the circumstances.

---

[159] Cf. BEYERHAUS, G., *op. cit.*, p. 20 f.

[160] BEYERHAUS, G., *op. cit.*, p. 23.

[161] *Comm.*, p. 89. For his views as a Reformer, when he broke with his youthful concessions, cf. BEYERHAUS, G., *op. cit.*, pp. 108–129.

## CHAPTER VII

## THE PRECIPITATE OF HUMANISM IN CALVIN THE REFORMER

THROUGHOUT our study we have hinted at the connection between Calvin's early humanism and his later work as a Reformer. It is our design in this chapter to study this subject more closely.

### Section 1. The Mental "Set"

It is remarkable that Calvin was converted to radical Protestantism rather late in life. He had been almost entirely committed to the humanistic ideal until his twenty-fourth year. As a rule young people experience their change before they are eighteen! To have experienced a conversion six years later than that meant much for Calvin, especially since he was unusually precocious. It may be said that at twenty-four he was a seasoned humanist, as a study of the *Seneca Commentaries* abundantly testifies. Sufficient attention has not been given to this fact. Generally his biographers exclaim over the extreme youth of the writer of the *Commentaries,* and in a way they are right. But from the point of view of his conversion, the same cannot be said. This, I believe, is of the utmost importance when we consider the precipitate of humanism in his work as a reformer.

The most striking result of this late conversion we can reasonably expect to appear in what may be called his mental "set." No longer a very young man, and having so thoroughly imbibed the spirit of humanism, his conversion could not possibly negative his acquired habits and attitudes of mind. A Loyola, also converted late, remains a soldier and disciplinarian, and retains the attitude that makes possible his unquestioning loyalty to the "generalissimo" of the Roman Church. So John Calvin does not shake off, and never shall, what had been years in the making of his mind.

His mental "set" determined his attitude toward tradition. That is, whereas the "old learning" had not been able to disengage itself from its reverence for the teachings of the

medieval doctors, the men who had undergone the influence
of the humanistic spirit reacted sharply against them. The
humanistic antagonism for the scholastics was developed
only when their failure to recognize them was criticized.
At first there was merely a devotion to the classics and the
early fathers, which in their own right stood above the
scholastic teachers. The latter were simply ignored. It is
true that Valla sometimes inveighs against the medievalists
by name but he generally passes them by, and shows his
contempt by not even quoting them. On the other hand he
exhibits a mastery of the early fathers, Jerome particularly,
as Petrarch had of Augustine. The Petrarchan reverance
for Augustine had been more than a weakness, contrary to
the belief of certain critics; it was in direct line with the
revived classical spirit. This line was taken up by Valla not
only, but by the Brethren of the Common Life, by Erasmus,
Budé, and was one of the roots of Reformation thought. The
Reformers did not just *happen* to appeal to the fathers; nor
they were the discoverers of their writings. The humanists had long before led the way. The opinion that Calvin
was largely scholastic in his method finds no support from
a fair study of his writings. He labored rather in the spirit
of the early fathers. In defining therefore his attitude
toward tradition one must guard against the idea that he
overthrew all tradition. It was only the scholastic that he
eschewed, while the ancient patristic literature found a
large place in his affections.

An earmark of humanism was its exercise of independent
judgment, its appeal, so to speak, to common sense. Facing
situations that could find no adequate direction from the
schoolmen, they were thrown back on their own resources.
The discovery of good style, for example, was something
that the scholastics could not guide, for they knew precious
little about it. A true appreciation of the classics as such
they had themselves never had, so the humanists had to find
their own balance there. Besides, a new vantage-point was
offered in the classics. The literature of a vital past, it
afforded a congenial climate to healthy individuals. It was
more stimulating to spend an hour with Plato than a month
with Thomas or Duns Scotus. Canvassing the idea of God,
or of the world, or of human responsibility under the tutor-

ship of the greatest Academicians, or of the Peripatetics, or of Plutarch, was infinitely more attractive and effective, than to listen to the disquisitions of the Sorbonne theologians. All this gave the young humanist a sense of intellectual superiority. He knew more than his teachers. And in later years the teachers never gave sufficient evidence to prove to him that his adolescent superiority-complex had been extravagant. The belief that truth is divine no matter where found called for the exercise of independent minds. This principle Calvin accepted, but it went beyond him. Unequal as we all are to live to the full the implication of any great article of faith, so Calvin was less than his creed. The creed is in a sense more important than any inconsistency Calvin may have been guilty of. In the main it gave moral authority to many of his progressive positions. So, for instance, we have his zeal for restoring the true text of Scripture, or textual criticism, by which he flew directly in the face of the conservative opinion of the age, and his respectful mention of the critical work of Valla and Erasmus. In exegesis Calvin's name towers above all that went before. His principle of interpreting the text in its natural sense was revolutionary, and is of significance still. So his mental "set" expressing itself in the use of canons of common sense, and thus arriving at independent judgments, is no mean part of his inheritance from humanism. Such a mind could be the organizing force of the Reformation in the midst of a mightily confused age.

Calvin also inherited from humanism a certain sophistication which may in a manner be called esthetic. There were crudities that he could not stomach. A certain elegance lies upon all he wrote, the light of classical clearness. He knows the power of a well-turned phrase and eschewed a barbarism as a poison. The clearest evidence of his good taste is found in his doctrine of the Eucharist. He was certain that the early church agreed with his interpretation of the "real presence." At the distance we today stand from him it is rather difficult to see how he could have been so terrifically at odds with Rome and certain Lutherans like Westphal and Heshusius, for in reality he held to a presence of the body of Christ in the partaking of the Lord's Supper. Metaphysically there was in his view nothing flagrantly at variance with the Catholics. It was just as hard to accept the Calvinistic as the Roman or the Lutheran, for the outsider at least. Let me quote what appears to me the clearest statement he ever penned on the subject:

In regard to the local presence, I wonder that our censors are not ashamed to raise a quarrel. As they deny that the body of Christ is circumscribed by local space, they (Lutherans) hold it to be immense. What do we hold? That we are to seek it in heaven, which, as the Scripture declares, has received him till he appears to judgment. There is no ground, however, for any individual to charge us with holding that he is absent from us, and thus separating the head from the members. Certainly if Paul could say that so long as we are in the world we are absent as pilgrims from the Lord, we may say, on the same ground, that we are separated from him by a species of absence, inasmuch as we are now absent from his heavenly dwelling. Christ, then, is absent from us in respect to his body, but dwelling in us by his spirit he raises us to heaven to himself, transfusing into us the vivifying vigor of his flesh, just as the rays of the sun invigorate us by his vital warmth. Their common form saying that he is with us invisible is equivalent to saying, that though his form is treasured up in heaven, the substance of his flesh is on the earth. But a sense of piety clearly dictates that he infuses life into us from his flesh, in no other way than by descending into us by his energy, while, in respect to his body, he still continues in heaven.[1]

Now it is important to realize that although he seeks to refute the "popish figment of transsubstantiation" on which the Roman Church stands or falls, and though he refutes the Lutheran view because of its approximation of the Roman, nevertheless there is no fundamental difference metaphysically. For after all he believes that the believer is invigorated by the very *body* of Christ, even though the believer has to be raised to heaven to experience this whenever he communes. There was no thought of a *mere* spiritual presence.[2]

Now it is significant that to Calvin the localizing of the

---

[1] Mutual Consent of the Churches of Zurich and Geneva as to the Sacraments, *Tracts*, II, p. 240.

[2] Yet by a new allocation, so to say, of the body, the Roman Church was attacked in its very heart, for the loss of priestly power to bring down, as it were, the Christ from heaven, to dwell in that local spot represented by the visible host, would have made an end of the Church.

body of Christ in the elements of the Supper is repugnant
to sound taste. It violated good reason. Heshusius had
berated him "with paying more deference to reason than
to the word of God."[3] Calvin resents this imputation
violently. But he insists that it is an elemental requirement
of rational man to distinguish between the sign and the
thing signified:

> If he refuses to believe that there is any reason with-
> out philosophy, let him learn from a short syllogism:
> He who does not observe the analogy between the sign
> and the thing signified, is an unclean animal, not divid-
> ing the hoof; he who asserts that the bread is truly and
> properly the body of Christ, destroys the analogy be-
> tween the sign and the thing signified; therefore, he who
> asserts that the bread is properly the body, is an un-
> clean animal, not cleaving the hoof.

Calvin had been carefully trained in logic, in the appreciation of literary figures of speech; and, given his animus
against the Roman theology, Scripture texts that seemed to
contradict literally what he defended, were no obstacle.
Metaphor, metonomy were there to take care of such inci-
dentals. Calvin never had got away from his humanistic
inheritance. A thing may be thus and so, but our conception
of it must not be out of taste. I do not assert that Calvin
let good taste govern every one of his concepts but this did
play a part in the eucharistic controversy. It is the same
sense of propriety that prevents many people today from
conceiving of the miraculous in terms of the "crude" things
they appear to them to be, both physically and philosophi-
cally, while they seek to distil some religious essence from
them nevertheless. The same reason inheres in many a
non-Roman Catholic's assertion that though he believes in
the real presence of the Lord's body in the sacrament, he
does not affirm necessarily that it is by way of transsubstantiation or consubstantiation. One quotation from the
same tract just cited will show concretely how both the
Roman and Lutheran conception grated on his good taste:

> .... How will he prove that the body of Christ is taken
> by the mouth both corporeally and internally? He has
> elsewhere acknowledged that it is not chewed by the

---

[3] True Partaking of the Flesh and Blood of Christ in the Holy Supper in order to Dissipate the Mists of Tileman Heshusius, *Tracts*, II.

teeth nor touched by the palate.  Why should he be so
afraid of the touch of the palate or the throat, while he
ventures to assert that it is absorbed by the bowels?
What does he mean by the expression "within us"
(intra nos)?  By what is the body of Christ received
after it has passed the mouth?  After the mouth, if I
mistake not, the passage of the body is to the viscera or
intestines.  If he say that we are calumniously throwing
odium on him by the use of offensive terms, I should
like to know what difference there is by saying that
that which is received by the mouth is taken corporeally
within, and saying that it passes into the viscera and the
intestines?[4]

I shall refrain from showing in detail how difficult Calvin
made it for himself by injecting the element of good taste
in his definition of the real presence.  Surely, the Lutheran
theologians were far clearer in their language.  Calvin had
the insuperable task to perform of showing how one could
in a sense really eat the flesh and blood of the Christ, while
at the same time the body was NOT consumed.

It will be of interest to show how this affected Calvin's
interpretation of early Christian writers.  There is abundant
evidence that he perhaps read into the Scriptures, but certainly into the fathers, thoughts that were his own but not
theirs.  He could not believe that the Bible and the very
early church could hold to something that was so quite out
of taste as the Roman and Lutheran churches affirmed.  I
have tarried so long to define clearly what caused Calvin to
differ from his contemporaries, for we have here the most
important instance of his projecting his own conception into
the records of the early church.

In the same tract in which he opposes Heshusius he comes
at last to answer his opponent for insisting that "all these
were common to the fathers."  (p. 532).  Reviewing briefly
this material, we come to page 535 where he says:
".... Oecolompadius ..... clearly showed that the figment
of the local presence was unknown to the early church.....
As far as Westphal's importunity compelled me, I believe I
have satisfied sound and impartial readers in regard to the
consent of antiquity."[5]

---

4) *Ibid.*, p. 518.
5) Cf. his tracts against Westphal, *Tracts*, II.

After refuting Heshusius on the latter's having quoted from a spurious letter of Ignatius, he passes on to consider his opponent's use of Justin Martyr.

He next comes to Justin Martyr, whose authority I willingly allow to be very great. But what in him is adverse to our cause? He says that the bread in the supper is *not common.* The reason is that he had previously explained that none are admitted to partake of it but those who have been washed by baptism and have embraced the gospel. He afterwards goes further: "As Christ was made flesh, so we are taught that the food which was blessed by him by the word of prayer, and through which our flesh and blood are nourished *through transmutation,* is the flesh and blood of Christ himself." (And then comes Calvin's strangely bold but inadequate answer, which looks mighty like a grand bluff by rhetoric.) But the comparison of the mystical consecration in the supper with the incarnation of Christ, seems to Heshusius to carry the victory: as if Justin were making out that the one was as miraculous as the other, while all he meant was that *the flesh which Christ once assumed from us is daily given us for food!*
.... Irenaeus is a clearer expounder of what is thus briefly stated by Justin. I will not quote all his words, but will not omit anything that is pertinent. He inveighs against heretics who maintained that flesh is not capable of incorruption. If so, he says, neither has the Lord redeemed us by his own blood, nor is the cup of the Eucharist the communion of his blood, nor the bread which we break the communion of his body. The blood comes only from the veins and other substance of the man in which the Son of God truly redeemed us. And since we are his members, and are nourished by the creature, and he himself confers the creature upon us, making his sun to rise and rain to descend as it pleaseth him, he declared that the cup which is a creature is his body by which he nourishes our bodies. Therefore when the mingled cup and broken bread have the word of God pronounced, there is formed *a eucharist of the body and blood of Christ,* by which the substance of our flesh is nourished and consists. How is it denied that the flesh is capable of the gift of God which is eternal life, seeing that it is nourished by the body and blood of Christ and is his member, as the Apostle says, We are members of his body and of his bones, etc.[6]

---

[6] *Ibid.,* p. 537.

And after this very clear exposition of Irenaeus Calvin still says:

> Let the reader attend to the design of Irenaeus. He is not discussing whether or not we eat Christ corporeally.........

There are fifteen more pages of this sort of thing. It would not interest us to quote further. I believe enough has been presented to show that Calvin could not, or would not, see what the early church really believed. It was not at all repugnant to the early church to believe that the eucharist is the "medicine of immortality." The whole atmosphere in which Christianity arose was consonant with this view. Calvin was so under the influence of the taste of humanism that he sought to adapt the early Christian position to one more agreeable to his own as a then modern man. If Calvin removed a pace or two away from the ancient church in this matter, and did so by injecting his taste into it, he has been one of the factors in promoting the rationalism that in two centuries would rise to power in the churches.

It were unfair to leave the impression that the only feature of Calvin's doctrine of the Eucharist was its confused metaphysics. Together with the other Reformers he rescued the sacraments from their abuse as the sole means of salvation. Not the elements, but the Christ mattered to them. It is true that they regarded the sacraments as necessary under normal circumstances, but there were other necessary means also; for example, the preaching of the Word. The power wherewith they preached on the sacraments for the purpose of exciting the believers to pursue sanctification, is one of the chief contrasts between them and their Roman Catholic predecessors. The sacraments were no longer merely the means of making the member ready for heaven, but to fit him for better Christian living on earth. The latter was also one of the fruits of the new spirit of humanism, whose ideal was the cultivation of the perfect man.

### Section 2.  Methods and Ideals

It is obvious to the student of the *Institutes,* the *Commentaries,* and the *Tracts* that he had inherited the humanistic mental "set" not only, but that Calvin is indebted to the Renaissance in many respects as to his methods and ideals.

In the matter of methods we remark that the critical
apparatus of Valla, Erasmus, and Budé to establish the true
text of Scripture has won the unqualified approval of Calvin. He uses their books as authorities, though he never
fails to challenge any of their conclusions when he thinks
they are erroneous. The important point is that he approves
their method as such. The human element played a goodly
rôle when Valla used his own judgment in determining
which codices were the more reliable, and much more so
when he made free use of conjecture in establishing the
"correctness" of the text. Yet Calvin concedes the rightness
of this method, which was followed so much more learnedly
by Erasmus.[7]    Budé's *De Asse* was also used frequently by
the Reformer, especially in the Commentaries, for explaining the value of coins, weights, etc.[8]    In this manner,
according to Budé's method, Calvin permitted the light of
the Graeco-Roman civilization to fall on the Scripture.
Calvin is also famous for his exegetical method; by which
he operated with Scripture in much the same way that one
is wont to do with any other writing.  Besides saying that
the "spiritual truth, which is all that concerns us" should be
drawn from the text, he frequently speaks of the sacred
writers "accommodating their doctrine to their times."[9]
All this is very significant.  The age of theological inbreed-
ing is past, at least for the present.  As we shall see, the
leading idea of Calvin's Genevan Academy is that the new
educational aim for students is to get a solid grounding in
the arts and letters before they enter the professions.  Even

---

7) A fair example of Calvin's refrence to the critics is in the Commentary on Acts 26:28, 29 [CRXLVIII, 548], Particulam ἐν ὀλίγῳ varie
exponent interpretes.  Valla putavit sic vertendum, Parem abest quin
Christianum facias.  Erasmus reddidit:    Modica ex parte: Simplicius
vetus interpres: In modico:  quia saltem verbum verbo reddens, liberum
lectoribus iudicium permisit."

8) Cf. CR XXIV, 302, siclus sanctuarii, XLVII, 40, XLVII, 132, de-
narius, XLVII, 278, XXIII, 325, XLVIII, 2, XLIX, 371, L, 18, L, 107,
LII, 49, 112, Col. 2:18, XIL, 343, 450, I Cor. 9:27.

9) *Opera*, VII, p. 44, "In Vera Ecclesiae Reformandae Ratio," "De-
nique, eiusmodi loquutiones quum legis paedagogiam sapiant, elicienda
nobis inde spiritualis verita, quae sola ad nos pertinent."    On this, note 1
by the editors, " . . . Versio gallica simpliciter habet: Or ceste façon de
parler est procedée de ce que les Prophetes accomodoyent la doctrine à
leur temps auquel regnoyent les ceremonies.  Brief, puis que telles façons
de parler sentent les ombres de la Loy et les figures anciennes, il nous
en faut retirer la verité spirituelle.

though you would be a preacher, be first a humanist, expresses his thought on the matter.

Calvin's recognition of great humanists like Valla, Budé, and Erasmus was in itself a long step for a theologian. Though he in no sense regarded their work as an end in itself, he was aware that no successful theologian could afford to work without their achievements as a background. To this must be added that he had inherited from them and from the classics a vast body of erudition. This alone lent him an authority that reformers throughout Europe could not fail to respect. Learning without godliness was of little profit in his opinion, but godliness without learning was liable to all sorts of error on the other hand. Calvin was perhaps the most sophisticated of the reformers. Indulging almost never in mystical excursions, his speech is always chaste. Informed on everything that touched his work, he did little that was not thoroughly premeditated. Of course, his learning suffered from important lacunae. It was limited largely to the classics, church history, Scripture, and such like. He appears to have had no taste for the sciences. His only possible reference to Copernicus is in his comments on Psalm 46, where he appears to criticize the new astronomy in his remarks on the earth not being moved and abiding forever. After all, he was a humanist, and though the humanistic movement prepared the way for the scientific revolution, the humanists themselves were not destined to take part in it. Servetus is said to have remarked that Calvin would not have been so severe on him, had he known something about the natural sciences. Whether or not this was said, it was substantially true, and after all Calvin did burn one of the few scientists of the age. The best that can be said is that Tagaut, a canny mathematician, taught in the Academy about 1559, and that he wrote a work that appears to have expounded ideas adumbrating those of Galileo, Kepler, and Newton.[10] At the same time only the most orthodox views of astronomy were permitted. Despite the fact that Copernicus's famous work had been published in 1543, the Genevan authority was the treatise on the *Sphere* by John Holywood, or Joannes de Sacro Bosco, of

---

[10] BORGEAUD, CH., L'Académie de Calvin, Vol. I. of the same author's *Histoire de l'Université de Genève*, p. 67.

the Thirteenth Century. In 1572 Mathieu Béroald was still using this same text (despite the fact that in 1570 Barozzi had published his criticism of it).[11] A century later, in the days of Robert Chouet, de Sacro Bosco's text is no longer used by the department of natural science, though the theologians presumably still do, for in an outline of the courses on this subject we find a "rather large part.......devoted to an exposition of Copernicus's system.......All objections to it are examined and refuted with care, especially the theological arguments based on Scripture passages seeming to presume the geocentric view."[12]     But this is in 1672. It is interesting to learn that the famous Peter Ramus was once invited to lecture at the Academy, but that Beza asked him to temper his severe anti-Aristotelianism, since Master Calvin had made the *Organon* the foundation of Genevan philosophy. Ramus was accommodating, lecturing on the *First Oration of Cicero against Cataline*.[13]     This was May-June, 1570. So Calvin had had his limitations indeed, some of which outlived him for a century. The rise of modern philosophy as well as the new natural science would, I doubt not, have been a horror to him, as they have been to so many of his spiritual descendants. He was a humanist and no more, one who had been in the company of the explorers of the lost classical world; he was not to help discover the greater contemporary and future world which lay just behind the horizon.

Under the head of methods and ideals in Calvin's later humanism we must certainly place his founding of the Academy of Geneva. For a full discussion of this subject the reader is referred to Ch. Borgeaud's *Histoire de l'Université de Genève*, the first volume of which treats about L'Académie de Calvin (1559-1789). Pp. 21-83 form the narrative of the work of Calvin particularly. Dr. Borgeaud's work is so full of pertinent detail and so well documented that any subsequent writing on the Academy need do little more than develop some general conclusions.

In the *Ordonnances* of 1541 Calvin had already expressed his desire for an institution of learning. Fresh from Strass-

---

[11] *Ibid.*, pp. 68, 175.
[12] *Ibid.*, p. 416.
[13] *Ibid.*, p. 112.

burg where he had taught in Sturm's school, he had visions
of establishing in Geneva something similar to it. His ideal
was not realized until 1559. A bird's-eye view of the more
significant features of the new institution reveals the following: First, that in line with the new educational theory due
attention was given to the proper training of the student
from childhood. The Middle Ages had been very careless
about primary education. The reforms of Cordier are so
great simply because he made it his primary concern to
teach the children their elementals from the ground up, bit
by bit, step by step. Accordingly, Calvin (who had been his
pupil) planned his school in such a manner that the child
got a thorough schooling from his fifth or sixth year on.
Secondly, it was his ideal to have the men trained for the
professions by grounding them in the arts and letters, that
is, he insisted that they know their Latin and Greek. This
training in the classics was a balanced one: "Side by side,
says Borgeaud, with the Latin, and with equal rank, he
placed the study of Greek, and gave to these courses, a less
rhetorical turn (than in Sturm's program), free from all
Ciceromania!"[14]) It was the day of the undiminished popularity of Erasmus's *Adages* and Cordier's *Colloquies*. To
meet the cultured world on its own level one had to have
proficiency in classical quotations and allusions. Even in
the next century Milton's poetry must have been quite in-
telligible to the college lads. If today we look for other
things in cultured people, say, proficiency in the social
sciences, it is because the educational vogue is different.
The point is that Calvin demanded that his protégés be
equal to the best in the world of his day.

Thirdly, special mention deserves to be made of the
importance Calvin attached to the *word*. The humanists
had been mainly philologians, who cultivated words. Calvin's force of expression lay largely in his complete mastery
of words. To his mind a word had a dignity that he ever
reverenced. This inheritance from humanism, which he
had developed so carefully himself, he wanted by all means
to pass on to the generations following through his Academy.
His zeal to purify and enrich the French language might

---

14) *Op. cit.*, p. 45.

serve as a model for his students to emulate, not to speak
of the elegance and force with which he used the Latin.
Fourthly, a leading principle of Calvin, one he had in common with the other reformers, was that of "libre examen,"
the right of the student to examine and prove all things.[15]
However weakly this ideal was actually realized, the fact
that it was one of their expressed aims is significant. I
hasten to add that Calvin made an important qualification
of this principle, as far as its actual fulfilment went, namely,
that this freedom was not to be exercised by all men regard-
less of their beliefs. His experience with Servetus proved
to his mind that this liberty in the hands of heretics was a
danger. Hence, according to the *Ordonnances,* the Academy
was to be controlled by the ministers only. The Genevan
Council refused to concede this, insisting that they be represented. The time was not yet ripe for truly free schools.
The world had yet to taste a great deal more of colleges
managed by clerics only before it was ready to relinquish
the idea. It is to the credit of the reformers, nevertheless,
that they practised freedom of investigation with respect to
the history of the church, the Scriptures, and the then reigning conception of monarchical absolutism. They were perhaps revolutionary enough for their times.[16]

---

[15] Cf. Scherer, H., *Die Pädogogik vor Pestalozzi,* p. 133.

[16] In the Dedication of the *Commentary on Genesis* we have an excur-
sion on what Calvin regarded as an abuse of freedom: "In the meantime audacious scribblers arise, as from our own bosom, who not only ob-
scure the light of sound doctrine with clouds of error, or infatuate the
simple and less experienced with their wicked ravings, but by a profane
license of scepticism allow themselves to uproot the whole of religion.
For, as if, by their rank ironies and cavils, they could prove themselves
genuine disciples of Socrates, they have no axiom more plausible than
that faith must be free and unfettered, so that it may be possible by
reducing everything to a matter of doubt, to render the Scripture flex-
iblee (so to speak) as a nose of wax. Therefore they who being captivated by the allurements of this new school, now indulge in doubtful
speculations, obtain at length such proficiency that they are always
learning, yet never come to the knowledge of the truth."

Cf. also Clément, L., *Henri Estienne et son oeuvre française,* Paris,
1899. Estienne, an admirer of Calvin, was one of those men who by
his genius and independence could not help running at cross purposes
with the Genevan order, especially by his frequent violations of the
ordinances with respect to libraries and the publishing of books. It is
interesting to know that though Calvin enforced these ordinances, he
had not introduced them (they had been enacted by the Council while
he was in exile in 1539), p. 11 ff.

### Section 3. Calvin's Justification of and Progress in Humanism After His Conversion

Calvin's experience with the classics had taught him that there is some good in the pagans. As a general proposition he advanced the idea that the providence of God is not only general but also particular, that is, concerns not only the church but also the world at large, the good and the bad, and not only the great issues of life, but the very smallest. Now the conclusion of this proposition was that the good things wrought by the heathen were a providence of God for his world. Again, he holds that the Image of God was not wholly wiped out by the Fall of man, that there are sparks of it left, which, though having no power of leading a man back to a saving knowledge of God, nevertheless were evidences of the fact that God had not abandoned his fallen creature. Again, the distinction he drew between sin and grace, instead of between sin and nature, so common among Roman Catholics, is significant. Now the theory which best interprets his conception of the good that exists in the world at large, even in the reprobate, is his theory of common grace.

The literature on this theory is available mostly to those who read the Dutch. An epoch-making work among conservative Calvinists was *De Gemeene Gratie* (3 vols.) by Dr. Abraham Kuyper. More scientific is *Gereformeerde Dogmatiek* (4 vols.) by Prof. Herman Bavinck, whose Introduction (vol. I) is a mine of information on the subject. The most recent book is by Dr. Herman Kuiper, *Calvin on Common Grace*.

We recommend of course that one read the *Institutes*. We refer particularly to the following passages: Bk. II, Ch. II, par. 12, 13, 14 (especially pp. 246, 247, 248, 249, 253, 254f., 263, 264); Bk. III, Ch. IX, par. 3 (p. 641). I quote some of the leading sentences from these parts (Allen's translation):

> Some sparks continue to shine in the nature of man, even in its corrupt and degenerate state, which prove him to be a rational creature; and yet this light is smothered by so much ignorance that it cannot act with any degree of efficacy.......Let us.....examine the power of understanding. To condemn it to perpetual

blindness, so as to leave it no intelligence in anything,
is repugnant not only to the Divine word, but also to
the experience of common sense. For we perceive in
the mind of man some desire of investigating the truth,
towards which he would have no inclination, but from
some relish of it previously possessed..... although this
desire, small as it is, faints even before its entrance on
its course, because it immediately terminates in vanity
(Bk. II, ch. II, par. 12).

A very significant paragraph follows (Par. 13):

Yet its attempts are not always so fruitless, but that
it makes some discoveries, particularly when it applies
itself to inferior things. Nor is it so stupid, as to be
without some slender notion also of superior ones, however negligently it attends to the investigation of them;
but it possesses not an equal ability for both. For when
it goes beyond the limits of the present life, it is chiefly
convinced of its own imbecility. Wherefore, that we
may better perceive how far it proceeds in every case
according to the degrees of its ability, it will be useful
for us to propose the following distinction; that *there
is one understanding for terrestrial things, and another
for celestial ones.* I call those things terrestrial which
do not pertain to God and his kingdom, to true righteousness, or to the blessedness of the future life; but
which relate entirely to the present life, and are in
some sense confined in the limits of it. Celestial things
are the pure knowledge of God...... In the first class
(terrestrial) are included civil polity, domestic econo-
my, all the mechanical arts and the liberal sciences....
Now in regard to this class it must be confessed that as
man is naturally a creature inclined to society, he has
also by nature an instinctive propensity to cherish and
preserve that society; and therefore we perceive in the
minds of all men general impressions of civil probity
and order...... Hence that perpetual consent of all
nations, as well as individuals, to the laws..... (and)
the original idea of equity (in settling disputes).

Paragraph 15 should also be cited:

Whenever therefore we meet with heathen writers,
let us learn from that light of truth which is admirably
displayed in their works, that the human mind, fallen
as it is...., is yet invested and adorned by God with
excellent talents. If we believe that the Spirit of God
is the only fountain of truth, we shall neither reject or
despise the truth itself, wherever it appear, unless we
wish to insult the Spirit of God; for the gifts of the

Spirit cannot be undervalued without offering contempt and reproach to the Spirit himself. Now, shall we deny the light of truth to the ancient lawyers who have delivered such just principles of civil order and probity? Shall we say that the philosophers were blind in the exquisite contemplation and in their scientific description of nature? Shall we say that those who by the art of logic have taught us to speak in a manner consistent with reason, were destitute of understanding themselves? Shall we accuse those of insanity, who by the study of medicine have been exercising their industry for our advantage? And what shall we say of the mathematics? Shall we esteem them the delirious ravings of madmen? On the contrary,.....we shall admire them because.....they are truly excellent.

These quotations are taken from the final edition of the *Institutes*.

Let us study the first edition, however, that of 1536, for the purpose of getting Calvin's reaction to the spirit of humanism directly after his conversion. Incidentally we shall point out certain interesting parallels and contrasts with the later editions. There are six chapters in the first edition. Let us look at them successively.

### CHAPTER I.  CONCERNING THE LAW.

Calvin points out that there may be some good in human nature, but that inwardly man is bad.[17] Though man may be ignorant of the things he ought to know, God has written his law in his heart. This law is conscience. The Lord has also given man his written law, which is a "testimonium duntaxat legis naturalis," which stirs up our memory more frequently, and teaches those things which the inner teaching of natural law does not lead us to speak of enough.[18]

---

[17] Christianae religionis Institutio (1536), *Opera*, I, p. 28.

[18] *Ibid.*, I, p. 29 f.  By the law Calvin means more generally the Scriptures.  The idea of "lex naturalis" in a wider sense would also include the works of the noble pagans which issued from the activity of that law in him.  At all events, the parallel to this passage in the 1539 edition of the Institutes appears to indicate this, *Ibid.*, I, p. 297, where he contrasts the pagan writings with those of the Scripture.  This is one of the finest passages of Calvin, showing how warmly he still appreciated the classics, while he gives an account of why the Bible impresses him far more: "Haec autem virtus quam propria sit scripturae inde liquet, quod ex humanis scriptis quamlibet artificose expolitis, nullum omnino perinde ad nos officiendos valet.  Lege Demosthenes, aut Ciceronem; lege Platonem, Aristotelem, aut alios quovis ex illa cohorte: mirum in modum,

The essentials of the idea of common grace are found in this first edition of the *Institutes,* in these words: "Whatever is praiseworthy in man is by the grace of God."[19]

## CHAPTER II. CONCERNING FAITH.

The full heading of this chapter reads: "Concerning Faith, in Which also the Symbol Which *Is Called Apostolic* Is Explained." This is interesting. The Apostles' Creed *is called* Apostolic. This is doubtless borrowed from Lorenzo Valla who had contested the authenticity of this creed. Calvin has accepted the critical opinion. It is also worth noting that the creed is defined as an epitome of the faith to which the "ecclesia catholica" consents.[20]

---

fateor, te allicient, oblectabunt, movebunt, rapient; verum inde si ad sacram istam lectionem te conferas, velis nolis, ita vivide te afficiet, ita cor tuum penetrabit, ita medullis insidebit, ut prae istius sensus efficacia, vis illa rhetorum ac philosophorum prope evanescat."

There are only two references in the 1536 edition to pagan writers. *Ibid.,* I, 233 (Solon), 237 (Cicero). In this respect the later editions are markedly different. Calvin appears to have continued reading the classics, for as he grows older his use of them for purposes of illustration increases. The 1539 edition speaks of Plato, Plutarch (*Ibid.,* I, p. 286), Galen (p. 287), Demosthenes, Aristotle, "aut alii" (p. 297). Besides that he praises "mirificam (Dei) sapientiam quae testentur, innumera sunt, tum in coelo tum in terris documenta: . . . astrologia, medicina . . Equidem qui liberales illas artes vel imbiberunt, vel etiam degustarent, earum subsidio adiuti longe altius provehuntur ad introspicienda divinae sapientiae arcana . . . " (p. 287).

Further progress is made in the next editions. For example, in the edition of 1541, the French, where occurs the passage, "Or comme les payens mesmes confesent, il n'y a nation si barbare . . . qui n'ayent ceste persuasion qu'il y a quelque Dieu . . . " (*Opera,* III, p. 47). This is an allusion to a saying of Cicero, though his name is not mentioned (the name ocurs in the 1560 French edition, *Ibid.,* III, p. 47). The best edition for final comparison is the 1560 Latin one, where (*Ibid.,* II, pp. 43–51) there is a long addition on the works of God in nature, with copious reference to the great poets and thinkers of antiquity.

[19] *Ibid.,* I, p 45. "In homine igitur, si naturalibus suis dotibus censeatur, a vertice capitis ad plantam usque pedis scintilla boni non reperitur. Gratia Dei est, quidquid in eo est quod laudem meritur." It is not our task to criticize Calvin's idea of common grace, only to register the fact that it was his manner of justifying his appreciation of the good in nature and man. We merely point out that the medieval metaphysics of the entire depravity of natural man lies at its base. Whatever in him is good does not derive from man's nature as such, but appears to be the result of a special infusion of virtue from above. It is common because this grace is extended to all men, in various measures. The possibility this idea offers for liberalizing one's views on all matters is tremendous. Cf. KUIPER, H., *op. cit.,* for a thorough study of all the textual references to the expression "common grace" in Calvin's works.

[20] *Ibid.,* I, p. 56.

## CHAPTER III.   CONCERNING PRAYER.

The one time humanist, ostensibly not interested in the vernacular, here makes a plea for the use of the vulgar tongue in public prayer. Let it be understood "that Greek should not be used among the Latins, nor Latin among the French or English, as hitherto has been done constantly, but let public prayers be made in the popular language which can be grasped by the whole congregation."[21]

## CHAPTERS IV AND V.   CONCERNING THE SACRAMENTS.

His discussion of marriage is interesting. He opposes the Roman Catholic conception of it as a sacrament. "Everybody admits that marriage is an institution of God (Gen. 2, Matth. 19); that it was bestowed on man as a sacrament no one had observed till the time of Gregory. And who in his right mind would ever have thought of such a thing? It is a good and holy ordinance of God. But farming, architecture, shoe-making, barbering have also been ordained by God; nevertheless they are not sacraments."[22]

## CHAPTER VI.   ON CHRISTIAN LIBERTY.

In connection with the idea of Christian liberty Calvin discusses ecclesiastical power and political administration. This is in many respects the most interesting chapter. One-fifth of the book is given to it. Few people have associated the name of Calvin with the idea of liberty. Let them study this great chapter.

Liberty for the Christian is, first, freedom for conscience with respect to the law (which has been fulfilled by Christ); next, it is freedom to obey God "alacri promptitudine"; and finally, it implies that we are free with respect to those things "quae per se sunt adiaphora." He adds that once it used to be forbidden "to laugh, to play, to add new possessions to the old and inherited ones, to delight in concert music, or to drink wine." All these belong, he says, to the adiaphora.[23] The rest of the chapter is devoted to questions of church

---

21) *Ibid.*, I, p. 88 f.
22) *Ibid.*, I, p. 192 f.
23) *Ibid.*, I, pp. 196–200.

government and political power, which is interesting enough as such, but not specially pertinent here.

The other editions of the *Institutes* have not seen as great an expansion of the chapter on liberty as the others have. As Calvin developed into the organizer of Reformed Protestantism he was confronted with many other questions. In fact, it sometimes appears as if there were fewer things regarded as adiaphora in Geneva than anywhere else in Europe. This should blind no one, however, to the fact that some of the outstanding principles expressed in this chapter on liberty have found wider and deeper development. Where he fell short it is our privilege to press on, to labor for more liberty that he ever dreamed it possible for man to enjoy.

# EPILOGUE

## AN ESSAY ON CALVIN'S DEFENSE OF
## SECULAR STUDIES: HIS DOCTRINE OF COMMON GRACE

On p. 108 of this book, I wrote: "The Reformation is largely a defense of the new age that the Renaissance had ushered in. Calvin did this in so many words when he propounded the theory of common grace." This seemed to be very true thirty-five years ago. But, the ground for his defense was seen to be Scriptural in the prevailing tradition of the church. This tradition was largely apologetic; that is, any secular phenomenon, like classical literature or like the humanist philological study of the literature, was defended for the reason that, e.g., it helped Biblical interpretation or to show that the faith was not contrary to reason. Some three decades later I made a fresh study of it, especially of *Institutes* II, ii, 13–17. This essay is the result. If it stands up under critical assessment, the Reformation may indeed be considered to have made, in Calvin, a significant break-through with respect to an age-old question of religion and culture. If so, Calvin laid a foundation for blessing modern "secularism." He could not foresee what forms this would take; had they been revealed to him he would perhaps have been shocked by some. But he might well have sought acquaintance with a Père Teilhard de Chardin.[1]

Our essay pertains to Calvin's post-conversion defense of secular studies, particularly the pagan classics. It involves a doctrine peculiar to Calvin, the so-called doctrine of common grace.

We begin with the fact that before his conversion he was a humanist and as such wrote the Seneca Commentary. Important as I had considered this to be in 1931, the fuller significance was not clearly seen till Prof. André M. Hugo published his *Calvijn en Seneca: Een inleidende studie van Calvijn op Seneca, De Clementia, anno 1532* (Groningen, 1957). Hugo and Prof. F. L.

---

[1] The main thrust of this essay has been put in a larger Renaissance perspective in my chapter on "Humanism and the Reformation" in *Essays in Divinity*, to be published by the Chicago University Press, 1967.

Battles have collaborated on a full-dress study of the Commentary, which I trust will appear soon. It is evident that only trained philologists like Hugo and Battles could properly appreciate the devotion and energy which their colleague of 1532 invested in his book. The evidence shows the excellence of it to be so great that one need not consider young Calvin over-bold to have hoped to be the successor to Erasmus himself. Humanism was to Calvin no passing fancy; his heart was in it.

His conversion took place about two years after the Commentary. For the present essay's purpose, the precise date is immaterial; for that matter, it could be twelve or even thirty months after April, 1532. What *is* crucial is that his conversion was not a turning away from humanism. So secular a literature as the classical continued to attract him. He could not but continue to praise it, for it never ceased to compel his admiration. So he never demitted his quondam humanism. But this essay has another purpose, namely, to show that Calvin discovered a religious defense of his post-conversion devotion to ancient literature. This religious defense is expressed in his doctrine of common grace which, in turn, may be considered as his charter of liberties for secular studies.

Calvin in effect distinguished between common grace and special grace. He himself did not invent this distinction in those words.[2] Reformed scholastics did that, and their more precise terms express his meaning very well.

Special grace is that grace which God gives to the elect, and

---

[2] See Herman Kuiper's *Calvin on Common Grace* (Goes—Grand Rapids, 1928) in which Calvin's *Institutes* and all his Scripture commentaries are combed for the idea of common grace, its terminology and the varied uses thereof. Dr. Kuiper has not found a single instance in which Calvin actually used the term common grace (gratia communis); he found only four in which gratia and communis are connected (pp. 177–8), but not as one term. There are adjectives, such as, "special" and "heavenly" grace, which the contexts show refer to "common grace". Besides, there are many synonyms for this grace: liberality, kindness, favor, gift, love, clemency, good will.

For the idea in the *Institutes*, the best help comes from the comments of Professor J. T. McNeill in the critical edition: *The Institutes of the Christian Religion*. Translation by F. L. Battles; Editor, J. T. McNeill (Library of Christian Classics, Vols. XX and XXI, London, 1961). Professor McNeill has properly footnoted some important common grace passages and supplied significant bibliography. See esp. Bk. II, Ch. ii, sections 15–17 (pp. 274–276); also, II, ii, 4 (pp. 293–294) and III, iii, 11 (p. 738).

Professors Abraham Kuyper and Herman Bavinck were the most distinguished champions of Calvin's common grace doctrine among the Dutch theologians of an earlier generation. Best known are Bavinck's *De Algemeene Genade* (Kampen 1894) and Kuyper's *De Gemeene Gratie*,

by it they are saved. Common grace is given to all men, the
non-elect and elect. The purpose was to account for the fact that
believers and non-believers have many good things in common;
in fact, it was evident to Calvin and many others that unbelievers
are sometimes so virtuous as to put believers to shame. In Calvin's view, these virtues are in unbelievers no "shining sins",
but genuine virtues, so genuine as to come directly as gifts from
God's grace—common grace, that is. But this common grace
does not save them.

Common grace is not only non-saving, but it bestows only
terrestrial goods. Special grace alone is saving, bestowing regen-
eration, justification, and sanctification. It gives only celestial
goods. Common grace restrains the power of evil in man's depraved nature; it also clothes that nature, which makes possible
public order, filial and parental affection, the development of
civilization, the earnest pursuit of the arts and sciences, and so
on. It does not regenerate or confer anything celestial. It is a
grace that has to do only with this earthly life. The elect are
also its beneficiaries so long as they are on earth and, of course,
to the extent they (as all men) are of the earth earthy.

To understand Calvin well, there are certain things we must
take in stride. To begin with, there is his doctrine of total depravity. To say it was meant to be an antidote for Renaissance
optimism begs the question of just what that optimism was. If it
was the humanists' belief that making classical literature the core
of educational curricula would improve men, Calvin (the old
Erasmian of the Seneca commentaries) certainly had no quarrel
with them.[3] It may be doubted that his view of human corruption resulted from a prolonged study of human psychology or
from any careful induction with respect to his contemporaries'
manners and morals. His descriptions of the evil human conditions are on the whole general, contrasting, say, with Sigmund

3 Vols. (Amsterdam 1902–04). These men were leaders of a Dutch revival
of Calvin studies. Kuyper was a man of varied (also literary) genius,
who provided imaginative, if sometimes out-dated, exegesis of Scripture
from the viewpoint of common grace. On his belief that Calvinism was
relevant to "every sphere of life," he founded the Dutch Anti-Revolu-
tionary political party and the Free University of Amsterdam.

[3] Calvin made the classical training the core of Geneva's college cur-
riculum. He could have subscribed to Vittorino da Feltre's view that his
school in Mantua was properly preparing students for graduate training
in the professional faculties of law, medicine, and theology. See W. H.
Woodward, *Vittorino da Feltre and Other Humanist Educators*, Columbia
University Press, 1963, p. 59; also pp. 37, 60–61.

Freud's researches with respect to the id and libido, and with the blow by blow accounts of human waywardness in our realistic drama and fiction. It is more comparable to the pronouncements of theologians influenced by Kierkegaardian existentialism. But let any who believes that all men have their price cast the first stone. Besides, there are religious geniuses who tend to see things either black or white, and Calvin may have had something of that. More credible, however, is that, influenced by Luther, he could magnify the grace of God the more effectively as the only source of good. This was, in turn, Calvin's reason for leading a grateful life. Gratitude was a most sensitive nerve of his religion. Ingratitude was to him the blackest of all the vices, for it claims goods that are unmerited as if they were man's possession owned by right of worth, labor, or seizure. Its offspring is hubris which claims the right to use them to satisfy ambition in disregard of the moral order or even common sense. This strikes a universal note heard in Sophocles' *Antigone*. Calvin has not been alone in having vivid awareness of a tragic flaw in man.

While recognizing that Calvin's doctrine of total depravity finds a mainspring in a desire to persuade men to regard grace alone, one will miss the significance of this (in his scheme of things) if his idea of depravity is disallowed because he does not argue it convincingly; a proposition may be true though its defense may be dubious.[4] With respect to man in general, his manner and tone is that of a prosecuting attorney. Disputing against freedom of the will, he found but one of the early fathers as a fully trusted witness, namely, St. Augustine (*Institutes* II, ii, 4); the others, especially the Greek fathers, were too much influenced by philosophy.[5] There is also his disinclination for sharply defined terminology. This can in part be the humanistic love of variety; saying the same things in synonyms and figures of speech. It sometimes makes for better reading than clear thinking. Thus on the one hand he deserves distinction as a Protestant theologian for recognizing creation and providence

---

[4] See my "Calvin and the Rhetorical Tradition," *Church History*, March 1957, pp. 3–21, in which Calvin's logic is characterized as rhetorical, enthymematical, rather than syllogistic; also, that his *Institutes* is a tissue of forensic, deliberative, and epideictic discourse.

[5] Whoever doubts that Calvin, in turn, was influenced by philosophy may profitably read a recent dissertation by Dr. Victor L. Nuovo: *Calvin's Theology: A Study of its Sources in Classical Antiquity*, Columbia University, 1964 (Typescript).

as a proper starting point of theology (as it was in the medieval period); yet in passages to be spoken of below his language is ambiguous when he discusses the relation of noble deeds of "natural" (carnal) man to that man's nature as a man. Let this suffice for such defects. We have to take him as he is, in order to understand our present subject matter.

It is not easy to live with Calvin's use of the word "grace" as shown to the non-elect while at the same time he denies that it is a divine concern for them as men. Commenting on Acts 14: 16–17 he says that "the Lord does not want for testimony while he sweetly allures men to the knowledge of himself with many and varied kindnesses"; yet, the end is to render men inexcusable (I, v, 14). Calvin stands as the only prominent theologian to insist on this with such boldness. Yet the basic paradox has troubled theodicy since Moses and the Prophets, especially as expounded by St. Paul. But to enlarge on this here will not serve our purpose. We should rather ask why Calvin calls these divine but non-saving kindnesses "grace". To Christian piety, grace is perhaps the loveliest word in the New Testament to describe the tender love of God toward sinners. That Calvin characterizes the terrestrial gifts to men as "grace" is to say that to him these natural gifts are in their kind just as holy as are the ones bestowed by saving grace in their kind. It is as if Calvin were saying that the non-elect are expendable,[6] but the gifts of God to them are not.

With this we strike our topic at dead center. The non-elect as beneficiaries of common grace's gifts are of no real concern, but the gifts are. Outstanding among these are secular studies. Presently we shall present a portion of Calvin's locus classicus on it, in which he singles out several kinds of learned pursuits, making clear that to esteem them lightly is an act of the gravest impiety, for to do so is to insult or disgrace the Holy Spirit.

In passing we must point to a common but curious fallacy. The gifts of common grace pertain to this present terrestrial life and have nothing pertaining to the celestial. The gifts are called good, but do not partake of "true" good. This would imply that

---

6) Zwingli felt differently. He expected as companions in heaven Theseus, Socrates, Aristides, Antigonus, Numa, Camillus, the Catos, and the Scipios. See Zwingli *Opera*, M. Schuler and J. Schultess, IV, 65. (Library of Christain Classics, XXIV, p. 275.) (Reference in McNeill's notes to the *Institutes* p. 342, note 8.)

terrestrial good is of less quality as good.[7] However there is more for our purpose than meets the eye in Calvin's denial of "true" good to the terrestrial. The latter is a good because it is from God. If intrinsically it has not the quality of the heavenly, it is still God's affair. For example, the sharp line he draws between the two appears when among the reasons for admiring with gratitude the secular knowledge there is not one that has to do with "heavenly" reasons. That is, the terrestrial goods have their own raison d'être. They are not slanted toward the celestial. Yet in their kind they are as holy as the other because of their common source. It is readily believable that had Calvin been pushed to his ultimate ground for it, he would have said: that is the affair of God, as sovereign. He is the potter, and who shall say to him: What doest thou?

If all this should be interpreted so as to confirm the opinion that Calvin was a cold fish, it was not so intended. The fate of the damned had been accepted for centuries as a matter of course, even among the gentlest. Nineteenth century survival-of-the-fittest evolution led some fine human beings to opposing relief legislation for the English poor. There can of course be no objection for one to make Calvin black as midnight, if only one judge oneself by the same standards. But this is not relevant to the present purpose, which is to show that by considering the non-elect to be expendable, Calvin puts in a sharper relief that the good manifested in them must not be lost.

---

[7] This distinction between a good and a true good may be vicious, for the piety with respect to the terrestrial could then be argued to be less important than that regarding the celestial. One may suspect that Calvin argued for the importance of the celestial in accents reminiscent of Monophysitism. Abraham Kuyper had found a way to bridge the two. With Calvin, he held that the world will someday be consumed by fire, so that nothing will appear salvaged. Meanwhile, men's bodies have disintegrated in the grave, their substance eventually becomes mere earth, or sustenance for other forms of life; as such they will not be resurrected. But on St. Paul's analogy of the seed (I Cor. 15), the dead will rise as new bodies; analogous to this, says Kuyper, there is a seed in all things terrestrial to survive the cosmic fire, to become the "new Jerusalem." This is Kuyper's interpretation of Rev. 21:24, 26. ". . . and the kings of the earth do bring their glory and honor into it [heaven]." See *De Gemeene Gratie*, I, ch. LXII, pp. 454–462. This is a bit of refined speculation, which one may take or leave. Nevertheless, the writer evinced a sensitiveness about the terrestrial as worthy of eternity. But perhaps it is too much to ask of 16th century Christians to put so high a premium on the terrestrial. To Jewish piety this was warp and woof of orthodoxy; but who then hearkened to a rabbi for aught but Hebrew? See also *Institutes* II, xi, 12, par. 2; and III, x, i with Prof. McNeill's note 8 on p. 724.

The *Institutes* has a locus classicus pertaining to our subject (II, ii, 13–17), of which section 15 is the part which particularly concerns us. It merits the attention of Renaissancists especially because Calvin in it includes some areas of classical literature as excellent gifts of the Holy Spirit, which to neglect or despise is a grave sin. Here it is:

> Whenever we come upon these matters in secular writers let that admirable light of truth shining in them teach us that the mind of man, though fallen and perverted from its wholeness, is nevertheless clothed and ornamented with God's excellent gifts. If we regard the Spirit of God as the sole fountain of truth, we shall neither reject the truth itself, nor despise it wherever it shall appear, unless we wish to dishonor the Spirit of God. For by holding the gifts of the Spirit in slight esteem, we contemn and reproach the Spirit himself. What then? Shall we deny that the truth shone upon the ancient jurists who established civic order and discipline with such great equity? Shall we say that the philosophers were blind in their fine observation and artful description of nature? Shall we say that those men were devoid of understanding who conceived the art of disputation[8] and taught us to speak reasonably? Shall we say that they are insane who developed medicine, devoting their labor to our benefit? What shall we say of all the mathematical sciences? Shall we consider them the ravings of madmen? No, we cannot read the writings of the ancients on these subjects without great admiration. We marvel at them because we are compelled to recognize how preeminent they are. But shall we count anything praiseworthy or noble without recognizing at the same time that it comes from God? Let us be ashamed of such ingratitude. into which not even the pagan poets fell, for they confessed that the Gods had invented philosophy, laws, and all the useful arts. Those men whom Scripture [I Cor. 2:14] calls "natural men" were, indeed, sharp and penetrating in their investigation of inferior things. Let us, accordingly, learn by their example how many gifts the Lord left to human nature even after it was despoiled of its true good.

This section appears first in the 1539 edition of the *Institutes*. Of all his praises of the admirable in pagan literature, this is the

---

8) "Ars disserendi." See below, note 10.

most eloquent. Moreover, it has a vehemence that suggests he is defending himself against talk of his viewing humanism as somehow inconsistent with evangelicalism, or that the classical literature might serve as models for style but not content, or that his view of human depravity could not be squared with the witness of common sense about learning. In 1539 Calvin was thirty years old. Only seven years before he had published his Commentary on Seneca's *De Clementia*, so to say as a declaration of faith in the Erasmian cultural idea of virtue through knowledge. Through his conversion he did not become a Christian, for he was a Christian before; rather it was a reassessment of the human predicament essentially in Luther's terms. It may have been a traumatic experience. While he had not ceased loving humanistic studies, it took him a long time to get clarity on how he could justify that love on religious grounds. I suggest that if he had achieved clarity by 1536 he would have put it in the first edition (1536). By 1539 he had indeed arrived at clarity.

Our locus classicus names certain areas of classical learning: (a) The works of the jurists, e.g., the thirty-nine whose writings are represented in Justinian's *Digest*. (b) The philosophers who have carefully observed and with art described nature. This could look as though he meant the pre-socratics and their like, but as likely he means the nature of things. Perhaps he echoes Aristotle's favorite phrasing, "What is a thing by nature?"[9] (c) The physicians: doubtless Hippocrates and Galen. (d) Those who so taught the art of discourse as to make us speak in accordance with reason.[10] (e) Mathematics (Euclid, *et al.*). Calvin here reflected the influence of the College of the Royal Readers in Paris (which he had attended for a year), where major emphases were the three languages (Greek, Latin, Hebrew) *and* mathematics.[11]

There had been a long history of question concerning the

---

[9] It may also be a deliberate omission of the Platonists.

[10] "Ars disserendi" is rhetorical discourse; "cum ratione" is ensured by dialectics. In the next section (No. 16) he expressly names dialectics. Calvin moves in the good sophistic tradition of Isocrates and Cicero, that the orator must have something to say.

[11] Oronce Fine (1495–1555) taught mathematics from 1530–1540 at the Lecteurs Royaux. He came a few months after the college's opening. He is described as no genius like Fernel, but he was a knowledgeable scholar. He was an exciting teacher. See, A. Lefranc, *Histoire du College de France*, Paris 1893, pp. 177–179. Bibliothèque Nationale, sub "Oronce Finée", lists a work of his which includes a Greek text of Euclid. He was a diligent publicist.

status of worldly learning: Tatian and his pupil Justin Martyr
came to opposite conclusions with respect to Greek philosophy.
Generally, the ground of justifying classical learning was its
usefulness for understanding Scripture, or for the enrichment of
a Christian culture. There was St. Thomas and his use of Aristotle. No one can reasonably doubt that St. Thomas delighted
in philosophical analysis and speculation as much as Aristotle
himself, but his over-all justification of using Aristotle was
largely apologetic. St. Thomas' handsome appropriation of "the
philosopher", like the glossators' bringing to light the Corpus
Juris Civilis, was of great importance for preparing the mind of
the West to receive the florescence of the classics on a vaster
scale during the Renaissance; but a clear acknowledgement of
classical learning having a proper raison d'être in its own right
as a secular or terrestrial concern would be hard to find. In
St. Thomas' case, it would at least have been contrary to the
constitution of the Dominican order.

Between A.D. 1300 and 1600, there were beginnings toward
emancipation for, say, poetry and mathematics, and scientific
observation. Poetry, of secondary status before, got an exaltation
through Dante that bespoke a dignity in its own right. Copernicus hazarded his views on the good right of observation and
mathematical calculation. The question of questions was: can
poetry and mathematics ring as true in their kind as the Law,
the Prophets, or the Gospel? Likewise, they who knew something of the depth and redemptive quality of the Greek *areté*
through knowledge, were compelled to accept it as a measure of
their own educational thrusts. But for Renaissance Christians,
like Erasmus, to confess such is one thing; quite another is to
justify it on the solidest possible religious grounds; so that for a
believer to be smitten with Homer would in its kind be as truly
pious as it would be an act of piety to forgive an enemy seventy
times seven times for Christ's sake. Such certainty about a terrestrial pursuit was not cogently expressed by Renaissance
humanists. Petrarch put his heart in the sonnets, he desired
post-mortem reputation, and climbed the mountain in obedience
to an irresistible curiosity. Yet if we may believe him to have
been even half serious about his imagined conversations with
St. Augustine and about his reading in the *Confessions* on Mt.
Ventoux, we must put him down as being of a double mind.
Rudolph Agricola, deeply in love with Greek, left Pavia to

study in Ferrara under Battista Guarino; yet he had not been settled a year in Ferrara but, feeling old age approaching (he was 36), he did not want to die without Hebrew. He even affects to depreciate Greek literature as of unworthy content; yet when he describes what he would do with Hebrew it was to give to the Old Testament a more polished version. Neither man was changed. After his brushes with St. Augustine, Petrarch went on as before. Having taken up Hebrew, Agricola's heart was still in style.[12] But the doubt diminished joy, and offered no balm for conscience.

Returning to section 15 quoted above, let us look at the context. In sections 13–14 Calvin acknowledges that in fallen man there is abundant evidence of his rational nature, that "he is by nature captivated by the truth". To deny this is "not only to go against God's Word, but also to run counter to the experience of common sense". Then he illustrates this in four areas of human endeavor: (a) "As a social animal, man tends through natural instinct to foster and preserve society;" and "there exist in all men's minds universal impressions of a certain fair dealing and order—hence arises that unvarying consent of all nations and of individual mortals with regard to laws." (b) "Household management" (economic life). (c) "All mechanical skills or manual arts . . . Thus we witness the energy and ability not only to learn but also to devise something new in each art or to perfect and to polish what one has learned from a predecessor". (d) "The liberal arts", which pertain to the "discovery or systematic transmission of the arts, or the inner and more excellent knowledge of them".

Section 15 begins: "Whenever we come upon *these matters* [italics mine throughout] in secular[13] writers, let that admirable light of truth shining in each of them teach us that the mind of man, though fallen and perverted from its wholeness, is nevertheless *clothed* and *ornamented* with God's excellent gifts." Contextually, "these matters" refer to the above four: respectively, they echo Aristotle's *Politics* and *Ethics*; Vitruvius; Quintilian;

---

12) I take for granted that the desires of Petrarch and Agricola respectively were proper to man's nature; e.g., the desire for reputation after death is a wish for a kind of natural immortality; and delight in language that will not grate on the ear is perennial. For Agricola's case, see my "Melanchthon's Sources for a Life of R. Agricola," *Archiv fuer Reformations-geschichte*, Jahrg. 52 (1961) Heft 1, pp. 68–73.

13) "Profani" is the word; the context would justify translating it "classical."

but especially Cicero. Calvin goes on to say that the truth in such writers comes "from the Spirit, the sole fountain of truth"; hence, to "reject the truth itself" or "to despise it wherever it shall appear" is to "dishonor the Spirit of God". In fact, "to hold the gifts of the spirit in slight esteem is to *contemn and insult the Spirit himself*."[14] Then in a series of rhetorical questions Calvin praises the admirable work of the Spirit in the classical jurists, in philosophers, physicians, rhetoricians and dialecticians, mathematicians. "We marvel at them because we are *compelled* to recognize how preeminent they are".

His climax is in these words: "But shall we count anything praiseworthy or noble without recognizing at the same time that it comes from God? Let us be ashamed of such *ingratitude*, into which not even the pagan poets fell, for they confessed that the gods had *invented* philosophy, laws, and all the useful arts."

In Calvin's locus classicus I have italicized certain words. Calvin is *"compelled"* to admire the classical writers. This is on a line with his statement of not wanting to go against common sense. In addition, it appears that his response to the Spirit's terrestrial gifts is as irresistible as his response to the Holy Spirit's witness to the truth of Scripture.[15] In each case his response is to the same Spirit. As a believer he accepts the Scripture on the testimony of the spirit accorded only to the elect; as one of the human race he is a theist because the Spirit has endowed him with a sense of divinity.[16] Calvin does not confuse these two.

Lightly to esteem or neglect, let alone to despise and reject, the gifts is to *contemn and insult the Spirit.* It is a base form of practical atheism. Calvin rejected a piety careless of learning, let alone a piety proud of its ignorance. To him it was impiety. Besides, for one to scorn learning was to live in the sin of

---

14) Hendrikus Berkhof, a Reformed theologian, has developed suggestive ideas concerning the relation of the Holy Spirit to the sciences and arts and, in fact, to modern "secularism." See his *The Doctrine of the Holy Spirit*, Richmond 1964, esp. pp. 100–104.

15) *Institutes* I, vii, 2: "How can we be assured that this (Scripture) has sprung from God unless we have recourse to the decree of the church? It is as if someone asked: Whence will we learn to distinguish light from darkness, white from black, sweet from bitter? Indeed, Scripture exhibits fully as clear evidence of its own truth as white and black things do of their color, or sweet and bitter do of their taste." See also I, vii, 5.

16) Edward A. Dowey, *Calvin's Doctrine of the Knowledge of God*, Columbia University Press, 1952, pp. 50–56 probes Calvin's idea of "sensus divinitatis" with great good sense, as he does practically all else in this book.

*ingratitude*, which put one outside the pale of even the pagans who confessed that "philosophy, laws, and all the useful arts" came from the gods.

Italics called attention to the words *clothed and ornamented* and *invented*.[17] God clothed and ornamented the fallen nature of man with the gifts of learning; also, approval is given to the statement that the pagans confessed that the gods had invented philosophy, laws, and the useful arts. It is possible to regard such language as a hyperbole of piety. Could this Protestant theologian of creation and providence have meant that the virtues in unregenerated man are not connected with his nature as a man, as if as to say, when Socrates was conversing in the market-place it was literally the Spirit thinking the thoughts for him and phrasing them? In II, ii, 16, Calvin, exercising more care, says that the "Spirit fills, moves, and quickens all things . . . according to the character that he bestowed upon each kind *by the law of creation*." But to a suspicious reader this may mean no more than that, say, the Spirit produces mathematics in a man via the head rather than the feet. More troublesome is II, iii, where he discusses two Romans, a bad one and a noble one: Catiline and Camillus. He poses a dilemma: "Either we must make Camillus equal to Catiline [i.e., in their nature's corruption], or we shall have in Camillus an example of proving that nature, if carefully cultivated, is not utterly devoid of goodness. Indeed, I admit that the endowments in Camillus seem rightly commendable if judged in themselves. But how will these serve as proof of natural goodness?" Calvin queries: "if a natural man can excel in such moral integrity, undoubtedly human nature did not lack the ability to cultivate virtue, yet what if the mind had been wicked and crooked, and had followed anything but righteousness? And there is no doubt that such it was, *if you grant that Camillus was a natural* [i.e., carnal] *man.*" Thus man's nature can produce only wickedness. The commendable deeds have no root in his nature. At least, that is what these words mean.

In this same section (II, iii, 4) he says this quite as clearly: The virtues manifested in the depraved natural man "are not common gifts of nature" but special gifts of God. "For this reason, we are not afraid, in common parlance, to call this man

---

17) These are metaphors saying that the gifts are adventitious.

wellborn, and that one depraved in nature. Yet we do not hesitate to include both under the universal condition of depravity". It appears, then, that to call Camillus wellborn is to make a concession to common parlance but is in fact not the truth. Again, "when the Lord wished to put Saul over the kingdom he formed him as a new man [I Sam. 10:6]. This is the reason why Plato, alluding to the Homeric legend, says that kings' sons are born with some distinguishing mark. For God, in providing for the human race, often endows with a heroic nature those destined to command. From this *workshop* have come the qualities of great leaders celebrated in histories".

What shall we say of this? In view of his overall teaching, the language [clothed upon, invented, workshop] is apparently contradictory, at least ambiguous. The reasoning [if you grant Camillus as a natural (or carnal) man] is from the general to the particular, without any induction anywhere. But we let the ambiguities and the enthymemes stand. We must take Calvin as he is. He got his theology straight from the Bible, as he saw it. Contradictions did not trouble him so long as content is drawn from Scripture.[18] Coming from God, these would have their explanation somehow, sometime. Moreover, through the doubtful reasoning and the ambiguities there shines his deeper purpose of justifying all terrestrial good as holy. His heirs may count themselves fortunate for his so specifically including the higher learning in the good. Calvin's case against ingratitude for, say, philosophy can be turned against him; at least to those who realize the indispensableness of philosophical analyses of and speculation about everything, including how men express their religious faith. Every thought, as every word, of every man is fair game. But to Calvin, e.g., the being of God is to be adored, not curiously explored. He reports with approval that "when a certain shameless fellow mockingly asked a pious old man what God had done before the creation of the world, the latter aptly countered that he had been building hell for the curious." (I, xiv, 1). As Dr. Nuovo has shown, Calvin's philosophical sources are mainly practical popularizing ones; yet what beginnings would they have had but for the great ones? Withal, Calvin had

---

[18] See F. Wendel, *Calvin, Origins and Development of the Religious Thought* (translated by P. Mairet), N. Y. and Evanston 1963, pp. 357–360.

a dim view of most scholastic inquiries as a frivolity and use-less.[19]

Withal, however, Calvin is on the side of civilization with respect to the secular studies which, in our parlance, is the higher learning. On the showing, there is reason for saying that he has given it a charter of liberties. What this means I wish to suggest.

By describing learning as a gift of God's grace, he intends to liberate the believer's conscience from a sense of guilt for par-ticipating in the same learned pursuits with men lacking in saving grace. Calvin would not be impressed with evangelists who preach anti-secularism. It is evident that he was aware of tragic flaws in man and would not condone abuse of the seculum; but the seculum is as such, through God's common grace, something holy.

Moreover, the higher learning is liberated from restrictions that would prevent it from being itself. It is free to operate on its own terms. Calvin is explicit in saying that gifts of common grace must not be confounded with those of saving grace. Re-generated men participating in a secular pursuit do not add one grain to its proper quality. It implies that the higher learning is free to exercise its proper role of critic even with respect to the church and the theologian.

Finally, it were a denial of the very genius of the Christian faith to set bounds to its "supernatural" or "celestial" thrust, whose nature it is to demand "our life, our all." But how does this square with a whole-hearted admiration and thankful use of the "terrestrial" gifts, an admiration which can become more fervent only through increased preoccupation with them? A venerable statement points the way: "Grace presupposes nature." The same truth is said by: "Special revelation presupposes gen-eral revelation." Sensitivity to the latter is prerequisite for sensi-tivity to the former. Such priority of the natural gives its freedom a new dimension. In the hierarchy of values the spiritual is the highest, but in man that highest would not even exist but for man's physical nature and his relation to the total of the ter-restrial; and the language of the Christian hope of a resurrected *body* and of a new *earth* would seem to say that the terrestrial will be eternally indispensable.

---

[19] See the impressive statement of late scholasticism's importance embodied in Heiko A. Oberman, *The Harvest of Medieval Theology*, Harvard University Press, 1963.

If Calvin did not realize the many implications of his doctrine as can we, as heirs of the modern era, the vehemence of his conception still justifies them.

# BIBLIOGRAPHY

# BIBLIOGRAPHY

ALCIATI, ANDREA—*De singulari certamine Liber*, Venice, 1548.
—Andrea Alciati *Emblematum fontes quattuor*, Namely, an Account of the Original Collection made at Milan 1522, and Photolith Facsimiles of the Editions, Augsburg 1531, Paris 1534, and Venice 1546. Edited by Henry Green, with a Sketch of Alciati's Life and Bibliographical Observatoins respecting Early Reprints. 1870.
—*In tres posteriores Codicis Iustiniani libros Annotatiunculae*, 1513.

ALLEN, P. S.—*Opus Epistolarum Desiderii Erasmi Roterodami*, Oxford, 1906.
—*The Age of Erasmus*, Oxford 1914.

ANGUS, S.—*The Mystery-Religions and Christianity: A Study in the Religious Background of Early Christianity*, New York 1925.

BACON, JAMES—*The Life and Times of Francis the First, King of France*, London 1830.

BAUMGARTER, A. J.—*Calvin hébraïsant et interprète de l'Ancien Testament*, Paris 1889.

BAVINCK, H.—*Gereformeerde Dogmatiek*, 1906.

BAYLE, PIERRE—*Dictionaire historique et critique*, Rotterdam 1720.

BEAULIEUX, CH.—*Catalogue de la Réserve XVIᵉ siècle (1501–1540) de la Bibliothèque de l'Université de Paris*, Paris (VIe) 1910.

BEROALDUS, PH.—*Commentationes* condite a Philippo Beroaldo adiecta paraphrastica M. Ant. Sabellici interpretatione *in Suetonium Tranquillum* . . . Louis Hornken, 1512.
—*M. Annei Lucani, Cordubensis pharsalia* diligentissime per G. Versellanum recognita. *Cum commentariis* . . . Philippi Beroaldi Bononiensis nuper repertis. Josse Bade, 1514.
—*Oratio de laudibus Gymnasu Parrhisiorum et poetices acta in enarratione Lucani.*

BEYERHAUS, G.—*Studien zur Staatsanschauung Calvins mit besonderer Berücksichtigung seines Souveränitätsbegriffs*, Berlin 1910.

BEZE, TH. DE—*Histoire ecclésiastique des églises réformées au royaume de France*, 2 vols., Ed. Vesson, 1882.
—*Les vrais pourtraits des hommes illustres* . . . Tr. de Latin de Theodore de Besze, Genève, de Laon, 1881.
—Vie de Calvin, *Opera Calvini*, XXI.

BORGEAUD, CH.—*Histoire de l'Université de Genève*, Genève, 1909.

BOSSERT, A.—*Calvin*, in Les grands écrivains français, Paris 1906.

BRANTÔME, PIERRE—*Oeuvres complètes*. Edited by Buchon, Paris 1838.

BROCKHAUS, F. A.—*Konversations-Lexicon*. 14e Aufl. Leipzig-Berlin, 1892.

BRUNOT, F.—*Histoire de la langue française dès origines à 1900*, Tome II, Seizième siècle.

BUDÉ, E. DE—*Vie de Guillaume Budé, fondateur du Collège de France 1467–1540)*, Paris 1884.

BUDÉ, GUILLAUME—*Annotiones in quattuor et viginti Pandectarum libros*, in vol. I of *Lucubrationes Budaei*, Bâle 1557.
—*Commentarii linguae graecae*, Josse Badius, Paris 1529.
—*De asse et partibus eius libri quinque*, Josse Badius, Paris, 1514–15.
—*De l'Institution du prince* . . . , Revue, enrichy par Jean de Luxembourg, Paris 1547.
—*De transitu Hellenismi ad Christianismum libri tres*, Paris 1535.

*Bulletin historique et littéraire de la Société de l'histoire du Protestantisme français*, Paris (Biblothèque du Protestantisme français). Referred to throughout as *Bulletin*.

BURCKHARDT, J.—*The Civilization of the Renaissance in Italy*, New York and London 1909.

ÇASE, S. J.—*Experience with the Supernatural in Early Christian Times*, New York and London 1929.

*Catalogue des actes de François I$^{er}$* publié par l'Académie des Sciences morales et politiques, 1887–1908, 10 vols.

CALVIN, J.—*Opera quae supersunt omnia*, Edd. G. Baum, E. Cunitz, E. Reuss, 59 vols., 1866 seq. (Corpus Reformatorum vols. 29–88).

—*L. Annaei Senecae . . . libro duo De Clementia . . . Jo. Calvini Noviodunaei Commentariis illustrati. . . .* Parisiis apud Ludovicum Cyaneum, 1532. Opera Calv., vol. V, pp. ix–lvii, 1–162. Referred to in the text as *Comm*.

—*Institutes of the Christian Religion*. Transl. by John Allen, Philadelphia 1841.

—*Tracts relating to the Reformation*. Transl. by Henry Beveridge, Edinburgh 1849–60.

CELLINI, BENVENUTO— *Memoirs*, numerous editions.

CHRISTIAN, M. A.—*Origines de l'imprimerie en France*, Paris 1901.

CLARK, W. R.—*Savonarola, His Life and Times*, Chicago 1891.

CLÉMENT, L.—*Henri Estienne et son oeuvre française*, Paris 1899.

CLOUZOT, H.—Chronologie de la vie de François Rabelais, pp. cxxiii–cxliii of *Oeuvres de François Rabelais*, éd. crit. publiée par Abel Lefranc, et. al., Paris 1912.

—Les amitiés de Rabelais en Orléans, et la lettre au bailli du bailli des baillis, Tome III, 156–175 of *Revue des Études Rabelaisiennes*.

COLEMAN, C. B.—*The Treatise of Lorenzo Valla on the Donation of Constantine*. Text and translation into English, New Haven 1922.

COMBET, J.—*Louis XI et le Saint-Siège*, Paris 1903.

COP, NICHOLAS—Rectoral Oration November 1, 1533, *Opera Calvini* Xb, 30–31.

CORDIER, MATHURIN—*De corrupti sermonis apud Gallos emendatione et loquendi Latine ratione libellis*, Paris 1530.

—*Exempla de Latino declinatu partium orationes*, Paris 1540.

—*Colloquiorum centuria selecta; or, A Select Century of Corderius's Colloquies*. English transl. by John Clarke, Boston 1770.

*Corpus Juris Civilis*, in quattuor partes distinctum, Dionysio Gothofredoje, auctore . . . Francofurti ad Moenum 1688.

CRÉVIER, J. B. L.—*Histoire de l'Université de Paris, depuis son origine jusqu'en l'année 1600*, Paris 1761.

CREIGHTON, M.—*History of the Papacy*, 1327–1527, 6 vols. 1892 seq.

CROISET, A. AND M.—*An Abridged History of Greek Literature*. Authorized translation by Geo. F. Heffelbower, New York 1904.

*Cyclopedia of Education, A*.—Paul Monroe, Editor, New York 1915.

DANTE, ALIGHIERI—*De Monarchia*. Translation by Aurelia Henry, 1904.

D'ARGENTRE (CHARLES DU PLESSIS)—*Collectio judiciorum de novis erroribus qui ab initio XIIII saeculi usque ad annum 1713 in ecclesia proscripti sunt et notati*, 3 vols. 1725–36.

DE FAYE, EUG.—*Clément d'Alexandrie, étude sur les rapports du Christianisme et de philosophie grecque au II$^e$ siècle*, Paris 1898.

DE LABRIOLLE, P.—*The Life and Times of St. Ambrose*. Translated from the French by Herbert Wilson. London 1928.

DELARUELLE, LOUIS—Études sur l'humanisme français: Nicole Bérault. Notes biographiques suivies d'un appendice sur plusiers de ses publications. *Musée Belge*, Tome XIII (1909), pp. 253–312.

—*Guillaume Budé; les origines, les debuts, les idées maîtresses*, Bibliothèque de l'École des Hautes Études, 1907.

—*Répertoire analytique et chronologique de la correspondance de Guillaume Budé*, Toulouse et Paris 1907.

—Une amitié d'humanistes. Étude sur les relations de Budé et de Érasme d'après leur correspondance (1516–1531), *Musée Belge*, IX, 321 ff.

DE LAUR, H. DURAND—*Érasme: Precurseur et initiateur de l'esprit moderne*, 2 vols., Paris 1872.

DE NOLHAC, P.—*Pétrarque et l'humanisme*, nouv. éd. Paris 1907.

*Dictionnaire des antiquités grecques et romaines*, d'après les textes et les monuments . . . , Paris 1904.

DORJAHN, A. P.—*On Readings in the Hand of Budaeus (i) inserted in Desk-Copy of Pliny's Letters* . . . Seminar Report, October 1922–June 1923, Chicago 1923.

DOUEN, O.—La Réforme: est-elle la fille de la réforme allemande? *Bulletin* XLI, 57–92.

DOUMERGUE, É.—*Jean Calvin, les hommes et les choses de son temps*, 7 vols., Lausaune, 1899–1919.

DU BELLAY, JOACHIM—*La Déffense et illustration de la langue françoyse* (1549). Édition critique par Henri Chamard, Paris 1904.

DUCHEMIN, NICHOLAS—*Antapologia adversus Aurelii Albucii defensionem pro And. Alciato contra Petrum Stellam* . . . Parisiis, ex officiana G. Morrhii, 1531.

*Église Gallicane, Histoire de l'*, par Longueval, Fontenay, Brunooy et Berthier, IVe Edition, 1827.

*Enciclopedia Italiana di Scienze, Lettere ed Arti*, Institui Giovanni Tuccani 1929. Article on Alciati with portrait.

ERASMUS ROTERODAMI, DISIDERIUS—*Opera omnia*, emendatiora et auctiora; cura F. Clerici, 10 vols., Lugd. Bat. 1703–6.

ERICHSON, A.—Bibliographia Calviniana, *Opera Calv.* LIX, 462–586.

FAGUET, ÉMILE—*Seizième siècle études littéraires*, Nouvelle Bibliothèque Littéraire, Paris 1894.

FAIRBAIRN, A. M.—Calvin and the Reformed Church, *Cambridge Modern History*, Vol. II, Ch. XI.

FRANKLIN, ALFRED—*Dictionnaire historique des arts, métiers, et professions exercés dans Paris depuis le treizième siècle*, Paris-Leipzig 1906.

GAGUIN, ROBERT—*De origine et gestis Francorum Compendium*, Pierre le Dru 1495.

FIGGIS, J. N.—*The Political Aspects of St. Augustine's City of God*, London 1921.

—*Studies of Political Thought from Gerson to Grotius*, Cambridge 1907.

GIARDINI, O.—Nuove indagini sulla vita e le condotto di Andrea Alciato, *Archivo storico lombardo*, t. XXX, 1903.

GIBBON, E.—*The Decline and Fall of the Roman Empire*, with notes by H. H. Milman, London and New York.

GODET, M.—*La congregation de Montaigu* . . . , Paris 1912.

GRAF, K. H.—Jacobus Stapulensis, *Zeitschrift f. d. historische Theologie*, Hamburg and Gotha, 1852, pp. 3–86, 165–237.

GREGOROVIUS, F.—*A History of Rome in the Middle Ages*, London 1894–1902.

GRESSWELL, W. P.—*Memoirs of Angelus Politianus, Joannes Picus of Mirandola et al.* Manchester 1805.

GRIMALDI, ALESSANDRO—*Funeral Oration, January 19, 1550, for Andrea Alciati.* Translated for the Holbein Society by Henry Green, 1871.

GUIZOT, M.—*St. Louis and Calvin*, Great Men of France, MacMillan, 1869.

HAUSER, HENRI—*Études sur la Réforme française*, Paris 1909.

HERMINJARD, A. L.—*Correspondance des Réformateurs dans les pays de la langue française*, Genève–Paris 1878–86, 7 vols.

HERZOG, J. J.—*Realencyklopädie für Protestantische Theologie und Kirche*, 3e Aufl., hg. von A. Hauck, 24 vols., 1896–1913.

HEUBI, W.—*François Ier et le mouvement intellectuel en France*, 1913.

KARLOWA, OTTO—*Römische Rechtsgeschichte*, 2 vols., Leipzig 1885.

HOLL, KARL—*Gesammelte Aufsätze zur Kirchengeschichte*, 3 vols., Tübingen 1927.

HOTMAN, FR.—*Francogallia*, 1586.

HYMA, A.—*The Christian Renaissance, A History of the "Devotio Moderna,"* New York and London, 1925.

IMBART DE LA TOUR, P.—*Les origines de la Réforme:* Vol. I *La France moderne* (1905), Vol. II *L'Église catholique et la crise de la Renaissance* (1909), Vol. III *L'Évangelisme 1521–38* (1914).

JANSSEN, R.—Principles of the Evangelical Reformers, *Onze Toekomst* (Editor, E. J. Tuuk), April 1, 1931, Vol. 34, No. 13, Section 2.

JOURDAIN, CAR:—*Index Chronologicus Chartarum pertinentium ad historiam Universitatis Parisiensis, ab ejus originibus ad finem Decimi Sexti saeculi . . .* Parisiis 1862.

*Journal d'un Bourgeois de Paris sous la règne de François Ier, 1515–1536*, Éd. Bourilly.

JOVY, É.—*François Tissard et Jérome Aléandre*, Vilry-le-François, 1899–1900.

KOLFHAUS, W.—Die Verkehr Calvins mit Bullinger, *Calvinstudien*, Editor, J. Bohatec, 1909.

KUIPER, H.—*Calvin on Common Grace*, Goes 1928.

KUYPER, A., SR.—*De Gemeene Gratie*, 3 vols. 1902.

LANG, A.—Die Bekehrung Johannes Calvins, *Studien zur Gesch. der Theol. und der Kirche*, Vol. III, Leipzig 1897.

LANSON, G.—*Histoire de la littérature française*, Paris 1922.

LAROUSSE, PIERRE—*Grand Dictionnaire universel français*, historique, géographique, biographique, mythologique, etc., Paris 1865.

LATOMUS (Jacques Masson)—*De trium linguarum et studii theologici ratione*, Anvers 1519.

LAVISSE, É.—*Histoire de France.* Tome cinquième: I. Les guerres d' Italie. La France sous Charles VIII, Louis XII et François I, par H. Lemonnier 1903.

LAVISSE, E. ET RAMBEAUD, A.—*Histoire Générale du IVe siècle à nos jours*, 12 vols., Paris 1884. Vol. IV: Renaissance et Réforme; les nouveaux mondes (1492–1559).

LECOULTRE, H.—Calvin d'après son Commentaire sur le De Clementia de Sénèque (1532), *Revue de Théologie et de Philosophie*, 1891, pp. 51–77.

—La conversion de Calvin. Étude morale. *Rev. de Théol. et de Philos.*, 1890, pp. 5–30.

LEFRANC, ABEL—*Histoire de Collège de France depuis ses origines jusqu'* *à la fin du premier empire*, Paris 1893.
—Idées religieuses de Marguerite de Navarre, *Bulletin* XLVI, 7 ff., 72 ff., 137 ff., 295 ff., 418 ff.
—*Oeuvres de François Rabelais.* Édition critique publiée par Lefranc et al., Paris 1912. Introduction: Étude sur le Gargantua, pages i–lxxxvii, par Lefranc.
—*Jean Calvin . . . Institutions de la religion chrétienne* (1541), réimprimé sous la direction de la A. Lefranc, par H. Chatelain et J. Pannier, Paris 1911.
—*La Jeunesse de Calvin*, Paris 1888.
—*Les dernières poésies de Marguerite de Navarre*, publiées la première fois avec une introduction et des notes, Paris 1896. Introduction pp. l–lxxvii.
—Les plus anciennes mentions du "Pantagruel" et du "Gargantua," *Rev. des Études Rabelaisiennes*, III, pp. 216–221.
—Marguerite de Navarre et le platonisme de la renaissance, *Bibliothèque de l'École des Chartres*, T. LVIII, 1897.

LAETUS, POMPONIUS—Pomponii Leti viri clarissimi *Opuscula.* De Romanorum magistratibus. De sacerdotibus. De iurisperitis. De legibus eorundum. De antiquitatibus urbis: qui tamen alterius videtur stylo scriptis libellis. . . . Opuscula preterea duo L. Fenestella de Romanorum sacerdotibus. Eiusdem de eorumdem magistratibus. Basileae 1535.

MACHIAVELLI, NICCOLO— *The Prince.* Many editions.

MARC-MONNIER—*La Renaissance de Dante à Luther*, Histoire générale la littérature moderne, Paris 1864.

MARGUERITE DE NAVARRE—*L'Heptaméron*, Ed. par Paul Lacroix avec Notice historique sur Marguerite d'Angoulême reine de Navarre, pp. i–xxxvi, Paris 1880.

MARMELSTEIN, J. W.—Calviniana, *Neophilologus*, onder redaktie van Proff. J. J. Salverda de Grave, K. R. Gallas, enz., J. B. Wolters, Groningen–Den Haage, 1930, 16e jaargang, 1ste afl., pp. 1–6.

MAROT, CLÉMENT—*Oeuvres Complètes*, par M. Pierre Jannet, Paris 1868.

MCNEILL, J. T.—*Unitive Protestantism, A study in our Religious Resources*, Abingdon Press 1930.

MATTHAEUS, ANTONIUS—*Andrea Alciati Jurisconsulti Mediolanensis Tractatus contra vitam monasticam*, Leiden 1740.

MICHELET, J.—*Histoire de France au seizième siècle*, 2e éd., Paris 1885–87. T. VII Renaissance, T. VIII Réforme.

MONNIER, PH.—*Le Quattrocento, essai sur l'histoire littéraire du XVᵉ siècle italien.* 2 vols., new edition, Paris 1912.

MOORE, M. W. G.—*La Réforme allemande et la littérature française; recherches sur la notorieté de Luther en France.* Publications de la Faculté des lettres, fascicule 52, Strasbourg 1930.

NIESEL, W.—Verstand Calvin Deutsch? *Zeitschrift für Kirchengeschichte*, XLIX Bd., III Heft, 1930, 343–46.

NISARD, C.—*Les gladiateurs de la république des lettres aux XVᵉ, XVIᵉ, et XVIIᵉ siècles*, Paris 1860.

OMONT, H.—Essai sur les débuts de la typographie grecque à Paris, *Mémoires de la Société de l'histoire de Paris*, XVIII, 1892.
—*Georges Hermonyme de Sparte, maître de grec à Paris*, 1885.

OORTHUYS, G.—*De Anthropologie van Zwingli*, Leiden 1905.

*Ordonnances des rois de France;* règne de François I<sup>er</sup>; publiée par l'Académie des Sciences morales et politiques, 10 vols., 1902–08.

OSWALD, J. C.—*A History of Printing; Its Development through Five Hundred Years,* New York and London 1928.

PANNIER, J.—Les Protestants françaises et l'Algerie, *Bulletin* LXXIX, 146 ff.

—Recherches sur la formation intellectuel de Calvin, *Revue d'Histoire et de Philosophie religieuse,* March–June 1930, 264 ff.

PAULY, AUGUST, ET AL.—*Real-Encyclopaedie der classischen Alterthumswissenschaft,* Stuttgart 1846.

PEROTTI, NICCOLO—*Cornucopia linguae Latinae,* Venice 1480.

—*Grammatica,* Venice 1471, 1505.

PHILIPPE, J.—*Guillaume Fichet, sa vie, ses oeuvres.* Annecy 1892.

PICHON, RENÉ—*Lactante, Étude sur le mouvement philosophique et religieuse sous le règne de Constantin,* Paris 1901.

PICOT, É.—Les Moralistés polemiques ou la controvers religeuse dans l'ancien théâtre français, *Bulletin* XXXVI, 169 ff., 225 ff., 337 ff.

PIPER, O.—Vom französischen Protestantisme, *Zeitwende* (Monatschrift), März, 1930.

POLITIAN, ANGELO—*Omnium Angeli Politiani operum . . .* Josse Bade 1519.

QUICHERAT, J.—*Histoire de Sainte-Barbe; Collège, Communauté, Institution,* 1860–64, 3 vols.

RASHDALL, H.—*The Universities of Europe in the Middle Ages,* 2 vols., in 3, Oxford 1895.

RAYNAL, LOUIS H. CH. DE—*Histoire du Berry depuis les temps les plus anciens jusqu'en 1789,* Bourges 1847, 4 vols.

REBITTÉ, D.—*Guillaume Budé restaurateur des études grecques en France;* essai historique, Paris 1846.

REICHLING, D.—*Das Doctrinale des Alexander de Villa-Dei,* Monumental Germaniae Paedagogica XII, Berlin 1893.

RENAUDET, A.—Érasme, sa vie, et son oeuvre jusqu'à 1517 d'après sa correspondance, *Revue historique,* CXI, 225–62, CXII, 241–74.

—Jean Standonck, un réformateur catholique avant la Réforme, *Bulletin* LVII, 5–81.

—*Préréforme et Humanisme à Paris pendant les premières guerres d'Italie (1494–1517),* 1916.

RENOUARD, PH.—*Bibliographie des impressions et des oeuvres de Josse Badius Ascensius, imprimeur et humaniste, 1462–1535,* Paris 1908, 3 vols.

—*Imprimeurs parisiens, libraires, fondeurs de caractères et correcteurs d'imprimerie, depuis l'introduction de l'imprimerie à Paris (1470) jusqu' à la fin du XVI<sup>e</sup> siècle,* Paris 1898.

—*Les marques typographiques parisiennes des XVe et XVIe siècles,* Paris 1926.

REUSS, E.—L'Histoire de la Bible française, *Rev. de Théologie de Strasbourg,* 1865, p. 217 ff.

REYBURN, H. Y.—*John Calvin, His Life, Letters, and Work,* New York, 1914.

RONZY, PIERRE—*Un humaniste italianisant, Papire Masson (1544–1611),* Paris 1911.

SAINT-AMAND, IMBERT DE—*Women of the Valois Court.* Translated by Gilbert Martin, New York 1893.

SAINTSBURY, G.—*A History of Criticism and Literary Taste in Europe, from the Earliest Texts to the Present Day*, 3 vols., New York–London 1900.

SANDYS, J. E.—*A Companion to Latin Studies*, 3rd Edition, Cambridge 1921.

—*A History of Classical Scholarship from the Sixth Century to the End of the Middle Ages*, 2nd Edition, Cambridge 1906.

SCHERER, H.—*Die Pädagogik vor Pestalozzi* . . . , Leipzig 1897.

SCOTT, IZORA—*Controversies over the Imitation of Cicero as a Model for Style and Some Phases of their Influence on the Schools of the Renaissance*, New York City 1910.

SENECA, L. A.—*Lucubrationes omnes*, additis etiam nonnullis Erasmi Roterodami cura, ab innumeris mendis repurgatae. In Basilaea 1515.

—*Opera Senecae* per Des. Erasmum ex fide veterum codicum tum ex probatis autoribus emendata. Basilaea, officina Frobeniana 1529.

SMITH, P.—*The Age of the Reformation*, New York 1920.

SOHM, W.—*Die Schule Johann Sturms und die Kirche Strassburgs in ihrem gegenseitigen Verhältnis (1503–81)*, Munich–Berlin 1912.

STINZING, R.—*Ulrich Zazius. Ein Beitrag zur Geschichte der Rechtswissenschaft im Zeitalter der Reformation*. Basel 1857.

STROWSKI, F.—*Histoire des lettres, Deuxième volume (De Ronsard à nos jours)*, in Tome XIII of Histoire de la nation française (Éd. Gabriel Hanataux), Paris 1923.

SYMONDS, J. A.—Machiavelli, *Encyclopedia Brittanica* 1894.

TAYLOR, H. O—*Thought and Expression in the Sixteenth Century*, 2 vols., New York 1920.

TEUFFEL, W. S.—*A History of Roman Literature*, Translated by W. Wagner, London 1873.

THOMAS, J.—*Le Concordat de 1516, ses origines, son histoire au XVIe siècle*, 3 vols., 1910.

THOMPSON, J. W.—*Economic and Social History of the Middle Ages*, New York and London 1928.

—*Feudal Germany*, Chicago 1928.

THOMPSON, J. W., ROWLEY, G., SCHEVILL, F., SARTON, G.—*The Civilization of the Renaissance*, Chicago 1929.

TILLEY, A.—*The Dawn of the French Renaissance*, Cambridge 1918.

TIMPERLEY, C H.—*A Dictionary of Printers and Printing, with the Progress of Literature, Ancient and Modern, Bibliographical Illustrations*, London 1838.

TIRABOSCHI, CAV. ABATO GIROLAMO—*Storia della Letteratura Italiana* Firenze 1805–13.

TRIWUNATZ, M.—*Guillaume Budé's De l'institution du prince. Ein Beitrag zur Geschichte der Renaissancebewegung in Frankreich*. Erlangen–Leipzig 1903.

VALLA, LORENZO—*Laurentii Vallae opera*, nunc primo non mediocribus vigiliis & iudicio quorundam eruditiis, virorum in unum volumen collecta . . . Basileae apud Henricum Petrum, MDXL.

VALOIS, N.—*Histoire de la pragmatique sanction de Bourges sous Charles VII*, Paris 1906.

VIÉNOT, J.—*Histoire de la Réforme française*, Paris 1926.

VILLEY, PIERRE—*Marot et Rabelais*, Paris 1923.

VOIGT, GEORG—*Die Wiederbelehbung des classischen Alterthums oder das erste Jahrhundert des Humanismus*, 2 vols., Berlin 1893.

WALKER, W.—*John Calvin, the Organizer of Reformed Protestantism (1509–64)*, New York–London 1906.

WATSON, F.—Mathurin Corderius: Schoolmaster at Paris, Bordeaux, and Geneva, in the Sixteenth Century, *School Review* XII (April, 1904), 284–98.

WEISS, N.—L'Institution chrétienne de Calvin, d'après "Études sur Calvin," par M. Lanson, *Bulletin* XLIII, 106 ff.

—Louis de Berquin, *Bulletin* 1918, p. 162 ff.

—Notes sur les traités de Luther traduits en français et imprimés en France entre 1525 et 1534, Art. I of La Littérature de la Réforme française, *Bulletin* XXXVI, 664 ff.

—Paris et la Réforme sous François Ier, *Bulletin* XLIII, 242–70.

WINKLER PRINS—*Geïllustreerde Encyclopaedie*, 3rd Edition, Amsterdam 1906.

WOODWARD, WM. H.—*Vittorino da Feltre and Other Humanist Educators.* An Introduction to the History of Classical Education. Cambridge 1905.

WOOLF, C. N. S.—*Bartolus of Sassoferrato, His Position in the History of Medieval Political Thought*, Cambridge 1913.

ZANTA, LÉONTINE—*La Renaissance du Stoicisme au XVIe siècle*, Paris 1914.

# INDEX

Accommodation in exegesis, 154
Accursius (1182–1260), 117
"Address to Francis I," 1536
  French version of, 130
Aequum, 142
Agricola, Rudolph (1444–1485), 111
  note 45
Albucius (pseudonym of Alciati)
Alciati, Andrea (1492-1550), 4,
  44–60, 83, 140
*Antapologia* of Duchemin, 37, 49,
  52–60
Augustine, St. (354–430), 75, 95,
  144
Aurogallus, Matthew, 65
Authors ancient & Renaissance,
  references to in Seneca
  Commentary, 94–96

Badius Ascensius, Josse
  (1462–?1535), 127–130
Barnosse, Arnould de, 32
Bartholus (1314–1357), 117 and
  note 64, 136f.
Barzizza, Gasparina da (fl. 1407),
  125
Basil, St. (330–?379), 116
Bavinck, Herman (fl. 1900), 159
Beda, Noel (d. 1536), 18, 21f., 29
Berault, Nicholas, 25
Beroaldus, Nicholas, 42, 129
Beza, Theodore (1519–1605),
  3 and note 8, 40 note 1, 156
Berquin, Louis de (d. 1529), 27–29,
  31f., 33–36, 38f.
Bible, references to in Seneca
  Commentary, 96
Bibliothèque Nationale, 117 and
  note 63
Billory, Pierre, 24
Borgeaud, Ch., 156f.
Bourges, University of, 44f.
Brethren of the Common Life
  18–21
Briçonnet, Bishop (1470–1534),
  27, 30f.
Budé, Guillaume (1467–1540), 3
  note 8, 14, 25, 35f., 44, 62, 72,
  83, 113–124, 139f. Works: *Annotationes in Pandectas*, 44,
  116–119; *Commentarii linguae
  graecae*, 62, 123f.; *De Asse*,
  119f.; *De transitu Hellenismi
  ad Christianismum*, 120. *L'institution du Prince*, 120–123;
  *In Novum Testamentum An-
  notationes*, 118

Calvin, John (1509–1564), *passim*
Carlstadt (Karlstadt)
  (1480?–1541), 31, 34
Castellio (1515–1563), 72
Cellini (1500–1571), 4 note 10
Charles VIII, Italian invasion of,
  100f.
Cheradamus, Joannes, 132
Christian philosophy, 79
Cicero, 72f., 94
Ciceronianism, 119, 129
*Ciceronianus* of Erasmus, 59 and
  note 32, 78
Clement of Alexandria
  (150?–?220), 76
Clichthove, Josse, 33
Common Grace, Doctrine of, 75,
  159f, 165f.
Concordat of 1516, 1–3
Connan, François de, 43 and note
  14, 87
Conscience, 73
Conversion of Calvin, 2, 12, 27,
  37f., 40 note 1, 42, 90; cf. 13f.
Cop, Dr. Guillaume, 14, 24f., 117
Cop, Nicholas, ix, 14
Copernicus (1473–1543), 155f.
Cordier, Mathurin (1473–1564),
  15–17, 30, 157
Critical apparatus, humanistic, 154

Danès, Pierre, 4 note 8, 63, 133
Daniel, François, 43
Demochares (Antoine de Monchy),
  24
De l'Estoile, Pierre (fl. 1530), 37,
  41, 43, 58f.
Digest (see Pandects)
Duchemin, Nicholas, viii, 37, 43
  (see *Antapologia*)
Durand, Nicholas (see
  Villegagnon)

*Emblems* of Alciati, 45, 47, 50–52
Epicureanism, 74, 108–113
Erasmus (1469?–1536), 20, 22, 25,
  27, 32, 34f., 59 and note 32, 62,
  72, 76, 77–79, 91f., 113f., 115,
  157
Erudition, French vs. Italian,
  113–116 and notes 53, 54, 55;
  of Calvin, 155
Escape, Seneca Commentary as,
  8, 13
Esthetic sense in Calvin, 148–153
Estienne, Henri (1528–1598), 133
Eucharist, 148–153

.